The Industry

The
Industry

LIFE IN THE
HOLLYWOOD FAST LANE

Saul David

Times
BOOKS

Published by TIMES BOOKS, a division of
Quadrangle/The New York Times Book Co., Inc.
Three Park Avenue, New York, N.Y. 10016

Published simultaneously in Canada by
Fitzhenry & Whiteside, Ltd., Toronto

Library of Congress Cataloging in Publication Data

David, Saul.
The industry.
Includes index.

1. Moving-picture industry—California—Hollywood.
2. Social customs—California—Hollywood. I. Title.
PN1993.5.U65D3 1980   384'.8'09794993   80-5783
ISBN 0-8129-0971-2

Designed by Sam Gantt

MANUFACTURED IN THE UNITED STATES OF AMERICA

*"I may not know where it's at,
but this ain't the place."*

—BUZZ HENRY

Contents

The
Industry

1

I Am
Summoned to the Coast—
and Fired

THERE ARE NO purely paranoid fears when you're working at a studio, only real disasters and narrow escapes. *They* are, in fact, *always* plotting behind your back, and when they can they kill you.

Years ago I worked briefly for a Mr. Kaufmann who was in the business of selling radio stations (chiefly FM-ers) to small-city-newspaper owners and installing them. The egos and bank balances of the newspaper men were apparently full and accessible—he had lots of customers. When I told Kaufmann that I wanted to settle down at one of those little stations and do local programming, he thought I was mad. He said something like this:

"See that console, kid? You know what makes it work—those tubes, right? Well, talent is like those tubes. The damn thing won't work without them, but they burn out. And when they do, you know what? You throw them away and get new ones."

I didn't take his advice. Instead, I took the job, burned out and was thrown away in a few months. But like the fellow behind the elephant, I had been caught by show biz. I was talent. Since then I've learned nothing to disprove Mr. Kaufmann's version of how it is.

I went to Hollywood in 1960 as a kind of hybrid executive at Columbia
—that is, I was hired for presumed story-finding talent with the built-in
understanding that this was to lead me toward production. It was a silly
and irritating job which sounded good on the East Coast, where it was
invented, but insane on the West Coast, where I simply appeared to be
a spy for both sides.

The Columbia contract was for several years, but by the time I got
off the airplane on the golden end, the situation had decayed and I was
viewed with discomfort and regret. Management's plans had changed
—in fact, management had changed and the powerful New York executive who had sponsored me was halfway out the door. Here in Hollywood, the people who had successfully yanked the rug out from under
him saw me as a hangover from another time—and a man whose loyalty
could not be counted on. They shook my hand and wondered out loud
what to do with me.

But I was listed as an executive and consequently invited and expected to appear at regular conferences in the office of the late Sam
Briskin, who had taken over the head of production job on Harry Cohn's
death. Sam was a genial man, quite unlike the stories I had heard about
Cohn—and he enjoyed the staff meetings at which all upcoming projects were hashed over, past or current success or failure analyzed and
ideas tried out. Ideas in such meetings are essentially of two kinds—
trend-spotting and remakes. Both stem from the unshakable Industry
conviction that picture-making is an industry like dress manufacture;
that all public taste moves in waves and cycles of different strength and
duration and that everything worthwhile has already been done—the
problem is to know when to redo it and in what contemporary style.

But sometimes a success would come along which no analysis could
explain—and everyone would worry until it was categorized. An out-
standing example of this kind of trouble was caused by the success of
Suddenly Last Summer, a Tennessee Williams play full of the playwright's obsessive fantasies and unorthodox passions, turning on a horri-
fying Oedipal relationship and winding up with a not very obscure
suggestion of cannibalism—just the kind of mess, Elizabeth Taylor and
all, that should have died at the box office once it got out of the sick
metropolitan centers. But this one didn't, and it worried our executive
conferences—especially Sam Briskin. We tried explanations but they
were obviously faked and halfhearted, and Sam was not looking for an
easy out—he took the job seriously and there was the Need to Know.

Sam Briskin's was a huge office, longer than wide, windows on Gower
Street at the right as you entered, his huge desk at the very rear (on a
dais?) and the rest of the room filled with comfortable sofas, easy chairs,

coffee tables and the oversize lamps which are a standard feature of Beverly Hills interiors, offices and homes alike. There was a marked tendency to make them out of *objets*—like imitation Ming horses with the light standards rising from the saddles—but I may be remembering another office. The seating arrangements, like most such, were complicated and meaningful. I never fully understood the precise significance of where you sat, whether on sofa or chair or how far away from the desk and on which side—but I was asked politely to move often enough so that I grasped the fact there was a meaning to it all, no matter how obscure. Such requests were always polite: "Why don't you sit over here by Harry?" But they were unmistakably noncasual and I always complied.

Sam usually sat beaming at us as we filed in and took our places. In front of him on the desk was a large ceramic dish filled with candies— hard candies and little chocolate miniatures. No matter how grave the business of the meeting, it was always begun informally with Sam tossing candies at us as we got into place. He always looked into the dish and selected the candy for the man—asking first if the color was okay: "You want a green one?" As the weeks went by I began to realize that this too had meaning. The chocolate miniatures were some sort of mark of favor—Sam never asked if you wanted one but doled them out very sparingly, and the receiver invariably said, "Thanks for the chocolate, Sam."

One afternoon the routine varied. Although we were usually allowed to gather in the outer office until we were all assembled, this time Sam's door was open and he stood in the doorway, cheerfully urging us in. Obviously he could hardly wait.

Once assembled, he trotted back behind his desk and, leaning on it with both hands, said, "Boys, I've got it!"

Naturally we all smiled, although no one was quite sure what Sam had got. But he wasted no time. What he had was the explanation of the success of *Suddenly Last Summer*.

He said, "Boys, we been making the whole thing too complicated. I asked myself, what's it about? What's it *really* about—forgetting all the bullshit about insane asylums and all that crap? And it came to me why the people like it. They can tell. When you throw all the other stuff away, what's left?"

We didn't know.

"I'll tell you. Mother Love. *Suddenly Last Summer* is really just a fancy story of Mother Love. You see?"

Motherlovers, we saw.

But they wanted me gone, and after a few months there seemed to be no place at all for me in the meetings. Everyone would be seated, gestured into place while I remained standing. Mr. Embarrassment. After a couple of those I stopped attending. Nobody inquired about my absence. Finally Briskin's executive assistant, a young man with a speech impediment who sat at the side of Briskin's desk and occasionally underscored a good point by saying, "You're so right, S-Samm," telephoned me and said someone would be in to discuss my contract.

The executive assigned to "settling" my contract was a pleasant young man named Gordon Stulberg, whose tenor voice unfortunately rose abruptly into a scream when the guy across the desk was too stupid to get the point. Since the point in question was for me to accept some twenty-five cents on the dollar for the contract's remaining time, and since I hadn't the foggiest idea of how to parlay my failure there into another job, there was a lot of screaming.

As discussions went along, I lost first my secretary, second my ability to make outgoing phone calls through the switchboard. It was very isolated. Even the agents stopped visiting—all except one.

His name was Arthur Landau, and when I met him he was already a memory of himself. Arthur was a tiny man, bone-dry, thin and energetic—a hawk's profile, deeply tanned and wrinkled, topped by an aggressive white brush haircut. He was very thin—thin so that you were conscious of collar bones and shoulder bones under his jacket, and the jacket was thin with wear. But the most striking thing about him was his voice, the voice of a man with a mechanical larynx.

It's a disconcerting sound coming from a human—an uninflected, reedy monotone, full of breath but jarringly without resonance. A computer voice, coming harshly from a fierce and impatient little man bursting with stories and opinions and demands which he could hardly articulate and which were inordinately painful to hear—let alone to understand.

Landau had been one of the great agents of the town once, the representative of such as Marie Dressler, the discoverer of Jean Harlow. "Thalberg used to come to the door to meet me in those days. Thalberg!"

When I met him they didn't come to the door anymore. He was barely tolerated by the men of his generation—uneasily ignored by younger men who were embarrassed by his assortment of old-time ideas and recollections. Landau had little or nothing to sell—no clients —only suggestions for remakes of remakes and the hope that if something worked he'd not be forgotten.

Once I asked one of the older executives about him and the man grimaced, shrugged and then said, "Look, he already owes me—I don't know—maybe a hundred bucks altogether. I'll never see it again."

So I knew that the worn jackets were how it was. The money had gone wherever it goes—a sick child, cancer—it was gone and here was Arthur Landau croaking and flapping his wings like an angry, crippled crow. His old friends were not happy to see him.

Neither was I, at first. But my own growing isolation fit in with Arthur's need to have someplace to call—someone to pitch—to be "in action." So he took to spending more and more time in my silent office and I got over the difficulty of his delivery and began to listen.

Most Old Hollywood stories are interesting but similar—fabulous deals, parties, fights and names, names, names. Everyone was in at the birth of everything and it was all casual and kingly—"I said, Irving, I won't tell you what the idea is, but I want your promise that if you use it I get fifteen percent. . . ." There was a lot of that. But when he talked about Jean Harlow, it was different.

In Hollywood, people talk about each other constantly—myth-making and myth-smashing are a constant process, and the eagerness rarely hides the hurt or the self-preserving contempt. The ones handled most roughly are the most successful, and of them the roughest handling is routinely given to the sex queens. The gush of O My God sentiment over the dead Marilyn Monroe was in striking contrast to the way she was talked about when she was alive. Then there was no story too vile, no perversion too sick to believe and pass along.

For a long time it was Raquel whose celebrated flesh was consumed at the parties and in the columns as Monroe was consumed and Harlow before her. But Raquel is tougher, and she came to the fair all grown up and with few illusions as to the prices and the trophies. Her wave seems to have crested, and all the people who've been waiting patiently for a headline-making tragedy so they can wallow, love, forgive, and then revel in talk about how *they killed her* may have to get off some other way. Only last week the girl was Farrah, and, even though the most they had on her was an addiction to tennis, the columns instantly glittered with cheap shots and one-liners. Hoping to escape accusations of being nothing but teeth, tits and razzmatazz, Farrah avoided sex bomb parts and was murdered instead for pretending to be Carole Lombard. It probably doesn't feel like good fortune to her but she lucked out when Bo Derek appeared. This week Bo's the girl, and the gusts of creative malice are already blowing through the hair salons and dress shops where they chopped up Marilyn and Raquel and the others. Right now Bo's ahead, but there's time. They'll think of something.

Still, the way Landau spoke of Jean Harlow was different—when her name was mentioned he would soften, remembering less angry times maybe. And when I asked him questions, I fell into an odd awkwardness about what to call her. Harlow? Jean? Because Landau rarely used her name—he called her the Girl.

It was the shameless sentiment of the silent films—I could almost hear the piano—but the old man was not trying to impress me or himself. I called her Harlow and Jean and finally Jean Harlow—and he would nod, twisting his head to look at me (he had formed the habit of pacing so he could have his back turned when he needed to clear his throat), and he'd say, "The day I took the Girl to see Hughes—did I ever tell you . . . ?" And I would hear about *Hell's Angels*—all of it. And about the mother and the stepfather and Paul Bern and the white bedroom and so on and on. . . .

Of course there had been lots of interest in Harlow—Columbia had tried, 20th Century-Fox had had a couple of screenplays written, but nothing had worked out. In truth, considering the richness of the material, it's remarkable and interesting how rarely Hollywood has been able to make a believable film about itself. *Sunset Boulevard, The Big Knife, The Bad and the Beautiful*—are there any others? *Day of the Locust* and *The Last Tycoon* were, in their separate ways, perfect examples of that vision of Hollywood which never dies in New York. The customers shrugged at both of them, and the only movie in recent years which hit the mark was probably *Shampoo*. But good as it was, *Shampoo* was not about Hollywood—it was rather about the Beverly Hills and Bel-Air culture which has grown up around the industry as Grosse Point grew up around GM. There are no films about Hollywood anymore. For that matter, were there ever any happy ones?

Movies were out for the moment—for me, anyhow—but what about a book about Harlow? I had come from the publishing business, and it was not hard to find a publisher who would put up the money for a writer who would get the story from Landau. I had nothing else to do.

About the time the book appeared, Columbia roused itself and sent for me. In characteristic studio style, the approach was not friendly, complimentary or seductive—these being approaches used toward people you don't already have under contract. Instead, I was informed that I was a conniving ingrate who had churned up a best seller behind their backs—that since I was stealing their bread I owed them everything, including the rights to *Harlow*. It was Arthur Landau's moment now—and he was equal to it. "We are taking bids," he said.

They get very angry about such things in Hollywood, hysterical with rage if the problem is of their own making. So I was not surprised at the rage caused by my connection with the book *Harlow*. Or to learn that another studio intended to sue me, Landau, the publisher—someone—

because they had repeatedly announced that they were going to film Harlow's life. Stuff like that is routine, it's called "casting a cloud on the project," and is the main way uppity types are brought to heel out here. (The function of studio legal departments is chiefly to employ the law in the way the Mafia employs a bomb—to make antagonists think twice and then collapse in fear. It often works.)

But the publisher had already been called an upstart, the author was a fierce little man whose earnings were not attachable by the studio, and neither Landau nor I had anything left to lose.

The book began to sell well, and the noise was unbelievable. Landau was to be barred from the lot (but how do you make a deal with someone you won't allow in?) and I was fired (but of course I had already been fired—they couldn't *erase* me) and it was terrible and a great joy to Arthur Landau, who told me one day that he would surely sell the book to Columbia for my sake—but he just wanted to "be in action" a little longer first.

It finally got to be time to make a sale, and after much huffing and puffing and phone calls amid go-betweens, an appointment was set for Landau to see his old friend Sam Briskin. I vividly recall that the time of the appointment was three o'clock—and that it was three-thirty when my phone rang. A hoarse voice which I barely recognized as Briskin's demanded that I "get down here right now," and I got.

In the outer office, through the closed and locked doors (Mr. Briskin's office had one of those doors which locks automatically and which he alone could open via a button on his desk), I could hear the sound of battle. The really frightened secretary shouted my name into the intercom, the latch clicked, and I went in to an appalling sight—two elderly, ill men (Briskin had had at least one heart attack) almost incoherent with rage.

Landau could only croak terrible sounds, but he was literally jumping up and down in front of the great desk, wheezing, flailing his arms at each jump. Sam Briskin, purple, sweating, veins swollen on his forehead, was pounding the desk, yelling, his voice almost as strange as Landau's. "Crook, dirty crook . . . crook" was all I could make out.

I think they were both glad for the interruption, and they both subsided, breathing noisily. I was scared. Really heedless passion is always scary, even when it's called—and this could not have been called—love.

I mediated. It was curiously easy—a matter of an option, a time limit and so on. They were not really in disagreement about Harlow, they were in disagreement about the pains and terrors of a lifetime—those two terrible old men.

In any case I scratched together a deal and each man nodded, still sobbing for breath, when I asked, "Okay by you?" They did not shake hands.

Then Briskin caught his breath. "Now," he said to Landau, "get the hell out of my office." Landau stared at him, turned and marched off across the carpet, down the long room to the door. There he paused, waiting for the latch to click. Briskin clicked it and the door opened. Then Briskin spoke again.

"Just a minute."

Landau turned.

"Remember me to your wife."

2

The Old-Time Hollywood Wild Men

WHEN I FIRST came out, the differences between working in New York publishing and the Industry were disappointingly smaller than I had been led to expect. For one thing, the dominant culture was that of the Hollywood New Yorkers. No band of far-flung Empire Englishmen ever clung together more lovingly or spoke of "home" more feelingly than they. But they don't leave because they *are* the Hollywood they moan about—a kind of anti-Establishment government in exile with its bags packed and its roots deep in the decomposed granite of Brentwood and Bel-Air.

Until lately, the Hollywood New Yorkers even set the dress code— the old rep tie look of Andover, Yale, J. Press and Brooks Brothers. Despite the climate, more New York executives wear Bermuda shorts in summer than their Hollywood counterparts. And when I arrived it was all button-down oxford cloth and tweed jackets in the heat—you want someone to think you're a cowboy? Or a grip? Indeed, the dominant octopus of that period, MCA, carried the point to the end. MCA's black-suited, french-cuffed, buttoned-up young men were snickered at —but cautiously, as a Florentine might have snickered at a Medici retainer. The local joke "Dress British, think Yiddish" was as much an incantation as a knock.

Hollywood New Yorkers all look like Midnight Cowboys now. The straphanger's pride is wearing Levi's and motorcycle boots and combing his hair forward.

Not everyone, of course. While it's probably true that the streets of Lubbock, Texas, display fewer denim riders' jackets than the sidewalk in front of Nate 'n' Al's deli on Beverly Drive, there are still a few conspicuous holdouts. They are the corny and flamboyant types who were already an anachronism when Brooks Brothers buttoned down the open range—the Old-Time Wild Men.

Old-Time Wild Men look like caricatures of silent-film directors. In fact, most *are* directors, but not all—the breed also embraces production men, stunt gaffers and cameramen (the ones who do not call themselves cinematographers). At one time I knew a publicist and one screenwriter who qualified, but real Old-Time Wild Men are mostly found in behind-the-camera trades. They are intensely physical men who make physical movies in a physical world. Strength is their religion, endurance their pride and alcohol their undoing. They are clannish and contemptuous of everything most of the world thinks is moviemaking. They are boorish and overbearing, tend to vote "wrong" and use socially unacceptable epithets in public. They are an unutterable pain to the Hollywood New Yorkers and a boon to caricaturists—but no one has yet figured out how to make big outdoor movies as well as they do without them.

The difference between movies made on sound stages and those made in remote jungles and deserts is the difference between a Fourth of July parade and an amphibious landing under fire. One neither prepares nor qualifies you for the other. In fact, much of the blame Soulless Hollywood gets for ruining fine and sensitive foreign directors is really a record of the failure of those directors to cope with the big, outdoor Hollywood epic.

There's something about those pictures which seems to hypnotize accredited European geniuses. When such a paragon is imported, given that corner office with the shower and artistic carte blanche, nine chances out of ten he suddenly reveals that he has always really thought of himself as the European John Ford and that what he really wants to do is a Big Western—enriched, you understand, with those nuances of character, those psychological penetrations which mark his work, monsieur—no insult to M. Ford intended. This has turned out to be an irresistible recipe for disaster.

Contrary to loving myth, those European auteur directors are usually given complete artistic freedom by Hollywood—that they have managed to blame their disasters on the Industry is probably only one more proof of genius, but it isn't so. The trouble is that the skills which served the director well in making his tender and meaningful award-winning film of three Vietnamese orphans saved from starvation by a U.S. Negro deserter, and how they learn from each other and all that, do not serve at all in Durango, Death Valley or Moab in the company of bad weather, animals, extras, equipment breakdowns and the cynical amusement of the Old-Time Wild Men who serve him. And when he flips and screams and makes ghastly left-to-right mistakes and stamps his foot and gets sarcastic in broken English, you can chalk up yet another time Hollywood has "taken a great talent and misused it."

I never met John Ford, idol and prototype of the Old-Time Wild Men, but the stories about him are endless. If they are to be believed, Mr. Ford has not always been pleasant company: Most John Ford yarns involve a show of brutal bad manners. But I have never heard one of those yarns where the teller didn't obviously worship the man, bad manners and all. "Every time the producer, poor bastard, would come on the set the old man'd just stop shooting. Now the guy would get nervous—what the hell, why aren't they working? And when he'd get up enough nerve to ask, the old man'd say, 'When I come to *your* office I expect *you* to stop working. Well, this is my office.' And you can bet your ass the guy would get the point right now."

Or of Henry Hathaway: "He gets mad, Hathaway does, when someone's dogging it. I see him go by a set painter one day—guy's asleep against a stage brace. Well, Hathaway just turns, goes back and jolts him one. Just pow!" True? No idea. The point is that the story was told with respect and affection. Moreover, the teller assumed that the miserable painter, belted awake, did not run shrieking to his union. Instead he is assumed to be somewhere now telling his friends, "Reminds me of the time Hathaway clobbered me with a two b' four . . ."

Sam Peckinpah, decades younger than Ford or Hathaway, is an authentic contemporary specimen. Every Peckinpah film is attended by stories of squads of assistants fired, vicious battles with the front office (Peckinpah tends to work in remote places like Durango where he can improve the odds) and predictions of final, utter disaster back at the Bistro, a peerless Beverly Hills hangout for the peers of Beverly Hills.

The Bistro Boys hate it, but they keep hiring him because a number of humiliating failures with their own have taught the Hollywood New Yorkers that only the Old-Time Wild Men can make those Old-Time Wild pictures. To be sure, they take the pictures away from him, recut them, break his back in the fine print—but they keep hiring him. And lately, the mean little plastic wild men of the new Cinema Criticism have been discovering Peckinpah, and his tide is rising. If he stays with it, he may even get to keep the money one of these times.

Old and new Cinema Criticism has trouble with Old-Time Wild Men because they are not only apt to be rude or drunk or both, they tend to talk only about what happened when they were shooting such and such, about the broad who showed up one day out of nowhere and gave the whole fucking crew the worst case of crabs you ever saw—not about Their Art.

The visions of the Frankenheimers and the Schlesingers, the Warhols and the Lumets, are vendable and chic on glossy paper with photos of the artist as a life-style. But Old-Time Wild Men look odd in the pages of *Vogue* and their views are depressing—they know neither Kafka nor karma and they don't care. They drink bourbon, some even rye. They are intolerant of homosexuals and coarse in their references to them. But how to make *The Wild Bunch* or *True Grit* in the bottom of that garden?

Until recently, the war movie was only another kind of western— with a squad where the sheriff used to be and with the Death of Young Men to stir the heart in place of Monument Valley and the music unfurling behind. There are "personal" war movies as there are inti-mate westerns, but neither is typical. It's no accident that *The Guns of Navarone* was instantly seen as an ideal design for a western. Or that someone suggested the ideal slogan for *The Longest Day* would be "If you liked World War II, you'll love *The Longest Day*."

So the men who make one kind are likely to make the other. One such is a small, joyful, tigerish writer-director named Samuel Fuller—the Boswell of *The Big Red One*, a man in love with an army division.

I met him during the '50s on one of my trolling-for-tie-ins expeditions to the West Coast. He said he had a book in mind. Sam Fuller's offices at Columbia looked like a private war museum. Shell cases, plaques, souvenirs of conquered towns, battle flags, helmets and mounted bits of weaponry were everywhere. And the walls were covered with unit photographs, smiling and autographed pictures of commanders, scenes of smoking devastation.

I remember that it was a hot day, the venetian blinds drawn against the sun and the air conditioning not working. The office held that special smell of canvas webbing and brass polish that brought back North Africa to me while I waited for Sam Fuller to put down the phone. Command.

The first time I saw a commanding general up close was in early 1943, in Cairo, Egypt, Middle East Headquarters. I had been sent with some kind of file to General Brereton's office. Brereton was a legendary Air Corps officer who had flown a handful of battered bombers out of the Philippines after the Japanese onslaught and patched and coaxed and nursed them halfway around the world to North Africa, where he and they were thrown into support of the British Eighth Army against Rommel. Brereton was a hero to us. He was said to be impatient, loudmouthed and tough—but he had *done* something.

I remember a long, curving flight of marble stairs (could they have been pink?) and lots of HQ people coming and going; the Egyptian employees all buttoned into their black summer suits, each with his red tarboosh, small smile on the face, fly whisk in hand. I had just gotten to the landing when a door crashed open just beyond me and two men charged out—a tall, stout, red-tabbed British officer followed by a small, angry, shirt-sleeved American who was yelling, "Don't give me that crap, you fat-assed son of a bitch—when I tell you to do something you goddam well do it, and right now"—with which he put his foot against the big man's rump and shoved him stumbling past me (paralyzed) on down the stairs. The smaller man turned and slammed back into the room. Now the closed door read *Maj. Gen. Lewis Brereton.*

I don't suppose the two men look alike—but when Sam Fuller charged around his desk to wring my hand, offer me a soft drink, ask how I liked it in Hollywood and had I ever met Ernest Hemingway, "that's him in that picture over there," I was reminded of my first glimpse of command. He gave me a detailed tour of the mementoes; each one came with an anecdote and each anecdote with a zestful point. Fuller saw himself as one of Mauldin's warriors—a pugnaciously permanent enlisted man who had been everywhere and seen it all. He was primarily a writer, he said, an old-time newspaperman who had turned director to protect his words. But now it was time for his Life's Work. It would be called *The Big Red One* and it would tell the story of the First Division in WWII. Of course the film would follow.

In a Hollywood which is traditionally suspicious of the written word because it's the weapon of the enemy and because it always costs money in front, storytelling used to be an important art. There were "writers" who never actually wrote a word—their profession was telling, doing voices, gestures, imitations and sound effects, conveying passion and actuality to people who were bored by the very act of reading and so rarely liked anything they had to read.

There were many storytelling styles—the trick was to find one suitable to both story and audience. I have seen men who sat quietly, spoke softly and fixed their listeners like hypnotists. I've seen others roar and jump around and cry real tears. Sam Briskin had a memorable style—

he told all stories in the present tense and used star names for the characters. "It's Sunday morning and we're in front of a big church— like St. Patrick's, classy. And there's a mob out front because a society wedding. Photographers and everybody. Now Doris Day comes out in her wedding gown. She's got a bouquet and she's about to throw it to some sweet old broad by the side there when Cary Grant breaks out of the line. They can't hold him back and he walks up to Doris. We see her face. 'Cary,' she says, 'I thought you were dead.' He looks. 'No, Doris,' he says, 'no such luck.' He walks away. Cut back to Doris. She faints. Now we go to titles. . . ."

Even among those legendary storytellers, Sam Fuller was unique. He had more energy and less shame, more joy, more urgency, a louder voice and a sense of timing that made him harder to interrupt than anyone else.

Now Sam pumped my hand and *talked.* He outlined *Big Red One,* prowling the office, turning swiftly to grab my arm in a hard grip, puffing his huge cigars, laughing ha-*ha* less in humor than out of a sort of ferocious, high-pitched glee.

I was overcome by the heat, the cigar smoke and the vitality. Without clearly registering what I was hearing, I was convinced that it was a masterpiece.

Next morning I phoned New York and told them—trying without success to recapture that hot enthusiasm in the quiet hotel room. Still, something got through, and New York urged me to stay over another few days and block out a deal "before someone else gets to him, right?"

Mr. Fuller's secretary said he was busy, would I wait on the line? I did and she came back and said I was invited to dinner that night.

When you're invited to someone's house out here, there's quite a fuss about directions. Many people have little printed maps which they send out with invitations. The reason is that most Industry people make a considerable effort, not exactly at privacy, but at being hard to find. Thus unlisted phones, houses concealed at the end of long driveways and behind blind gates, mailboxes without names and streets without sidewalks or adequate lighting.

Sam Fuller's house was at the top of one of the steep, winding canyons which link Beverly Hills and the Valley. Following directions, I slowed down exactly five and seven-tenths miles from Sunset, found the stone gateposts on the left and turned the rental car into a quarter mile of curving blacktop driveway, rimmed with tall hedges and lit only by my headlights. It was a dark night, full of the smell of flowering shrubs, and slightly misty. Out here, when you leave someone's house after a late party, it's usual to need to run your car's wiper and defroster for several minutes because of evening mist and chill. Although the Sunset Strip is always studded with efforts to start sidewalk cafés, by nine o'clock of a summer night no one would mistake a Los Angeles evening for a Roman one.

The driveway ended at a turnaround, a closed garage and a high chain-link fence with a locked gate. Far beyond, the bulk of the house was barely visible in the dark; but out in the turnaround there was just me and the car headlights splashed on the garage door. It was very quiet.

I rattled the locked gate, found a bell and pushed the button. Nothing. I called—"Hello, hello?"—but without much spirit. It takes someone quite different from me to stand in a dark driveway in another country and yell through a fence at a dark and lifeless house. I called, but I gave up.

Having to stay over had created a clean-shirt problem, and two new ones were at that moment in the car. For some reason, it seemed appropriate to change shirts then and there—one of those deeply meaningful gestures, I suppose. I had fetched a shirt out of the car, gone around into the theatrical glare of the headlights, taken off my drip-dry seersucker jacket and my wilted New York shirt and begun pulling pins and tissue from the new one when someone said, "Can I help you?"

I was rattled. There was now a man on the other side of the fence, wearing dark pants and a T-shirt and holding a flashlight.

I said, "I was just changing my shirt."

Then I said, "Mr. Fuller is expecting me for dinner."

Pause.

"I couldn't get in," I said.

The man said, finally, "The bell doesn't work. I'll unlock it."

He unlocked the gate and waited while I finished with the shirt, standing in the headlights before a silent audience of one. Then he opened the gate for me and shone the flashlight down a path toward the house.

"That'll take you to the door."

I guess I expected him to lead the way with the flashlight, but as soon as I moved the light went out and he was not behind me.

Once past the garage there were garden lights and finally a long arched and timber-pillared portico. A wrought-iron gate, unlocked—and I faced a pair of massive wooden doors, carved and studded and very Spanish. They opened, and there stood the same man, but now he was wearing one of those horizontally striped butler's vests over his T-shirt. His chin was up and his eyes cast down, but he was breathing hard.

"Good evening, sir," he said.

The point was not worth arguing. He led me off to the right, down a wide hall, trowel-plastered and lit by those black iron sconces shaped like torches, to a broad archway and a sunken living room.

"Mr. Fuller worked late," he said. "If you'd like to wait in here."

The Hollywood Hills, which divide the outer world of Los Angeles from the inner world of the San Fernando Valley, are full of huge old Spanish-style houses built in the '20s. For some gothic reason, the really enormous and fanciful ones are never found on the flatlands but are tucked away in the canyons. (Even today, those canyons have hundreds of acres where no one goes but deer and coyotes. When the houses were built, the roads were dirt and there were wolves and cougars too—suggesting that the canyons were a kind of subtropical Transylvania to the builders of those great houses.)

They are often extravagantly ugly—two- and three-story entrance halls, unexpected bursts of stained glass, twisting narrow stairways, pointless little levels and endless multicolored tile. There are vast, unappeasable fireplaces, beams (extra-rough-hewn) on every ceiling that isn't vaulted and muraled, and small windows with grilles, all over-grown with shrubbery. The walls are often as much as three feet thick —in them is hidden the long-lost cast-iron plumbing which quietly rusts and clogs and waits for a new owner to come along to make some plumbing contractor wealthy. (At dinner recently, a well-known actor told me he had bought such a house a year before for $150,000 and, as of that dinner, had already put $75,000 more into plumbing repair.)

Anyway, it was one of those houses. And the living room where I was left was large—large enough so that an ordinary tract house could have fit right into it, one end against the fireplace, the other against the arch, the ridgepole grazing the beamed ceiling. A big room.

What I could see of the furniture was also Spanish—dark wood, dark leather, high backs and unyielding cushions. To sit alone on a sofa in that immense room was impossible. I found an armchair with a back taller than I, by a lamp table with some magazines—*Reader's Digests*, the kind you find in summer cottages. The bulb was too dim for reading.

Time passed—maybe ten minutes, maybe forty-five. Then I heard a distant voice— "Hey David—where in hell are you?"

It was Sam Fuller, hunting through the rooms for his dinner guest. I called back and he came to the archway, laughing.

"Jesus," he said, looking around the room as if he had never seen it before. "What in hell do you suppose made him put you in *here?*"

He led me off to a small, comfortable study with a little bar and a lot of wide furniture covered in print and strewn with pillows, scripts, magazines and the trade papers. Sam made me a stiff drink, didn't take one for himself (he'd been working like hell and one drink would just put him away, he said) but kept puffing on one of his long, thick cigars and talking; taking up right where we had left off, hugging me intermittently to make a point, talking, talking, talking. He was shooting some small war picture at that moment and it was interpolated into the story somehow—with an appetite and gusto and a relish for the work which I found irresistible.

War stories. Try as I may, I cannot remember the details of his stories. But I remember how he drove home the sense of that *Big Red One*— a tide of men bound together, a heavy hammer smashing at the German wall. There were sharp, ironic anecdotes, full of explosions in the dark, the savage humor of the booby trap that blew out the wrong wall and killed the silly bastards who put it there, full of O. Henry twists and surprises and sudden tears. It was the storytelling of an Old-Time Newspaper Wild Man, tight, artificially compressed, and full of that sentimental cynicism which heightens what it mocks. *The Big Red One,* starting out in North Africa and pushing on from first blood into every major engagement in Europe, was and is a hell of a story. And if Sam Fuller made Kasserine Pass into Thermopylae, he would get no argument from me—not then when all of us remembered what the dying had been about, not now when that Future they died for has arrived full of withering contempt for both the saviors and what was saved.

We were approaching the Rhine when Mrs. Fuller appeared—slim, elegant and dressed so as to make me glad I had changed my shirt. Sam broke off at the sight of her and introduced us warmly by first names, then we went in to dinner.

There was a refectory table which memory makes twenty feet long. Maybe not, but it stretched away like a bowling alley, dark and polished and set with a great bowl of flowers in the center, and three places. Two were at the head end, the third was at the foot.

Sam gestured me to the side chair at the head and escorted Mrs. Fuller to the foot of the table, held the chair for her and then trotted back to me. Before sitting, he turned another side chair so he could put his feet up. He was wearing bright-red slippers.

"Jesus, what a day," he said. "Gotta put my feet up after one of these days." He beamed at me. "Hungry?"

From the far end, Mrs. Fuller, half seen behind the flowers, rang a table bell. Instantly a door opened behind me and in came the butler carrying a silver platter and followed by a middle-aged lady in an apron, carrying another one. On his was a tall glass of milk, on hers was a large glass bowl filled with tuna salad and a plate heaped with Ritz crackers. The milk went to Sam, who waited while it was placed on a paper doily before him.

"Hate to eat anything after a day like this," Sam said. He sipped at the milk between puffs of the cigar. The lady with the tuna salad served Mrs. Fuller and then came down the table to me, behind and to the left.

"Hey," Sam said, "put the whole thing down. This guy is hungry—right? Ha *ha!*"

She put the bowl and the crackers on the table and waited. Sam nodded at them.

"Okay, people—that's it!" They left. Sam turned to me.

"Okay, baby?" I nodded. "Where were we, hey? Come on—don't stand on ceremony, dig in!"

3

---§---

Enter Rick Bankable
and the World of
Sexual Extras

I N H O L L Y W O O D, career anxieties are such that practically any girl will answer the phone even in the midst of balling—if it just keeps on ringing. To initiate a call under those circumstances is considered bravado, but it happens. When it does, the acceptable line is "Oh, Jesus, honey—I forgot to check the answering service."

The Casting Couch is only the most vivid metaphor for a practice which began before Central Casting. "Which secretary did I hire? The one with the big tits, of course."

Which is not to say the Casting Couch doesn't exist. It does, and it makes more sense than selecting a secretary by cup size. When a given part calls for a girl described in terms of engorged male tissue, the man making the choice has other thermometers available, but he's not about to ignore his own. If he does, he abandons his claim to talent and instinct and the rest, in favor of "track record" and what, in the end, turns out to be someone else's thermometer. Of course, using one's own fever chart that way has sometimes been unfortunate. "The broad turns me on so she's got to turn *everyone* on" made Bella Darvi's name bright, for instance, but the light never got into the box office. But the negative ploy is far more common—"The broad's great, but she just hasn't got it for me, y'know?" He means the mercury never got out of the bulb and, all other things being equal, let's keep looking.

What people really mean by Casting Couch is not exactly that—it's the flesh exchange. "Is it true that most of those girls out there . . . ?" "Sure." "Which girls? Them?" "Sure." They really mean Bits and Extras.

One legal year to the legal day after my legal residence in California, I was processed through the local divorce mill, turned inside out, cleaned and clobbered by the judicial vacuum cleaner in Santa Monica —a shrine for attorneys, a vault for ex-wives. When I was served, my gladiator asked me how much money I had. On hearing, he said, "You haven't got enough dough for justice, friend. You'll have to settle for law." Ten years later I was still settling. The Santa Monica Domestic Relations courts used to be famous for decisions which turned highly paid movie men into parolees with empty pockets and life sentences. For these men, and there were lots of them, no-fault divorce came too late. When one of them dies and is found to have left little or nothing, people remark that he must have squandered all that money.

One of the girls I got to know after renting the furnished one-room apartment ("That's okay, Mr. David, a lot of our men have their kids with them on weekends") was an extra and bit player named Ellie.

Bits and Extras are lumped together on a standard movie budget somewhere above (but not far above) Mechanical and Spring Devices. They are not considered members of the cast, rather mobile furniture to be herded back and forth, placed foreground or background and told when to be animated, when to sit frozen so as not to distract from the actors. They are there to be used.

Of course, they don't think of themselves that way—but they don't exactly *not* think of themselves that way either. Generally, extras don't expect to become featured actors, let alone stars. They are a separate group with a unique professional problem: Their chances of steady employment are best if no one notices them, so the director doesn't scream, "For chrissakes, are those your cousins? They're in every damn shot!"—at which point those cousins are finished on that picture. Consequently, many extras make the effort at invisibility. Some have been known to check in, disappear and reappear only to be checked out— giving rise to legends of extras who hold nine-to-five jobs which fit neatly into their eight-to-six movie careers. But invisibility is a problem too. The way for an extra to become a bit player (at a sizable boost in pay) is to be noticed, established in a scene or involved with a principal player in one. So there's as much pushing as pulling, with the result that extra girls live in a unionized harem where booking arrangements are made by second assistant directors—with the inevitable sampling. Nothing is compulsory—not eating, rent, car payments or the installment on the debt at the dress shop. "Keep smiling, honey. There may be something going early next month and I'll keep you in mind. Sure, call me. Why not? Got my home phone?"

Ellie was always smiling. When you spoke to her she turned to you expecting to laugh, and whatever you said came out applauded by that wide, open-mouthed smile which broadened and bubbled into breathy laughter as you spoke. "Beautiful," she'd say, the way they say it here —half-growled and intimate with shared wit—"Byoo-oo'd'ful, baby."

Movie sets crackle with ritual one-liners and an air of gallant irony which dissolves in the drab studio streets and bores the hell out of people who weren't there.

"Gawd—the way he *said* it, you know that *dopey* look he gets? Well, crackup. *Crack*up."

Extras like to say they are fired at the end of every day, and it's almost true. The moment they are dismissed they charge at the nearest telephones to call the service, to call casting, to call that second assistant they met at that party over to whatsis' house who said "call me." They always do call.

Ellie knew lots of seconds, and she was a pal of many "gophers," which meant she also knew a lot of Names. Gophers, or go-fors, to be exact, come in all sorts of titles and jobs. But their real function is to be Man Friday to a Name, to go for—coffee? girls? Whatever. When Tony Curtis was busted at Heathrow airport, the Hollywood reaction after jokes (which head has the Tony?) was a mild indignation that the star should have been caught holding. Where in hell was his gopher?

It was important to Ellie. Aside from the practical questions of employment, she really dug Names. Fame and money turned her on, and she was not pretending when her breath shortened in a tight two-shot with a Name. She would kid about it, pretending it was simply the money, but it was more. There ought to be a valentine for it, but Ellie's form of heterosexual hero worship is known inelegantly out here as Name-fucking.

Ellie would say, rolling her eyes, "It's just that hundred-dollar bills make me sexy." But it wasn't that. Name-fuckers are embarrassed by their own compulsive romanticism. Ellie would rather have been thought a kind of hooker than what she really was—a small-town girl playing cool, but prisoner to an imagination formed by fan mags, a coin on the flesh exchange. I think it was Dr. Johnson who pointed out that but for imagination a man would be as content in the arms of a chambermaid as in those of a duchess. Name-fuckers are incandescent with that kind of imagination.

Since Names are medals and trophies they must be displayed. Another problem. Every male star who isn't gay is married, or both. So inevitably there's an afternoon world. Again, imagination—because it's not located in his great house in Bel-Air; either "she" might be coming home today or you know how Jap gardeners are and "what the hell, didn't whatsis say your pad is around here somewhere?"

Ah, distinctly I remember it was 24 December and Columbia's Christmas party on Stage 12 was fading fast. There was more water than ice in the cardboard buckets and Kim Novak hadn't even put in an appearance. About five o'clock and thinning and the executives in their dark suits were gathered by the card table with the sandwiches, talking shop. Time to go.

My Date showed up late. She'd been working on another lot where there was no Christmas party and they had just knocked off.

"Hi honey the traffic was terrible on the freeway that's why I'm—hi Lou, hi Charlie, Merry Christmas, you guys." All that while crossing the stage to me, greeting friends, waving. She was a pretty and popular girl with a high, clear laugh. The executives at the sandwich table took note that the prettiest girl in the room was looking for me. Point? I nodded a modest acknowledgment of prowess. She finally reached me, kissed me with enthusiasm, broke, flashed a smile over my shoulder to someone and said, "Somebody die, honey? This place is a morgue wait a sec I just want to say hi to . . . be right back."

"Let's split, okay?" she said when she got back to me after kissing three guys I had never met. "Split" was a very advanced word in those days, but My Date used all the hip words (she had kindly explained why I should stop saying "hep"), only she used them in sentences and enunciated clearly. When I didn't know, she enjoyed explaining. We had a good time together.

Hollywood is not a cheerful place at Christmas or Thanksgiving. In this unsentimental business which makes its living wringing out other people's handkerchiefs, *they* always turn to blood ties when the sentiment is real. So while the great houses of Beverly Hills and Brentwood are full in that season, the guests are mostly from back East, relatives come to revel and marvel.

That leaves the army of young people, the beautiful, greedy, shaking with look-at-me people who don't go home, can't go home, wouldn't go home if they could. The reasons are as corny as the lies they wrote and the money they haven't got and gulpings like "They didn't know I had the kid—nobody back there knows," a grinding of clichés that no swinger has to look at squarely except at Thanksgiving and Christmas. It's not their best time.

I had a tree in my one-room apartment, an aggressively large, family-large, spruce tree waiting to be trimmed. There was a gaudy pile of presents I couldn't afford all waiting for tomorrow and the kids. ("The girls ought to be with their mu-ther on these occasions, don't you agree? You can pick them up about ten on Christmas day if you like, but be sure you have them back for dinnertime. Their grandmu-ther will be expecting . . .") Divorced kids score on Christmas—two trees, two sets of presents from the competitors. And then there are those extra things from Mommy's Friend and from the Lady that Daddy Met that time in the restaurant.

But that would come later. Now we were going to Ellie's place for a Merry Christmas drink.

"She's kinda down, hon," My Date said. "That damn Larry claims he hasn't got the money." She brooded. "I told her he's a bastard."

I waited for a clue.

"We're all bastards," I said, expecting her to knuckle my arm and laugh. But she was serious.

"He gave her a hundred bucks and said that's all he can get right now. He wouldn't give a shit if she wound up in Tijuana. Turn left here, hon —there's no left turn at the avenue. Right at the corner and then left again. Know where you are now?"

Ellie met us at the door. I suppose I stared, because she looked down at herself, then back up at me, and laughed. "My Gawd—the way you looked I thought it must show. Come on in. Larry's here. Larry Go-pher." A voice change to lower register. "Rick's going to drop by, you know. You've met him. No?"

Rick was the Name for whom Larry gophered. And a big one too. There's one of those Yiddish-mama jokes about celebrity which winds up, "By me you're a captain, by your papa you're a captain, but tell me —are you a captain by another captain?" Rick was and is. A major male star about whom the magic word is used. Bankable. As they say out here about the bankable few: With him and the phone book you've got a *Deal.*

A Deal is the beginning of everything, yet by itself the term is mean-ingless. A *Firm* Deal is better; it means both the contracting parties have heard of the arrangement and the one with the money may be seriously considering giving some to the one with the Package, in which case he would expect to get Commitments. A Commitment (skip a step and say a *Firm* Commitment) is an absolute promise by a star of some magnitude that he or she will deliver the talent and the body to a given production during a given time span provided that various other demands and terms are met, various satisfactions guaranteed and money paid by such and such a date. Whereupon the receiver of these fragile promises puts them up as a kind of collateral. If it all hangs together, someone goes to the bank—hence *bankable.*

Bankable Rick arrived attended by a supermarket delivery boy carrying a bag full of stuff from the gourmet section and a couple of bottles—and instantly we became a party. The girls' voices rose and they talked at once, Larry Gopher smiled and seated and carried things, the record player clicked on. Gaiety Now. I noted, without delight, that Rick and My Date were old friends, kissing friends, friends with "remember" jokes and stories. Ellie seemed to be saying "My Gawd" and laughing constantly. Ice cubes clattered and the star's bright, square smile traversed the room like an enamel searchlight. All those famous teeth, the familiar manner—the inescapable, enveloping, thirty-times-larger-than-life-and-filling-the-room-with-everybody's-ambitions—probably even mine. Hiya, Rick Bankable—I recognized you right away. How does it feel to be you, Rick, you probable bastard who knew My Date a hell of a long time before I did and probably better? Fuck you, Rick.

"Glad to meet you at last," I said. The trouble with most of them is that it really works—whatever it is that happens on the screen happens in rooms too. It was no use telling myself it was just another lifeguard.

"I've heard of you too," Rick said, turning the great smile full in my face. "I think you're a menace."

Everybody laughed. Me too. The star thinks I'm a menace—ha, ha. Rick, you're beau-tiful.

"You want to know why?" The smile never dimmed, he just talked through it. "Because you're the guy from New York who tells writers what to write—I read a piece about you in the trades. Manufacturing best sellers, I think it said." That much-mimicked, breathy, overprecise enunciation—"Man-u-facturing best sell-ers."

It had gotten much quieter.

Rick noticed the hush, scanned us, spoke to My Date.

"This *is* him, isn't it?" Back to me. "Of *course.*"

"How about a drinkie?" Ellie said. "Who's for a martooni?"

But Rick hadn't finished with me. Now he prodded me lightly in the breastbone with a forefinger brown as wood and polished. Still smiling, and speaking softly.

"Nonbooks. Isn't that what the critics are calling that kind of man-u-factured garbage?"

"Hey, take it easy," My Date said—apparently to both of us. I didn't need the advice.

I was confused and embarrassed. Finally I said, "I hope you're kidding, Mr. Bankable."

Instantly he came forward and put his arm around my shoulder. "No, no. Call me Rick. Please. Nothing personal. Nothing. Larry, get him a drink—of *course.*"

Then he said, "It's just that I despise pseudointellectuals. I despise the idea of anyone interfering with the creative process, you understand?"

I said, "Maybe you don't realize what editors actually do, Rick. I mean, lots of times an editor has an idea—sometimes he even rewrites —you'd be surprised how many famous—why you take Thomas Wolfe and Maxwell—"

Rick waved me silent. "You people shouldn't touch a comma," he said. "Not a single comma." He turned the light off. "Hey, Larry, what happened to the music?"

After that I kept my distance. Party. Food. No, I don't dance. Ellie disappeared into the bedroom with Larry. Rick, dancing with My Date, watched and laughed. They reappeared, Ellie first, Larry hanging back. Both looked at Rick. He laughed more.

My Date checked the play. "You're kind of a bastard," she said, and he beamed at her. The record stopped and he sat down again.

"You're right," he said. "Nevah denied it—*nev*-ah."

Like every actor he borrowed himself from himself without warning. Rick had scored unforgettably as a Southern courthouse lawyer a few seasons back. Now he invoked the man, the film, the award—with a gesture and a slurred pronunciation.

I said, "Bravo," and applauded lightly. Just trying to stay in the room, but oddly, it was the right thing. He laughed with real amusement for the first time, looked over at Larry Gopher and, following his look, I suddenly saw how anxious Larry was. He and Ellie were talking, always seeing Rick out of the corner, and although it was smoky and the records were playing they were standing in some kind of line. . . .

Rick looked at his watch, and Larry Gopher broke off his conversation with Ellie and stood.

"Hey, buddy," Larry said, "can I have a word with you?" He meant in the other room. Rick put down his drink, making the small move a piece of marvelous control.

"A word?" he said. "Of *course.* It's Christmas Eve." The smile brightened a notch—his hands were held in a characteristic gesture in front of him, about to conduct an invisible orchestra. The scene where he turns to the jury, of course.

Ellie drew her breath. "The courtroom scene," she said. She turned to me and whispered, "He's gonna do the courtroom bit, I bet. . . ."

But Larry Gopher ruined it by moving. He was very nervous. "I know you have to shove off, Rick—but there's something . . ." He was at the bedroom doorway, talking over his shoulder. "Could we . . . ?"

"In the bedroom? You and I—a little man-to-man talk in the bedroom?" Rick came smoothly to his feet—a little half-bow, smile unaltered, the familiar springing walk. "Back in a moment, ladies."

When the door closed, Ellie stopped smiling. My Date said, "Don't worry, hon. It's nothing to him." She didn't sound convinced, but Ellie brightened.

The bedroom door opened again. I couldn't tell a thing. Rick crossed the room briskly, picked up his topcoat and went straight to the front door.

"Ah what a tangled web we weave," he said, "when first we practice to conceive." His look gathered us, stayed on me. "Corny, you think? A bit tasteless for the circumstances?" He looked at his watch and opened the door. "Now that everyone's on the defensive maybe I can leave all you lovable parasites. I know you must have things to talk about. Merry Christmas." He made the exit and the door closed. Then it opened again. He looked in. All in place.

"I hate to ruin an exit—but," he turned to Larry, "did you order the car?"

"Pick you up at seven-thirty," Larry said. "I told him to wait and there's a table at the Polo Lounge later if you want to use it."

Rick beamed. "Good, good—they'll probably want to talk. Why don't you and Adele join us there?" Again the smile. "Later, everybody."

Ellie turned with the sound of the door and went straight into the kitchen. Larry followed. I turned to My Date and asked, "Who's Adele?"

In the kitchen Ellie said something angry and Larry Gopher said, "Oh shit—don't be like that," and then the water ran.

"I think the party's over, hon," My Date said, then, "Adele Gopher, Mrs. Larry." She began picking up glasses, emptying ashtrays, moving quickly and efficiently. When the glasses were all on a tray she went to the kitchen. The swinging door was closed and I started for it.

"See if you can find my purse, will you, hon?" She disappeared into the kitchen. I found her purse on the record player in plain sight and waited. In a few minutes all three of them reappeared. Everyone was smiling. I handed her the purse and kissed Ellie on the cheek and said Merry Christmas and it was time to go. To my surprise Larry Gopher was leaving too. He kissed Ellie warmly and patted her rump and we all chorused Merry Christmas in the doorway and then out and down-stairs by the pool. It was dark already—after six. The pool lights were on and the green garden lights in the shrubbery—and the traffic was quieter than usual for that time of night.

Larry walked us to the car and opened the door for My Date.

"I don't care what you say," he said. "He's going to lend me the dough."

"Bullshit," said My Date. She got into the car.

"I'm telling you," Larry said. "I know him. When he stuck his head back in—that cinched it. I'm telling you."

I got in on the driver's side. Larry came around and put his hand through the window, and we shook. "Awfully nice to meet you," he said. "Sure heard a lot about you."

That seemed to about do it. I nodded, grinned—another jumble of Merry Christmases and we drove off.

"Do you mind going over the canyon to my place while I change?" she asked. "I'm beat and I'd like to get comfortable before we tackle the tree. Okay? Turn left then at the light, there's a no-turn sign on Sunset, you know. Stay on it to Crescent and over Laurel Canyon, okay?"

"Sure," I said, slowing for the light. "Left here and then up Crescent and over Laurel. Gotcha, chief."

She punched my arm lightly. "You'll get your wings yet," she said. She leaned back and relaxed. The light changed and I made the turn, thinking about it all.

"Say, hon," I said, "that was kind of a tough scene at Ellie's. Did Larry really leave when we did?"

She sat up, surprised. "Of course. You don't think he had a pass for Christmas Eve, do you? Adele and the kids, I mean." She peered over at me. "You're kind of funny, hon. Square nice funny."

"Thanks for the nice," I said. "But what I meant was what about Ellie? I mean Christmas Eve and that—you think she'd like to come and do the tree with us?"

My Date laughed. "She'd be bored to death, you know. Besides, she's got a heavy date tonight—the Grove, the whole works. That's why she borrowed my fur stole—didn't you notice I left it there?"

I hadn't noticed.

"Well, pay attention, sweetie pie," she said, settling back again. "We ask questions later."

———

The other day the L.A.P.D. raided a club called Plato's Retreat (West) and the usual civilibertine news stories lit up the tube and the papers

—minus names and identifiable pictures. There wasn't much of a stir compared to what such items used to cause. Los Angeles is uneasy about sin. Even though it has always had the most publicity, it has probably never really ranked with Sodom, Gomorrah, Phoenix City or San Francisco. In New York, Plato's Retreat apparently functions as publicly as Bloomingdale's—perhaps with some of the same customers. But Los Angeles—Hollywood—has always been a little nervous because it's so obviously in the flesh business.

I have heard enough stories about orgies to believe—"Honest to God, we opened the front door and there was all this dim, red light, and when I could see, damned if everybody wasn't bareass naked"—but I've never made that scene (never invited as far as I know) and the only deliberate orgy I actually attended was not much.

A successful TV writer drunk on *Playboy* pictures and that all-out vision of perfumed sweat hired a purveyor of such entertainments to set up an orgy. "We rented this house on Mulholland Drive just for the night," he reported. "Be there before it gets dark, man. It's going to be wild, *wild!*"

"Why before dark?"

"Come *on,*" he said. "Don't you want to pick yours out?"

That sounded promising. He told me the whole event had been set up by a prominent girlie photographer whose credentials in such matters were unassailably impure.

In fact, I had met the man once at a Sexy Hollywood Party which I attended as a visitor from the East. It was a film-launching party at the producer's home. The movie was an upper-class skin flick, which is to say it wasn't very daring but the Names were recognizable. It was a summer afternoon. There were green lawns and trestle tables and the rental tents were going up when I arrived—early, because the producer was anxious to discuss a book-movie deal with me "before the action starts and I lose you." Yeah!

But there wasn't that much to talk about and he was quickly called away, so I wandered around, admiring the establishment. The attractive action was at the swimming pool, where a cadaverous, bearded fellow slung with cameras was clicking off pictures of a girl in the pool —bending, snapping, "Now jump up as high as you can! Great! Now on your back, eyes shut—smiling." Laughter and the pleasant sound of splashing water.

As I got there he was helping her out of the pool and onto a gaudy towel laid out by the diving board. It took me a minute to register that she was naked. The photographer was cordial, but the moment the girl heard I was a visitor from New York she tuned me out. Besides, she was busy arranging and rearranging herself on that towel while the photographer clicked away

All this time he had been hovering over her, of course. But now he put in a new roll of film, moved down to her feet and crouched. "Okay," he said, "let's do the beaver stuff now."

I had moved and crouched with him and now found myself gaping as she snapped her knees apart, twisted up onto one buttock and called, "How's that?"

Fifty feet away the workmen were staking and guying the clear-plastic tent walls: "Gimme a little slack this way, willya?" The sun was still high and I was sweating in my drip-dry cord suit. This was a while ago—but it's still one thing on your coffee table and another in the backyard.

I rose, but—was it insulting to look away? Besides, I didn't actually want to. So I moved up to the head end of the girl. She flashed me an automatic smile and took another pose. "Wider, honey," said the photographer, and she complained as he moved in close.

"That's the best I can do without dislocating it."

"That's good!" he said. Then, "Just stay there while I reload. Last roll —it's getting orange out."

She relaxed and I lit a cigarette for her. "Can I ask you a question?"
"Sure."

"I know it sounds dumb—but are you an actress?"

"Trying to be."

"Well—these pictures, do they help?"

She focused on me for the first time. "Help? How the hell do I know? It's publicity!"

So respecting the orgy, I could see that the photographer was qualified.

"It's costing me a bundle," my friend said, "but goddammit, I've been hearing those stories all my life, so when I got this chunk of dough I figured now or never."

"You mean the girls are hired to . . . uh . . ."

He was unsure. "It's a package deal. He quoted me a price to set it up and I'm damned if I know who gets what. Liquor, glasses, everything. Cheese sandwiches. Dip. You know?"

"Sounds great."

"Costing me a bundle. Every dime *Playboy*'s paying me. Oh, didn't I tell you? I sold them a story. They're paying good dough. Poetic?"

"I'll be there."

Mulholland Drive, a winding scenic road which runs along the crest of the hills separating Los Angeles city from the San Fernando valley, is dotted with romantic views and romantic houses. This was not one. It was a bony-looking two-story, white-painted clapboard house. So close to the road that cars were strung out along the highway, the house looked narrow and very upright and bare—in an area where everything else is horizontal, shrubbed and hidden. It was like having an orgy in a lighthouse.

It was bare inside, too. No curtains and drapes—just window shades through which the hot late-afternoon sun poured greenly. Aquarium light. Card tables, folding chairs and pillows. Floor pillows, hassocks, sofa pillows, bed pillows. Fringes and tassels and a lot of those huge cotton India print fabrics in tablecloth sizes and printed in discouraged reds and yellows and blues—mostly badly off register.

The girls were clustered together like dance-hall girls in a western, flanking a couple of card tables loaded with bottles and stacks of plastic glasses. There were a couple of big sacks of popcorn, and a radio was tuned to a pop station. There were more men than women—twice as many, it seemed to me. There was a certain amount of conversation and some laughter, but it was as if nobody there had ever met before. I stood for a while at the edge of first one and then another conversation group. Then I gave up. My friend was nowhere to be found, and I left without saying goodbye to anyone because I didn't know anyone to say goodbye to. As I drove away more cars were pulling up.

He phoned me next day. "What happened? I looked everywhere for you."

I explained that I had showed up, been discouraged, and gone. "How about you? Did you get your money's worth?"

"Did I! It was a blast," he said. "Took a little while to break the ice, but once it got dark and everyone got a little loaded—man, you should have stayed!"

"I was embarrassed," I said. "Let's face it. Some people have a talent for that kind of stuff and some don't. I felt like an idiot, so I took off."

"Yeah. You're right about that—I mean different kinds. . . . Well, it was an idea."

"Wait a minute," I said. "I thought you said . . ."

"Yeah. I mean no."

"No? But it was your party."

"Shit," he said, "don't I know it. There was this nice little blonde and I was talking to her—before it got dark, you know? And I explained it was my party and I even handed her some crap about casting in the next show . . . and I figured I had it made."

"So?"

"So after a while I ask if she wants another drink and she does so I say, 'Just stay right there and I'll be back with it,' but by the time I get back she's not where I left her. And by now it's getting dark and—no shit—some of them were really scoring, right there on the goddam floor and out in the cars."

"What about the blonde?"

"Oh," he said, "I had been putting it away and I was getting pissed about the whole thing. So I went stumbling through the joint looking for her. Every time I see some blonde hair I take a close look. You can imagine not everybody dug that—right? Anyway, finally I found her. I mean she's in the little bedroom and there's some joker all over her. So I bend down and I light my cigarette lighter so she can see me and I say, 'Hi—remember me?' And she looks right at me and says, 'Yes. But go away, will you? Guys like you make me nervous.'

"It's like a secret society," he said. "And I just don't belong."

Me either.

Maybe there is no secret society, no high sign and no passwords. But there are divisions which defy explanation: betrayers and betrayed, liars and the gulled. It is traditional to insist that the treacherous are, in the end, themselves betrayed—but as between men and women, I'd like to see some evidence, Lord. The impassioned arguments on behalf of women's rights are not easy to refute. But the betrayed wife attracts sympathetic understanding and legal support while the cuckold attracts snickers. To get through life without humiliation, it may be better to have the kind of mind which is suspicious of the habits of Arcadian shepherds.

I once asked Sinatra why he associated with riffraff. It wasn't a serious question, but the answer was straight. "It's relaxing," he said.

Therapy:

A fellow I know went through one of those brutal and never-final divorces which began with his humiliation and wound up with permanent servitude. He tore at his chains for a while, then grew sullen and morose. It's not unusual. But he didn't enjoy hating himself, so he went into psychiatry, reducing his standard of living to subsistence, and after some years emerged with a wisecrack and a slogan.

"My shrink said to me, 'You know, you're always talking about one kind of man with just as much fear and hatred as you talk about ex-wives. Agents. So I have a suggestion for you. When you're dealing with some woman, and you know she's probably as much a cheat and a liar as the others but you don't know how to cope with her, ask yourself this: *'What would an agent do?'* "

"What would an agent do?" But how does anyone know except in embarrassed retrospect after having made a fool of himself again?

Agents *know,* and they are not bemused by elegances about roads not taken, and that has made all the difference.

It's a kind of magic trick, I think. Only a week or so after moving west with a soured wife, a sick child and a toddler, the trick was demonstrated for me, and if I had had the wit I'd have become an agent then and there.

We were living near the ocean in a little shake-roofed house perched on a cliff. It gets misty out there at night and very quiet—far from city lights. About three in the morning the sick one started to cry, and it was at once apparent that we were out of the special formula. Something called Mul-Soy, I think. At that hour you don't waken the neighbors you haven't met to ask if they happen to have an exotic milk substitute— but I remembered the Hollywood Ranch Market. Eighteen or twenty miles away, but all you have to do is follow Sunset and turn right when you get to Vine. The Hollywood Ranch Market never closes. In fact, it has no front doors at all.

It was getting close to four when I arrived. The market was nearly empty at that hour—bus drivers drinking coffee and a couple of old ladies with those string shopping bags picking out vegetables.

The clerk rubbed his eyes and remembered that there were a few cans of Mul-Soy in the back room.

While waiting, I strolled into the magazine and paperback enclosure, a kind of high-walled pen made of wooden racks, with all the books and magazines on the inside.

There was a girl in there reading some large magazine or newspaper, holding it up before her so that she was hidden from the waist up.

I browsed without focusing, waiting for the clerk and the Mul-Soy. Then for some reason I turned toward the girl—and as I did, she lowered the magazine. Slowly, slowly. Her dark hair appeared, then her eyes, dark, heavily made up, looking straight at me. The magazine kept moving down. Her chin, her neck, her breasts. The magazine stopped moving and she stared at me without expression—two dark eyes and two dark nipples. Then her mouth twitched, she shrugged, and magically there was a halter top in place. She raised the magazine again and the clerk said, "Oh there you are. One can enough?"

What would an agent have done? I don't know. I went away and marveled and remained outside, maybe forever.

4

The Producer and the Hollywood Expert

MOTION-PICTURE producers are regularly asked a question which is never asked of directors or screenwriters. "What does a producer do?"

There are lots of answers, but the question is tough because the questioner probably wouldn't be asking it if he didn't believe that an honest answer would be, "Nothing much."

Several sad facts contribute. First, there's a confusion in terms. Studios and distributors—the people who put up the money—are also called producers. The MPPA, the Motion Picture Producers Association, the group which negotiates Industry contracts, deals with such matters as censorship and generally speaks for Hollywood, is known as the Producers, but its membership does not include those producers who actively make movies. Those fellows, also called "line" producers, are members of PGA, Producers Guild of America, and they are simply employees of the Producers in their corporate capacities. It's confusing enough so that even in Hollywood quite a few people think the groups interchangeable and producers are often taxed with the sins of the Producers.

Since the producer's functions are most effective when least visible, he's unlikely to get any creative credit even from the well-meaning critic or spectator or even actor, because they see no evidence of his contribution, if he made one. But the director's contribution, whether brilliantly creative or purely mechanical, is highly and publicly visible, while the screenwriter's is on record in black and white and multicolored pages. Somewhere there may be a screenwriter who tells his friends that the biggest improvements in the script—the best jokes, the most telling moments—were contributed by a patient and creative and sensitive producer. Somewhere . . .

And, of course, such paragon producers are probably no more common than such paragon screenwriters. It is also quite true that some pictures have been made without the services of a producer. Often as not they look it—but not always. There are directors who take over the whole function—people like Richard Brooks and others who make fine and difficult films without producers. Not without the function—without the title.

Stanley Kramer, a man of great reputation and one of the few producers generally credited with the films he produces, once told an industry gathering that the definition of a producer should be "The Man with the Dream."

Most impressive, and we attending dreamers sniffed our appreciation. But I notice that Stanley Kramer assumed the baton and became a producer-director as soon as possible. Now he directs all his stuff. Maybe he got tired of that look on people's faces, maybe he noticed that there's no Best Produced Academy Award. Of course, there's a Thalberg award for producers credited with a great record of film achievements—each of which was credited to the director when it happened.

Oddly enough, the second most often asked question is "How do you get to *be* a producer?" I've never been asked the question without wanting to turn it around and ask the questioner the first one—just to find out what *he* thinks a producer is and does. But something stops me. Guilt?

How does anyone become anything in an Industry which has no serious apprentice program, will admit no standards and does its best to keep outsiders outside? The essential difficulty is that the Industry is in love with its own dream of dazzling luck—the magical explosion of fame and money from nowhere! "Yesterday they told you you would not go far . . . next day on your dressing room they've hung a star. . . ." They want it that way.

Later on, when I was a working producer at 20th with a new wife and a big house in a canyon, the real-estate broker across the street from us asked me if I could find some summer work at the studio for his eighteen-year-old son, Bert. I knew Bert, a short, blond, mouthy, good-looking kid who asked a lot of questions about movies, wanted to take acting lessons and did a fair day's work from time to time helping me keep the ivy ahead of the crabgrass at a buck and a half an hour.

Maybe he could work as an extra? I phoned an agent I knew, asked him to introduce the boy to extra casting, then phoned casting and told them he was a friend of a friend, the usual thing, no arm twisting.

I'm not sure exactly what wires crossed, but the agent took young Bert into feature casting instead—and the next thing I knew, my buck-and-a-half-an-hour weed puller was cast as Robin, second lead in *Batman*. Whoosh.

Batman was hailed as a hit before it was seen on the tube. It was simply one of those times when everybody knew that this was going to be one of those freaky sensations—a Hula Hoop—zap—powie—maybe good for two seasons and then nothing. Everybody was right too. Except young Bert.

It takes a lot of experience or wisdom or plain pessimism for someone who suddenly makes it in Hollywood to believe it can ever end. The belief goes against the natural conviction that Goodness has finally triumphed, and Bert was not going to bite Fate's finger. Within a couple of weeks he had moved out and married (he was draft age, of course), and there was a child expected. Next, he had his father, mother and little brother barred from the set and from the lot because they made him nervous with all that winking and beaming. My agent told me Bert was quarreling with the Barrington Tower apartments because of their inexplicable reluctance to accept his baby gorilla as a housepet. Sadly, the gorilla died and was replaced by a lion cub—which was accepted. At this point, my agent friend was fired—"Bert said he has nothing against me but he needs more high-powered representation." By then the commissary was buzzing with stories of trouble on the set—bad words between Robin and Batman plus the usual challenges to the directors.

Since *Batman* was a full-time job for all hands and Bert had moved out of my neighborhood, I saw him infrequently—generally trotting between sound stages in costume, cape floating behind and followed by many people. Once he appeared quite unexpectedly at my office and talked excitedly about his production plans. He was going into feature production in a few months and he had always liked my ideas and he had never forgotten how I had been helpful in getting him started. . . .

Then there was a divorce. The other girl was one of those pretty people you hear about, and I gather it was a tough settlement—one of those "Give her whatever she wants only get her and the kid off my back so I can breathe" settlements. The series was peaking about then and the imitations had not taken hold—a sign that the fever had passed —but he was making large sums doing personal appearances at county fairs and such. How could it ever end?

It could and did, the way it always does—abruptly. There were debts and loans and even some racehorses which never got to carry Bert's colors. He had married the other girl and there was another baby and another divorce. Then his family sold the house across the street and moved away, and I didn't hear much more. My teenage daughter, in high school with the younger boy, reported one day that Bert had come home to live for a while and then left again.

As nearly as I can make out, *Batman* was all of it—when the series stopped and the personals ran down, that was that—but for the diminishing residuals as the show plays off into infinity. If Bert ever got another job in front of a camera, I haven't heard about it. Start to finish —maybe two and a half years. By now, he must be old enough to vote.

About "going Hollywood." You don't really need to buy a baby gorilla —someone will do it for you.

There's no grace period for newcomers, either. When I had been in Hollywood only a few weeks, attending staff meetings at Columbia and trying to figure out what I could do to justify my existence, I got a script from a writer friend back East. It arrived airmail special along with a letter wishing me luck in the new job and offering first crack at the enclosed. My friend had collaborated on the screenplay with a well-known television director, and they were sure it was exactly right for such and such a star under contract to Columbia, and they wanted me to be the first, etc.

No matter how vague my status, there was no question that I was supposed to be some kind of story expert. Unfortunately, what the Industry means by an Expert is not someone who knows his craft (except on the back lot) but rather someone with entree. The "inside track" to a best seller, the unlisted phone numbers and the friendships with "the one he *really* listens to," the private knowledge of who is "hungry" and where they need something right now to use up a pay-or-play commitment—that's what we mean by expertise. It's the procurer's game, of course—and while there's lots of talk about talent and quite a lot of respect for it too, the terrible dependency on collateral finally makes every decision. Even now, with all the brave and excited talk about the end of "The System," that dependency has only become more obvious and the demand for collateral more pressing all the way down the line. The numbers are larger, and some of the names may have changed, but the first question everyone asks is still "Who's in it?"

So my New York publishing credentials, while culturally impressive, had no practical use. Still, there I was, and the downtrodden, sourly skeptical story department waited to see what "New York's latest genius" would do.

Heading Columbia's story department at that time was Bill Fadiman, a man with scars of his own to display and whose welcome to me had been understandably muted. It's a sure thing that Fadiman had had it from some infallible source that I was there to replace him—it was more credible than the truth, anyhow, and it had just that believable touch of insult added to injury. Fadiman is a quite accomplished man; he has produced films and written and edited books, and his literary connections were at least as good as mine. My loudly heralded, vaguely titled advent must have struck Bill Fadiman like a sharp stick in the eye.

I could have said, "Listen, Bill, I'm not here to replace you," and made an enemy for life. Besides, after three months of uneasy discussions which left me without a title or a status as a member of some department or other, I wouldn't have bet on anything. The fact that Bill Fadiman was pleasant to me says a lot about his quality. Or maybe he didn't give a damn.

But meanwhile I had gotten this red-hot screenplay from my friend, who knew nothing about the game of Office Kafka in which I had found myself. To him, I was a West Coast movie exec—sitting within sight of the combination to the safe.

I read the screenplay and didn't like it, but rationalizations come easy when you need them. "Here's something a couple of friends of mine sent along—hot out of the old portable, y'know?" So I sent it along to Fadiman with a little note burning with modesty.

Three days later I got it back with a memo from Bill Fadiman which said, "We have seen this tiresome crap three times now. Your try makes it four. Since I don't seem able to convince your friend we're not interested, maybe *you* want to tell him this time."

I wrote my friend a somewhat overwrought letter saying for chrissake and what are you trying to do to me. And back came a telegram: MIGHT HAVE KNOWN YOU'D GO HOLLYWOOD STOP

5

§

"We're in the Monster-Making Business"

THE WISECRACK that history is written by winners is immensely satisfying to all of us injustice collectors. But except for historians Julius Caesar and Winston Churchill, both of whom were abruptly removed by the stockholders after they had made and written their versions, history, like everything else, is written by writers, a group who never think of themselves as winners no matter what they win.

Was there ever a Kipling's India? Were those deep white London winters a snow job by Dickens? Writers invent and reinvent history, tell us who we were and uncover sins and glories we only recall upon reading. In that sense, Hollywood, even more than Troy, is a bardic myth, a literary invention like Sherwood Forest and wicked King John.

The problem is that the stories are all told by disenchanted and rejected lovers. It's no accident that almost every Hollywood story deals with a brilliant and sensitive writer who *sells out* and gets a mouthful of ashes for his pains. Except Sammy Glick, of course—he sold out early and often, and even though he got his mouthful at the end of the book, Budd Schulberg seems to be saying that he was such a monster that he

40

didn't care. Probably *What Makes Sammy Run?* is the best of the Hollywood novels because Schulberg was too honest and too angry to pretend, as most have done, that the monster looked in the mirror and saw despair. Also, unique among those who have written seriously about Hollywood, Schulberg, son of B. P. Schulberg, had had a look at how it really works—how the decisions are actually made and the big jobs really filled. Most novelists, critics or even screenwriters are reporting the circus from ringside. They rarely know how anything happens to *be* there in the ring. The result is a Hollywood literature like grand opera, full of wicked barons and boundless depravity and the devil in a shower of gold. Arias: The house goes, the cars go—and so on. So they do. What do you expect from idealism overwhelmed by guilt?

At the end of one of those really awful days of shooting when the actor wept his inability to read that shit, when his agent couldn't be found and the director insisted on thirty takes and the cameraman took three and a half hours to light a simple two-wall interior because "that goddam idiot [the art director] didn't leave any place to hang the goddam lights," the whole thing was put succinctly by Richard Zanuck.

"We're in the monster-making business," he said.

So, with every screenwriter playing Beowulf to the Industry's Grendel, it's not surprising that the literature tends to be heroic and partial. Hollywood screenwriters, banded together in a guild of considerable wealth and astonishing militancy, are fervent champions of the Little Man. Perhaps the stridency of the attitude comes from an uneasy recognition that they are firmly and finally married to the enemy, as the eagle to Washington on the twenty-five-cent piece. Drenched in liberal-Democratic politics, sponsoring every minority crusade and passing flaming Jacobin resolutions for the press, these talented creators in their fierce tug-o'-war with the moguls have perfected a major contribution to culture—the blockbuster social drama, the lucrative rubber sword of safe controversy.

History's tidal change has left *Birth of a Nation* high and dry as almost the only major film example of *unsafe* controversy. What is usually billed as fiercely controversial is one of the innumerable variations of the same old snowball and the same old silk hat. It takes little enough courage to attack Moloch or the Military Industrial Complex or man-eating sharks and boy-eating mothers. But it is possible and profitable to be very publicly brave while doing so. In Hollywood, the Joe McCarthy era, the Blacklist and the Unfriendly Ten are Valley Forge —or the Sierra Maestra years, depending on age and hair length. That time of terror and exile and loss has become almost a race memory. It comes up in every political argument, even between people who weren't there or who weren't touched by it. There *was* a blacklist, and many people were broken for their political beliefs, and some talented artists lost productive years and suffered anguish (then and now and probably whenever politics and moralities become one). But as the wisecrack runs: Not all were talented, some were just unfriendly.

History says that for a while during the McCarthy decade, Evil triumphed in Hollywood. Certainly the ideological civil war of those days bred the spectacular invective and overreactions of these days. But even then, passion had to struggle with neatness. Jewish Jack Warner and Louis B. Mayer were prominent among the *fascisti.* Outspoken bigotry then and now was not confined to the wicked exploiting classes. It was and is loudest among the blue-collar, backlot union brothers, white, proud and impregnable in their immense beds of feathers. In Hollywood, it's always hard to get a clean shot.

During one legendary strike of those years, Warner Bros. is said to have manned the walls and parapets of the studio with armed guards, ready to fight off any attempt by the Reds to take over the empty sound stages. What would they have done with them? No one seems to know. But I've been told about those armed guards again and again by speakers to whom their existence proved "how close we came to a right-wing takeover."

The only proper test of it all is the films themselves. Did McCarthy-era Hollywood turn out a bunch of McCarthy-slanted films? As nearly as a fair judgment is possible in this very different, sadly similar time, nothing much happened in spite of the personal brutalities. A few baldly anti-Red films were released without making any lasting impression on awards or customers. Some of the major social-problem films of the time were *The Court-Martial of Billy Mitchell, Cry the Beloved Country, From Here to Eternity, Judgment at Nuremberg, The Man in the Gray Flannel Suit, The Naked and the Dead, Patterns*—none of them Joe McCarthy's vision, many of them skirmishes on the road to enlightenment.

It is only fair to note that during those years there were at least seven Abbott and Costellos, perhaps four Andy Hardys—but aren't there always? There was also *Baby Doll,* which drew more shooting and shouting then than *Deep Throat* later on. John Wayne's *The Alamo* was ideologically assaulted and defended much as his *Green Berets* a decade later. The interesting point is that in spite of Hollywood's well-documented passion for imitating success into infinity, *Green Berets* is childless. What major star or director or other breathing collateral would consent to ornament a promilitary, win-in-Vietnam war film? This is principled self-censorship. What else? Research reveals that during those years Ronald Reagan top-lined an undistinguished western called *Law and Order.* Aha?

Screenwriters come by their paranoia honestly. They are first hired and first fired in the long, loosely connected chain which is big-studio filming. If he has written an original story, novel or screenplay, a screenwriter has only a just-better-than-even chance of finishing the job and retaining a "solo credit." Screenwriters often suspect that there are other screenwriters hidden away from sight working on the same project at the same time. They call it "writing behind me," and it does sometimes happen. Screenwriters suspect that the producer to whom they're pitching an "approach" is listening only for the purpose of (a) stealing or (b) corrupting the idea. When a screenwriter is asked to do a "polish"—to touch up dialogue, point a few scenes in a screenplay which someone thinks nearly perfect—he will shake his head glumly and say, "Uh-uh. You got to throw the whole thing away and start fresh. Nothing usable here." But he's likely to be as quixotic as he is venal. Give him a screenplay thought to be hopeless and he's quite likely to come back with "You really want to know what to do with this thing? Shoot it."

Either way, he improves his own image at the expense of the Bosses.

Screenwriters are apt to combine sentimental toughness with unbearable loftiness. Ask a comedy writer why his guild is making some screaming demand and he is quite likely to answer, "In the beginning was the Word." And he will not crack a smile when he says it.

The problem is that he's more right than wrong, however painful his union militancy and his King James rhetoric. A really good story and a really well-written screenplay will survive poor direction, inadequate production and dull acting. In fact, it will often transform them, and many a one-shot genius owes that shot to a script he couldn't dent. But the reverse is not true—even in the old days, when audiences were said to have come just to be with their idols, there were idolatrous flops, and no star guarantees success today. The great directors have all lavished their touches and insights on dumb, dull pictures. The talent didn't fail, but no director can do more than generate a little spurious excitement for a few minutes at a time to hide the defects of an uninteresting story.

So how do you become a producer? The best way is to control a story or screenplay which everyone wants—actors, directors, Money. International best sellers preferred and no previous experience required.

6

§

A Brief Fling as In-House Procurer

I HAD ONE, *Sex and the Single Girl.*

My connection with that book, as with *Harlow,* was a by-product of my two concurrent divorces—broken home, broken office.

When Columbia turned off the phone, my days were left to isolation, Arthur Landau and the ghost of Jean Harlow; my evenings were being shaped by other limitations. Any studio executive being divorced by a wife of long standing is an automatic cad who has discarded her for one of those light-headed popsies—the ungrateful bastard. If the verdict is accurate, he's not too badly off. If not, he is exposed to a lot of dreary head-shaking without the compensations of sin.

David and Helen Brown were sympathetic, hospitable to me and My Date and cheerfully unsentimental about Shattered Lives. We were often there for dinner and for an endless, ferocious Scrabble tournament: the four of us wedged and intent around a huge coffee table in a little room windowed by a vast view down the seacoast palisades to Santa Monica, the bay and the flat Pacific.

Along with the letters, we matched problems. David was a story executive at 20th Fox—left over from the *ancien régime* of Darryl

Zanuck. Day by day he watched the water rise around Spyros Skouras as the studio wallowed and sank under the sodden weight of *Cleopatra*. Helen was a copywriter at a local ad agency, gritting her teeth about one of her bosses who bullied and undervalued her in the traditional way.

We were not a group of hot prospects. Among the four of us we had already racked up five or six divorces, so jokes tended to be a bit edgy. At some point of an evening My Date was likely to announce that if she had to hear another goddam word about my goddam ex she was going to goddam kill herself and/or all of us. She knew a lot of five-letter words for plaintiff.

The Hollywood of those what-the-hell divorce jokes like "how-do-you-like-your-new-father, we-had-him-last-year" is in the actor, fan mag and column world. It's the only one that makes the papers, and it's perfectly real, even as actors are perfectly real, but it is quite separate from the ordinary citizens of the Industry; part of the product, not of the process. That separation, in a world where everything is brilliantly visible, can be bewildering. But the laws for caterpillars are altogether different from the laws for butterflies.

About six weeks after the Great Silence descended, I was summoned to the office of a studio executive. He did not want to talk about my career; he wanted to know if I would get him a date. The question struck me as more insane than flattering—the executive was a young man, good-looking and a chief assistant to the head of production. He was married, but they were quarreling and she'd gone East. How about it?

I said, "Why me, Mel? If I was in your spot they'd have to put in a laundry chute for the traffic."

"The hell you would," he said. "That's what all you guys think. Anyway, I saw you at that Christmas thing on Stage 12."

"So?"

"So I asked around," he said. "She works extra, right?"

"Okay."

"So what the hell. They always have friends, don't they?" Us-guys-together time. I knew who *they* were, and, of course, I thought of Ellie.

"As a matter of fact . . ." I said, and his cheeks glistened. He got up and came around the desk. Us guys together. What the hell, she'd probably get a kick, and who am I to and everyone takes care of and—

"You're pretty sure about her?"

I was pretty sure about her and him and me.

I said, "Look Mel, she's just a girl I know—a friend of my friend, you know? I mean, how do I know?"

"Sure thing," he said. "I rely on your taste—I mean, she's probably got a little class—like your friend on Stage 12, right?"

Now I knew why me. Type-casting. You want a classy hooker, patronize a classy pimp.

I said, "She's an actress."

He looked wary.

"Nothing serious," I said, "but I can tell her you'll help out—a leg up, so to speak?"

He ignored my comradely leer, got up, went back behind his desk, sat, fiddled with a pencil and then leaned back. His smile had become pensive. Automatically I leaned forward, and there we were in the classic negotiation tableau—I pitching, he catching.

What in hell was I negotiating?

"Tell you what," Mel said. "Why does she have to know who I am?"

"Why not?"

"Well—you said about a job. . . ." He frowned. "I can't do that—I mean, call up Quine or Goetz or someone and say, 'Listen, I got this girl here . . .' I mean, it looks like hell, doesn't it?"

"I suppose so."

"Of course. You can see how it is, can't you?"

"Sure." I got up.

"Where you going?" Mel said. "Jeez, you got a short fuse." He paused delicately. "No wonder it's hard to get you squared away here."

Right in there.

I said, "Mel, you know that Jacob Adler joke—about the girl who comes backstage, and afterward he says to her, 'I'm an actor, I give tickets. You want bread, go fuck a baker.' So she's an actress, she wants to work, what's the matter with that?"

"I heard that joke," he said. "You know who tells that one great? Lou Holtz. You ever hear him tell it?"

I had not.

"So what are you getting sore about?"

"Sore?"

"Come on. Sure you are," Mel said. "And I don't blame you, hanging around all this time . . . nothing off the ground . . . rough." He hesitated. "And the divorce thing, I can imagine. I got a little headache of my own in that department. Probably you heard?"

I nodded.

"Sure," he said. "Everyone knows. What the hell does *she* care? Everybody."

"All I heard was she went to New York," I said.

"Sure." He went dark with it. "And where do you think she goes in New York—the St. Regis? Shit."

"Not the St. Regis?"

"Ha," Mel said. "Not her. She goes straight to the company's apartment, so everybody will hear about it right away. Already Sam calls me —why don't I fly in over the weekend? A lot she cares if I look like a jerk."

I bicycled in the suddenly deep water, unprepared for the burst of intimacy. I needn't have worried.

"So I have to be careful, you see?"

The intercom buzzed. He flipped the switch, flashed me a smile. "Gloria, hold my calls a couple. Who? Well, tell him I'll call him right back. Five minutes."

Now me. Wrap-up.

"Why don't you fix it up, kid? Anytime next week. I'll tell you what —why don't we double? I could send a car for you and you could pick her up and we'd meet somewhere—"

"Hold it," I said. "You're losing me. I'm not supposed to tell her who you are—just make a date and pick—"

He broke in. Whoever had called was clearly important. "It was just an idea. Go ahead, tell her who I am. But listen, I'll leave it up to you, okay?"

"But no job promise? So what do I tell her—Perino's, Chasen's, what?"

"Chasen's!" The brakes squealed. "You kidding? You might as well put it on the tieline. Come on, quit the crap. Check out someplace out of town—Pasadena. I hear there's some great places to eat in La Jolla —you pick one, let me know, and I'll meet you. Okay?" He was looking anxiously at the intercom.

I said, "Should I tell her dutch?"

He laughed and then stopped laughing. "You're a big-headed son of a bitch, aren't you?"

"Right," I said, getting up.

He stared at me, shrugged. "Have it your way, kid. Now beat it."

I went to the door, opened it and tried a last shot. "You want to know her name?"

He was already on the intercom. "Get him back, Gloria."

That was on a Thursday. That night I told My Date, who took a cool view of my righteousness.

"You could have asked Ellie," she said.

I said, "Wait a minute. You understand what that bastard was doing —playing me like—"

"So it's not Bible class," My Date said. "What have you got this way?"

On Monday Mel wasn't in the studio. Then word got around that he'd gone to New York to bring her back.

I may have saved that marriage.

Now that Sunnybrook Farm has been turned into a commune it's hard to remember that *Sex and the Single Girl* was turned down by several publishers as too rough—"just asking for censorship problems." Published by Bernard Geis, it was bitterly reviewed as a "nonbook," attacked for its "brazen vulgarity" and denounced by a literary elite which even then was ready to die for Lady Chatterley's right to ball the gardener but contemptuous of the dime-store clerk's hunger for the ass of the married assistant manager.

The book's huge success, the elevation of Helen Gurley Brown into absolute celebrity and the subsequent success of *Cosmopolitan* magazine with her at the helm took a while to impress the literary upper classes.

The book is unforgivably middle-class, nonideological and without spiritual agonies. It is full of tips on how to win the game, not how to kill the umpire.

Having played literary obstetrician to *S&SG*, I got custody of the motion-picture rights. At first, that was roughly equivalent to the breakfast rights to a china egg—but when the book took off, we all got thoughtful. *They* had bought many another book just for its title, hadn't They?

I concocted a yarn—something about computer programmers who use the machines to find out where the men are and program a sensational marital heist—told it to a friend, who told it to Max Bercutt, publicity chief of Warner Bros., who told it to Walter MacEwen, executive head of that company's story department, who sent back along the vine an invitation to come in and talk about it.

Late one afternoon I went in and sang my song to Walter MacEwen, who nodded pleasantly when I finished, buzzed an intercom and said, "Can you see the guy now about *Sex and the Single Girl*, Colonel? Yes. David."

Affirmative. I was led through an adjacent office belonging to executive assistant Steve Trilling into a book-lined corner alcove, one wall of which abruptly opened. Down a short passage, a couple of stairs, another door, and I was in another office. Facing me, behind a desk, Jack L. Warner. I was announced and left alone.

Mr. Warner stood up smiling, holding out his hand. From the waist down he was undressed to his shorts. I missed his hand first try. He followed my look.

"They're in Wardrobe getting pressed. Got to go out from here," said Mr. Warner.

I think I said, "Thank you."

The rest of the interview blurs in memory except for two moments. The first came when I launched into a pitch about the book. He waved me off.

"Know all about it," he said. "I even know it's dedicated to you."

The book is dedicated "to David." David Brown.

I didn't argue, and he flowed cheerfully on. Mr. Warner laughed a lot, told rapid-fire jokes and expected a response. Later on, listening to him carry on in the dining room, I was able to distinguish words from music —and, in fact, he was pretty funny. But during that first meeting I laughed every time he bared his teeth.

The second clear moment came when he broke off, reached under the desk and came up with a record album, still crisp in cellophane. He handed it to me.

"Can you understand this?"

It was a German version of *My Fair Lady.* On the back side, all the lyrics in German, no English translation.

"Sure thing," I said. He waited. I read one verse of something or other in my high school Yiddish-flavored German.

He took the album back. "Great, hey? You're okay, kid."

That was the end of the interview. He pushed a buzzer and MacEwen's voice said, "Yes, chief?"

"Come on in," J. L. Warner said.

Walter MacEwen reappeared and I stood, uncertainly. He gestured me back through the doorway. "Wait in my office."

I waited about ten minutes, and back came MacEwen. Very cheerful. "Let's talk deal for the book," he said.

We haggled, arrived at a number within the limits the Browns and I had discussed. I said I would have to check with them and let him know.

"Fine," said MacEwen. "Now what's your deal going to be?"

"My deal?"

"Aren't you going to produce the picture?"

I was.

As a matter of fact, I almost did.

7

I Exit
Sex and the
Single Girl

WARNER BROS. gave me two offices connected by a secretary and a pleasant, energetic comedy writer named Ben Starr to translate my "story idea" into a screen treatment and then, upon approval, a screenplay. It's what's called a "step deal." I myself was hired for one year as an employee assigned to the development of *Sex and the Single Girl.* Glazed in euphoria, I nodded when it was explained to me that I had no rights in the project itself, that I could be reassigned, fired or whatever. After all, why would They have hired me if They didn't intend . . .

My name went onto the hall door on a card inserted into a bracket—which stuck out at right angle, visible from quite a distance. At Columbia my door had had only a number.

Starr now shines brightly on television, but then this assignment was the big league for him—a solo credit, a best-selling book, a major feature! We adored each other and we brimmed with creative hilarity and we churned out pages and scenes and sequences at a great rate and in gusts of mutual approval. I would hear Starr laughing in the adjoining office, then a chair scrape and then his voice approaching, still full of laughter. "Testing, testing," he would call out, reading as he came. "Remember where she's stuck at the airport and they give her the wrong bag? Right? With me? Okay. Well, now hear this . . ."

I listened, applauded, suggested—and the pages rolled on. One day MacEwen congratulated me on how much work we were getting done. "Good stuff, too," he said.

I was so pleased I forgot to ask him how he knew.

A standard lunchtime gag in every studio commissary is for someone to follow a caustic or irreverent comment by picking up a table item (water glass, ashtray, vase or what have you) and whispering into it as if it were a microphone, "If you're listening, Darryl"—or J. L. or Mr. Mayer or Harry or Sam, etc.—"I didn't really mean it."

We laugh, not disbelieving. Every studio is full of "swear to God saw it with my own eyes" stories of peepholes, bugged telephones, hidden cameras and recorders and so on. Most of the stories are at least preposterous, at most insane—but they may be true for all I know. At Warner Bros. there was said to be a fellow who went through desks, just to make certain management was getting everything to which it was entitled. It was a house rule that every rough page, every sheet of notes, every false start on every screenplay had to be turned in to management. Why? Did anyone read it all? It is unimaginable except for the fact that it was demanded and usually ignored. But Starr and I, marveling how MacEwen knew about the pages, did the stuff with spilled powder, hairs across drawers, pages arranged just so. And we were convinced, angry —and delighted by the heady, mean excitement of it. It gave us a great sense of persecution and of consequence.

"Testing, testing . . ."

The weeks clicked on. I began to think of myself as a word on a screen credit. The guard at the auto gate learned to recognize my car so I could just slow down and wave graciously as I entered Troy each morning. I had a parking space with a nameplate.

Then one day I turned in the screen treatment to a cheerful Walter MacEwen and only a day later was summoned and beamed at and told to "go ahead into screenplay." Starr and I were jubilant and we told each other we were an irresistible team. "Testing, testing . . ."

One day MacEwen phoned to tell me I was expected to take my meals in the executive dining room—"The Chief told me to tell you he expects to see you there."

Of course, Starr was not invited—and our long, hilarious lunches came to an end. He was graceful about this evidence of caste, happy for me and satisfied with this confirmation of his militantly union-labor attitude. "The goddam bosses, they should only drop. Not you, bubbe —They."

J. L. Warner's executive dining room was located far from the commissary, and served from a separate kitchen presided over by a chef named Emilio, said to have been imported from some famous European restaurant and giving every indication of same. To be welcomed to the quiet, wood-paneled, crystal-and-china-set dining room by him was an unsettling experience after the brassy cafeteria atmosphere of the commissary, full of table-hopping actors and the loud jokes from the writers' table and the constant flash of teeth and eyeballs as everyone cased everyone else—"Who's she?"

In the executive dining room it was quiet, the cloth was white, and the long refectory table was flanked by a sideboard loaded with sweets, great bowls of fruit and cheeses and boxes of cigars. Emilio greeted everyone by name (he knew mine before we were introduced), and after cheerful inquiry as to health and disposition he discussed the day's menu. "Mr. David, today we have a choice of consommé, jellied madrilène or lobster bisque to start," and so on right through the meal, individual orders taken and filled for each course right through to dessert and cheese. I'm probably not the only cultural aspirant to learn that cheese and biscuits come at the end of the meal—and learn it at J. L. Warner's table.

I also learned a good deal about the care and selection and preservation and cutting of cigars, although I never learned to savor them myself —maybe because I never learned to lean backward in the chairs, an attitude indispensable to cigar smoking in the Company of Men.

Admission to the private dining room was by invitation, not by right, and was said to be limited to executives, producers, directors and honored guests. I never saw a star there—rumor had it that J. L. had said, "I don't need to look at actors when I eat," a remark which has his style, true or not. The sole exception is said to have been Jimmy Stewart, and he, according to my informant, was invited as an Air Force general, not an actor. Having heard Mr. Warner speak his mind a few times, the story is credible to me.

Mr. Warner sat at the head of the table and told jokes. Since the rest of us tended to cluster at the far end, there was sometimes a gap of half a dozen chairs between Mr. Warner and the first laugher. Fortunately, MacEwen and Wm. Orr (a son-in-law in charge of TV production) and a couple of others had permanent places near the head of the table. Sooner or later one or more of them would turn up to block J. L.'s view of the chorus, and we could stop trying to eat through a fixed grin.

Mr. Warner was not unkind to me personally. Not then when I was a new bulb, plugged in and burning bright; not later when I was discarded, still burning, because WB needed my socket.

Hollywood raconteurs have made J. L. Warner legendary. A widely told sample has him onstage with a group of Japanese dignitaries at an Industry Let's Be Friends Again right after WWII. Speeches were made, toasts were drunk, and the main Japanese guest acknowledged them all in an emotional and graceful pledge of eternal friendship.

Then it was J. L.'s turn, and he is said to have turned to the speaker and said cheerfully, "Great . . . great . . . and no more of that Pearl Harbor shit, right?"

I wasn't there, but a lot of people say they were. I myself once saw him introduce Lana Wood onstage by saying, "I don't know why she's here—I guess we're trying to make a deal with her sister." The sister is Natalie, of course; but the point worth noting is that all of us laughed. All of us. Including Miss Wood.

Nothing so grand in my case. Although I sat at that table for many weeks and listened attentively to lots of jokes, I don't think Mr. Warner ever actually knew my name. He called me something else—memory fails, but it was simply a name, not a nickname or a joke name, maybe Ralph. "Hey, Ralph, you know I used to direct two-reelers?" Like that.

It was part of the odd streak of impersonality out here—an impersonality which crops up in strange places. One of my favorite directors is a guy who gets laid a lot. (This is not hearsay, I have shared a location bungalow with him.) But he has met so many pretty and willing girls in so many offices, hotels and dressing rooms that their names—and sometimes their faces—blur together. He once asked me to do a favor for a blond girl working for us and, unable to remember her name, described her graphically:

"Comes up to about here, kind of green eyes and a funny laugh, you know"—an imitation—"and this white, white skin, you know which one I mean—beautiful skin, white like powder or something, I mean, her ass on a pillow like you'd have to use dulling spray. *You* know"—snap fingers—"the little one that made breakfast the other morning *You* came in—right?"

I knew her name and I knew her clothes had been in his closet for two weeks.

Well, the nameless girls have come and gone (literally, one hopes), and when I meet one of them, she speaks of him with real affection and always asks to be remembered. They worry about his health, his college-age daughter whom he openly adores, and the grosses of his latest. They invite him to all their weddings. They say of him, "He's nice—you know? Nice man." He is. But he doesn't remember their names.

Mr. Warner's impersonality was more like that. He had seen so many of me come and go that he dealt with me generically—just one more pretty face laughing it up in the executive dining room. "Testing, testing . . ."

Starr and I were diligent and optimistic, and I reported to him regularly on the whims of the upper classes. He worried for a while about Warner's calling me Ralph, but finally concluded that the name indicated affection. "Look, bubbe—he doesn't *have* to call you *anything*, does he?"

The screenplay grew, we visited each other's houses on weekends and talked about casting. Why not? If J. L. didn't know my name, he surely knew the book was becoming a huge best seller, and MacEwen beamed regular approval of the pages. So we were optimistic while remaining cautiously professional.

"What do you think about Natalie Wood?"

"As a lady computer programmer?"

"Yeah—but she's under contract here and they're supposed to be looking . . ."

"I think she'd be great."

"Well, I can go either way too."

One day I lingered outside the executive dining room until MacEwen came out.

"Got a minute?" he said.

"I was waiting for you."

We strolled.

"How much longer do you figure?" he asked.

"Couple or three weeks."

"Think you can finish by the first? That's a little over two weeks."

He was brisk and cheerful. "J. L.'s been asking."

"Sure thing," I said. A good sign. They were in a hurry because the book was hot.

"He's going to the Springs that weekend and he'd like to take it with him, okay?"

I pledged.

"Good," MacEwen said. "So we'll close Starr out on the 30th. Right?"

I nodded, not having thought about that part of it and not having mentioned Natalie Wood, either.

Starr was philosophical. "They're a bunch of cheap pricks," he said.

"That makes it exactly eight weeks and *They* don't want to pay for an extra week on my deal. That's how *They* are."

He was right. It was and it is.

"They've got fourteen days' reading time," Starr said, "then one set of changes. Two weeks. Maybe Gloria and I will get out of town for a week."

I said, "Let me know where you are, just in case."

"Don't worry," Starr said. "The screenplay is great, the book is hotter than a dollar pistol—everything's going our way. Tell him Natalie Wood. MacEwen."

We wrote FADEOUT three days ahead of time, sent the pages to Mimeo, and on the appointed day I said goodbye to Ben Starr and brought ten fresh mimeographed scripts of *Sex and the Single Girl,* screenplay by Ben Starr, to Walter MacEwen, who promptly buzzed Mr. Warner.

"David's here with *Sex and the Single Girl,* Colonel. Shall I send him in? Right."

He turned to me. "J. L.'s on his way out," he said.

"I'll take one in to him. See you next week."

He headed for the passage to J. L., I for the outer door. At the passage entrance he turned. "Good work," he said. "You're going to do all right around here."

Late Monday afternoon MacEwen summoned me. The smile was altered and he was holding out a script as I approached. "Haven't heard from J. L. yet," he said, "but meanwhile I'd love you to read this script. Got the time?"

I took it. The working title escapes me, but it was a comedy by David Schwartz, a writer with a number of good feature credits and a reputation for being much in demand.

"Right away," I said, and left with the script. Home free. They're looking for more projects for me.

Bright and early next morning I reported to MacEwen, enthusiastic but cautious.

"The script is very funny," I said, wondering exactly how to put it, "but it's quite a lot like *Sex and the Single Girl,* isn't it?"

He beamed. I went on. "I mean, the story's not the same, but it could easily *be* the story, couldn't it? This lady psychiatrist who writes a best seller about sex—"

MacEwen nearly embraced me.

"Exactly right," he said. "You could shoot this just about the way it is, call it *Sex and the Single Girl* and have a hell of a picture, right?"

"Testing, testing . . ."

A full minute is a long time for a decent burial in these matters. What will I tell Ben Starr? You'll think of something.

"This script's fully approved," MacEwen said. "See?"

He showed me another copy with a scrawled approval on it from Mr.
Warner.

"And I think we can give you Natalie Wood for the girl," he said.
"She's under contract here, you know. She likes it."

Ben Starr took it well enough. Like most screenwriters, his assump-
tions about executive perfidy were simple and complete. He didn't
suggest that I should have gone down in flames with him and he didn't
ask the obvious, embarrassing, painful and pointless questions normally
asked at this point: Did you fight for our script? What did they say when
you told them they were making an idiotic mistake? Maybe he was kind,
maybe numb.

Enter David Schwartz, older, balder, small-spoken. An obviously decent professional. He knew what had happened and spent no time on
it, which was merciful. What did I think of his script, *Sex and the Single
Girl II?* In fact, I was awed by it—uncertain as to whether I was really
expected to do more than nod.

"It's all approved," I said. "MacEwen told me so."

Schwartz shrugged. "It's your picture," he said.

When something goes wrong for you at a studio, you become aware
of it first by a kind of cone of silence around you. People respond when
you speak to them, but they never speak first. And, of course, no one
ever calls you back.

I forget what I was waiting for—a budget meeting, a casting callback
—but whatever it was, it didn't happen. Nothing happened.

For about a week. Then I called my friend MacEwen, my sponsor, the
unfailing returner of my calls. It took him a day to get back to me.

"You want to come in?"

"Yes. You busy now?"

"Uh, I'm afraid so. Could we make it late Friday afternoon?"

Two days away.

Late Friday afternoon I watched MacEwen fiddle with the pencils for
a while. Finally he told me he had bad news for me.

"We've decided not to make the picture."

Flabbergasted. Big best seller. Approved script.

Natalie. Tony. What? What?

"And we won't be picking up your option when it comes up nine
weeks from now."

Fired.

"I know how embarrassing this must be for you, so I've talked them
into giving you half of your remaining salary."

Fired again.

"So you can leave this afternoon."

Fired Fired Fired Goddam.

I said, "I'll have to think it over."

"We can send the check to your home?"

I said, "I'll be in on Monday, Walter."

He shrugged.

I am something of an expert on getting fired. Since coming to Hollywood, I have never quit a job—the best I can claim is a draw on one —but out here it's not much of a claim. You've heard jokes: Don't let that son of a bitch on the lot again unless we need him, etc. They are generally expressive of the root belief of the people who own the business that it's all a huge scam—that anyone allowed room at the trough should slurp and be grateful. So the major reason for firing is rarely incompetence—after all, who knows? It is usually ingratitude in one of its myriad forms.

Or simple necessity. I soon learned this was my case at WB.

I was told that William Orr, Mr. Warner's son-in-law and head of the TV operation, was being pushed out of his berth in some intercorporate coup and the only alternative for the company was to make him a producer of feature films. *Sex and the Single Girl* was ready and I was expendable.

It made sense to me—at least it explained the inexplicable aspect of MacEwen's story, the statement that they were not going to make the picture. They were, but not with me.

Knowledge was hardly power in this case, but it was important to me to know that I was not being fired for incompetence. On the other hand, the most I could hope for was full payment—WB could easily wait me out, fire me and *then* make the picture.

On Monday I told MacEwen I proposed to sit out my contract in hope of better things. He looked pained.

I said, "Walter, we've been friends, haven't we? So admit to me you want the picture for someone else and I'll take the money and go quietly. Okay?"

He looked hurt. He protested. He temporized and soothed. He understood my ill temper and he wanted to keep me from doing anything rash—anything that might jeopardize my future in the picture business.

"Just admit it," I said.

He asked me to leave his office. Dignity, man.

There was another full week of this. MacEwen never admitted anything. Finally he told me he'd been able to get the studio to pay me the full amount left in the contract—the condition being that I sign the paper and be off the lot by five o'clock that day. I did and I was.

It seems to me that this was on a Wednesday—and that before the week was out the trade papers carried the announcement that William Orr was the new producer of *Sex and the Single Girl.* The cast announcement followed by a few days. Tony Curtis, Natalie Wood, Henry Fonda.

Next I heard from my Friend Who Knew that David Schwartz was doing an extensive rewrite—and after him, someone else was called in to punch up the laughs. The film I finally saw was a broad farce. The script I left behind was a straight comedy, Ben Starr's was a satire. Proving?

Interviewed on TV recently, Henry Fonda was asked whether he had ever appeared in any pictures whose memory still makes him shudder.

"Sure," he said. "Quite a few."

"Would you name just one—maybe the worst?"

He didn't have to think. *"Sex and the Single Girl,"* he said.

So I was out in the street again, having come pretty close. I had been named a producer in the trade papers, which made me free to announce upcoming projects in the hope someone would bite. I had several weeks' salary and a handshake option on an unpublished manuscript, *Von Ryan's Express.*

8

I Enter
Von Ryan's Express

DAVID WESTHEIMER came to Hollywood from Houston, Texas, where he had grown up talented and mildly Jewish. That meld had brought him, by stages, to newspaper work—television editor for the Houston *Post*. He learned to smoke cigars, tell funny stories and write clear, easy, storyteller's prose. He began to write novels and came to Los Angeles. Later on, when *Von Ryan's Express* had become a best seller and while we were working together on the screenplay, David would peer over his glasses at me and the furniture of a producer's office at 20th Century–Fox and beam. "Damn. If the boys on the paper could only see me now!"

Westheimer has a famous joke. He has it because he's swarthy, dark and curly-haired—a Texan Cushite with a high voice and querulous drawl. When his deal on *Von Ryan's Express* was announced in the trade papers, a delegation of Screen Writers Guild socio-paladins welcomed him clamorously, "A breakthrough—a black screenwriter!"

It occasioned embarrassment—and some suspicion. Westheimer is always being hailed as a brother—and he rarely argues the point. Which brings me to his joke: "I'm passing. But nobody knows which way."

I first saw *Von Ryan's Express* while sitting among the ashes at Warner Bros., waiting for MacEwen to drop the other sabot. The sign over the door still trumpeted my name—a friend had talked me out of substituting the word "unclean." So when David dropped in, it was the visit of a wistful writer to a going producer. (He had no way of knowing just how going I was.) We'd been friendly for some time—after all, he was a book writer trying to be a screenwriter and I was a producer who spoke book.

I asked about the manuscript he was carrying.

"It's a war story," he said, adding, "I think Doubleday's going to take it. They're damn nice—considering they've been having a hard time making my advances back." I remember doing the traditional publishing joke. I took the manuscript from him, hefted it and said, "Feels like a winner."

"Want to look at it?"

I wasn't doing anything else.

Von Ryan's Express was marvelous—an obvious best seller and, most rare, a perfect film story.

Given adequate light, a camera will photograph anything it's pointed at. Still, the kind of story which is called filmic is not common in spite of guilds and workshops and college courses. Instead, endlessly, films are drunk on camera virtuosity—dazzling-blind, evocative images which feed the sense while the mind rejects boneless events and speeches. The photographers who can elevate the foaming of a poured beer into orgasm on Olympus are helpless when she speaks and he speaks and—shit—it's Dick and Jane.

Of course, any story is a movie story—and even though we no longer make those films where time dissolves in a riffle of calendar pages and the snowy branch sprouts first a bird, then a bud, and so on back to snow again, we revel in different clichés. "A story should have a beginning, a middle and an end—but not necessarily in that order" only gave words to what the flow of images had long since made intelligible. Once the camera got behind the proscenium and into the mind, everything was possible. Technically there's no story film can't tell. But there are stories which fit the medium as the sonnet fits the page.

Von Ryan's Express was a fantasy fulfilled. The real David Westheimer had been one of a plane crew shot down in southern Italy early in the war. After a time in Italian POW camps he and the others were loaded into boxcars and taken north to Germany, where they spent the long years behind the wire.

In *Von Ryan's Express* a similar bunch of POWs are crammed into boxcars and headed north, but—led, frightened and inspired by steel-

and-whipcord West Pointer Ryan, they capture the prison train and, in a series of breathtaking and just barely possible adventures, take it across the border into neutral Switzerland.

In *Von Ryan's Express,* escaping prisoners were helped by valiant Italians. In Westheimer's express, the prisoners actually did escape from the train during an air attack. David says the valiant Italians helped round them up and put them back onto the prison train.

Ryan must have been born on that train ride. They could have used him. (He was *such* a martinet, so ruthlessly hard on his own men that they called him Von Ryan. "You'll get the iron cross for this, Colonel *Von* Ryan," and so on. Hate him, fear him, follow him. Kill the guards, capture the train, "Does one of you speak German? Here, put this on.")

Later on David wrote another book about the prisoner-of-war experience. It is called *The Song of the Young Sentry* and there is no derringdo in it, only a series of portraits of men he knew, what they ate, how they dreamed and squabbled over food and tiny scraps of possession. What it was like. It is a true and touching novel of a fat boy, imprisoned by his fears and the uniform and the war and the captivity, making prison a home and growing up anyhow. It's a quiet book and no one has filmed it.

I told David what I thought about *Von Ryan* and he was pleased. He asked if I liked it enough to do the film.

"Absolutely."

"You got a deal."

No numbers were discussed, no papers were ever drawn between us. Only once before the production deal was made did he ever ask a question. There are not many Texan Jewish novelists here or anywhere.

I was elated. The evidence of *Sex and the Single Girl* was conclusive —any inexperienced idiot with the screen rights to something They want is a producer; it's the only screen credit the studios hold negotiable. After all, as any producer's kid will ask him sooner or later," a writer writes, a director directs—what does a producer do?" So any number of jugglers and trained bears have been called producers—credited the same way as David O. Selznick. But a trained bear with *Von Ryan's Express* is well on his way. PRODUCED BY URSA D. MAJOR.

Through a well-placed friend in publicity I let the information leak through to MacEwen. "Tell you what, Walter . . ." I was not going to hold a grudge. "Maybe a two-picture deal—*Ryan* first and then something we can mutually agree on." In fact, generous. "Let's not talk about *Sex and Single*—but I *own* this one, right?"

MacEwen bit. In typical style, he asked my friend to get him a copy

of the manuscript without my knowing. I obliged, told Westheimer the
game. He promised to act surprised.

A weekend later my friend called. "You're in, kid—MacEwen *loves*
it. He'll be calling you."

I waited all that day and the next. No call. My friend was surprised
but supposed They were probably embarrassed. "You know how it is,
kid—after this other thing. They probably want to get the whole deal
worked out. One bite—y'know?"

In the evening of the third day I got the phone call. It was from David
Westheimer. I wish I could reproduce that gentle, querulous pitch—I
still hear it.

"Saul? Uh, hey—I sure hate to ask you this kind of a question, but—
are you really pretty sure you can make a deal for *Von Ryan?*"

What? "I've never been more sure of anything. *Von Ryan* is a natural.
You know, I'm just waiting . . ." Then I said, "Why? Something happen?"

"Just a second," he said, and I heard him laughing and saying something to someone else. Then he came back on.

"I'm sure glad you're all that confident," he said. "Y' know, Dody's
on the floor, but I told her it would be all right?"

Dody is David's wife. Red-haired, Texan, enthusiastic, a great maker
of chili with a laugh to make the quail fly all over the state.

"Dody?"

"It ain't nothing," David said in the mother tongue. "Only that guy
MacEwen just called me here and offered me fifty grand for *Von Ryan's
Express.* When I turned it down is when Dody hit the floor."

"Turned it down?"

"Well," David said, "I told him it was your option and MacEwen said
did I have any papers with you and I said no. So he said—well, you know
what I mean . . . they didn't want you to do the picture. . . ."

"So you turned him down flat?"

"Hell, Saul—we got a deal, don't we?"

David had once told me that no book of his had earned more than
five thousand dollars. He lived (and lives) in a modest pool apartment
and has two young sons, who were younger then. No wonder Dody hit
the floor.

I said, "Give me two weeks. If I can't make a deal you can always go
back to MacEwen."

"Naw," said David. "Take all the time you need. I wouldn't want to
make a deal with anyone who'd do that."

To me, one of the great movies is John Ford's *The Long Voyage Home.* In a picture full of indelible images, perhaps the strongest one I carry is the vision of the men just come ashore—met and greeted by the smiling, anxious, servile little man in a bowler hat who lures them down to Joe's Place. Bobbing, ducking, grinning, whining along, touching an arm cajolingly—harmless and terrifying as he lures them to the drugged whiskey and the crimp's blackjack. Remember? Nemesis. Rubbing his hands and helping. "Whatever you want, gents . . ."

My helper was large, plump, rosy-cheeked and young. He didn't wear a bowler hat. But he came in grinning and bobbing, full of good will, humility and scorn for my enemies. Harris the Agent was always brisk and cheerful. Like many people out here and most agents, he had a disarming joke. Disagree with him and his gums would flash, his pale eyes roll upward. "Hey, pal—I can go either way."

Like all agents he was tuned in—he not only knew I was on my way out of Warner Bros., he also knew that I had a "hot" property. Doubleday had indeed accepted *Von Ryan's Express*—and along with that good news came better. The Book-of-the-Month Club had gone for it too. In publishing that's the jackpot. With that news, *Von Ryan's Express* was an anointed best seller. By Hollywood-agent standards it was already a smash hit, exquisitely ripe for the agent game.

Who in his right mind would buy anything less than a best seller, Manny? No one. So don't buy anything that hasn't sold a bunch of copies, right? Wrong. They cost too much—sometimes you gotta, but Jeezus, the exposure, I mean, who can do that without something to sweeten the package, improve the odds? So in modern Hollywood, best sellers are usually optioned by stars, directors "package elements" to improve the odds. What the hell, Manny, the fucking actor is gonna cut a chunk right off the top anyhow—you know the bastard's deal. So let him come in with the goddam thing—we're screwed either way.

So the best time to sell a best seller is before it actually is a best seller —at that magic moment when the seller is hopeful and his ambition still small, and the buyer is aflame with the hope of getting a big one cheap, nervously hoping to screw 'em all this time. You've got something their tongues are hanging out for—then you talk deal. Forget the gross, baby, if you want the part. Dreams—the natural nobility of the art which is not quite its own reward.

Naturally, young Harris didn't say any of those things. It would have been unbecoming. Instead he said, "I'd like to introduce you to a friend of mine. I think you two guys would like each other. Dick Zanuck."

I was shrewd. "You know Dick Zanuck?"

"One of my best friends."

"Why would he want to meet me?"

"Well," said Harris, almost shuddering with his respect for me, "I know what kind of a guy you are—your background and all—so I took the liberty. I mentioned you to Dick—not that he didn't know about you. . . ."

The hook went in. "He did?"

He made an appointment for me. Tomorrow morning, nine o'clock. I was impressed, while Harris showed quiet joy to be of service to a major figure like me.

"I told you I know him," he said. Then, "Mind if I come along?"

Dick Zanuck, famous son of a famous father, is a short, athletic young man with a tight, low-keyed manner and a profile like Dick Tracy's. His office then was in a wooden bungalow on the lot at 20th. The main administration building was still closed—the studio had been empty and vacant for nearly a year before Zanuck Senior took command in New York and appointed his son to run the studio. Grass was sprouting through the cracked asphalt, and great clumps of ragged, overgrown hibiscus and oleander scratched at the flaking stucco stage walls. Yucatan or Beverly Hills, the jungle reclaims its own.

Deferential Harris introduced us, backed off and sat on the sidelines while I pitched *Von Ryan's Express* to Zanuck, who listened intently, asked a few questions about the plot (as I recall, he was concerned that the ending was complicated) and then said, "I think it's terrific. Do you own it?"

"Not exactly," I said.

In my life so far, the speaking of six optimistic words has cost me more than my father earned in his entire lifetime. The words are, in order, "I do," "I will" and "Not exactly."

Zanuck heard and understood instantly. He looked at me and gave me one more chance. "Who represents you?"

I fell to the occasion, turned to Harris the Agent and said, "He does."

It was a heartwarming moment. I have thought of it many times, in many courtrooms, trying vainly to convince a series of judges, lawyers, Internal Revenue folks and even friends that I never participated in the enormous profits from *Von Ryan's Express.* Or *Our Man Flint.* Or *Fantastic Voyage.*

So my very own agent made me a deal as a staff producer for 20th Fox. That meant that for a weekly salary, I was at the studio to do its bidding. I was assigned to *Von Ryan's Express.* He told me it was a good deal, and I did not complain. Knowing little, delighted to be working,

I signed the paper and said thanks, making only one condition—that David Westheimer be employed to write the screenplay. Actually, David's deal and the deal for the novel itself were not negotiated with me, so I was without say in the matter. Had I said the option was mine and hired any attorney to close the deal for David and me . . . those two shares of Coca-Cola stock would have . . .

So now I had a contract and a project and an agent who was a friend of the boss. I could see how that friendship would be a great help to me —give me an inside track. And with the killer instinct of a lemming, I had just remarried. The future (as we once headlined a book jacket) lay ahead.

9

§

The Author as Disposable Tissue

"**W**HY DO YOU guys always change everything?"

"Like what?"

"Everything, damn near. The only movies I can remember where the story is the same as the book are *Gone with the Wind* and *The Wizard of Oz*. I suppose those were just too famous for you Hollywood geniuses to screw around with."

"Wrong. Read the books. We screwed around with them too!"

Out here the expression is "You can just about shoot the book." It is used a lot by grand old filmmakers like Mervyn LeRoy and top-echelon studio executives who have approved the purchase of a novel and then waited, drumming fingers through weekly production meetings, while the months roll by and the screenplay is "not quite ready to show yet, J. T."

"We had to get another writer, J. T.—Luke Quiverlip just wasn't getting the relationships you liked in the original material. . . ."

"Who'd you put on it?"

"A new kid—dynamite writer—did all the changes on the new Paul Newman picture, without a credit, of course, but they tell me he saved the thing. Meiklejohn Haze—Maze, that's it, Mike Maze."

"The Newman picture looks like a bomb."

"Oh—?"

And so on, as the costs mount. MGM owns a little book—*Forever,* by Mildred Cram, a novella, really, which the studio bought a decade ago for something in five figures. By now, accrued script costs—that is, the cost of attempts to wring an acceptable screenplay out of this story— have mounted to close to seven hundred thousand dollars. You may be sure that when they bought it—in the rush of euphoria that accompanies the purchase of "hot properties"—someone was saying, "We'll have the goddam thing in the theaters by Labor Day. Shit, you can just shoot the book."

Producers die of coronaries, agents of cancer. The people who live forever are the professional counterpunchers and nay-sayers.

The rationale is clear enough. Pictures being what they are, a prophecy of doom is odds on to be correct. Should the unlikely occur, jubilation erases all scars. "It's gonna do twenny million domestic, baby. Love ya."

When I came to 20th with *Von Ryan* the Zanucks were still plungers in a game increasingly dominated by wrong-bettors. They were a remarkable team, compulsive, competitive filmmakers to whom the way out of every disaster was straight ahead. "Make the picture."

So when Dick Zanuck said "Go," he meant it; when he said "Stick with the book," he was saying what we all believed. Only that highdiver's belief would have allowed him to make a deal putting a producer who'd never made a picture in charge of a writer who'd never written one. Mission: Make an epic.

The screenplay unrolled swiftly and easily. From time to time I sent pages down to Zanuck. He read them at once, scrawled comments and suggestions (with a Pentel pen) on the margins, invited me down for a talk if the matter was complicated. It went well, and iᴸ was the book, compressed, edited and simplified. David took to typing in one corner of my office while I paced and mowed the air for inspiration. "Wait, hold it—how about this?"

Jokes. Collaborative work on screenplays breeds a kind of running hysteria, and the by-product is either murderous hatred or a series of "killing" inside jokes.

One day David came in laughing around his cigar.

His younger son had finally focused on the change in Dad's life.

"Dad," he'd asked, "the man who runs the place where you work— is that *Darryl* Zudnick?"

So we started feeding the leader's name into the screenplay. A village, scene of an action sequence, was called Zudnicci. If the prisoners saw an old movie, it was *Zanook of the North*—terrific stuff like that. We cackled and wrote. It was summer, and the main administration building had been painted and refurbished. Zanuck now inhabited a majestic suite on the first floor—a suite that went on to a small kitchen and a john and a private staircase leading down to the steamroom and pool and executive barber shop below. From my window the view stretched west, over rooftops of sound stages, through tall eucalyptus out to Santa Monica and the sea. On a clear afternoon I could see the distant glitter of water, the shadowy blue bluff of Palos Verdes rimming off to the left in the blue sea haze. The studio was filling with people and projects, the commissary began to be noisy, the shrubbery was clipped and fragrant. In the morning there was a pungent smell of manure and wet earth as the rehired gardeners labored to rebuild the lawns and restock the flower beds.

The script grew. We argued, laughed, rewrote, acted out the parts and felt great.

David was intoxicated with the language of film writing—the abbreviations and the traditional jokes. MOS—*mit*-out sound, a transliterate dialect tribute to the days of Central European Herr Direktors in puttees; fades and dissolves and traveling shots and closeups and cutaways—the high signs and secret grips of Them. In that draft of the screenplay we had a scene in which a bridge collapses, and when David showed me his version of it, I read a page and shouted, "Christ no. You can't do that! *You can't cut away to Fincham when the bridge is falling!*"

I must have struck an attitude—Horatius at the literary bridge or whatever—because David looked up from the typewriter over his steel-rimmed half-glasses and suddenly capsized into a fit of laughter, whooping and yelping like the Alamo. "You can't cut away to Fincham when the bridge is falling"—over and over in a gasping falsetto. Screams of laughter. And finally, when breath returned—"Ain't it the truth. . . ."

It is, but sometimes there's no choice—as we would learn. So we pounded out the pages, and Celia D., the beaming maiden lady secretary who had followed me from job to job, typed and approved and sent the pages downstairs, where Dick Zanuck cried encouragement.

Then one day we were done and the typed pages transformed into blue-covered, mimeographed scripts.

"Terrific," Dick Zanuck said. "We'll make final changes later, when we get a director and some cast, so we won't have to do too many rewrites."

"Can we start budgeting?"

"Why not? Ask Stan to throw an ax at it."

So I took a script across to the production bungalow where I had first met Dick—where now Stan Hough presided over the tools and personnel and costs of actual filming, a job of enormous complexity and responsibility, chief of staff to the studio commander.

Stan is a tall, rangy man with the style of an ex-baseball player—which he was—plus great competence and an exasperated sense of humor. In those days he had two vices. He was a secret writer of screenplays and his personal loyalty to Zanuck was absolute.

Everyone knows that loyalty is a virtue most often honored in the breach—but out here that has a special flavor. *They* expect and get loyalty from underlings who don't expect and rarely get it back. Like prayer and incense, studio loyalty rises to heaven from a missionary position.

But even among the centurions and janissaries, Stan Hough's loyalty was notable. He revered Darryl and loved Dick—not blindly, but unswervingly. So when I brought him the screenplay, Stan said only, "Let's just hold off for a couple of days until we hear from the old man."

Darryl Zanuck. I had never seen him—studio gossip had it that there was a legal/domestic reason why he couldn't show up at the studio. But a huge suite of offices bore his name anyway, and to most of the Industry Zanuck meant Darryl. To me, Johnny-come-lately, it meant Dick.

In fact, especially in the early days, it meant both. Dick told me once that he and "D. Z." spoke at length every day, sometimes repeatedly—that every problem and every opportunity was discussed at length. I didn't know that then, but Stan Hough did.

He was wise to wait. In about a week there began to arrive a series of letters and cables from New York, Paris, London, Rome—all from "D. Z.," all addressed to Dick, all containing criticisms, comments, suggestions for *Von Ryan's Express*. With the first of them it became apparent that he wanted large changes.

Dick was mildly embarrassed. He could not pretend the changes were his idea, but he tried to adopt and endorse them. Only once did he betray the exasperation he must have felt—that time he sent me a copy of the cable with "(!—RDZ)" scrawled on the margin with his Pentel pen. That cable contained one of D. Z.'s wilder improvisations—the suggestion that somewhere in this prison train "there ought to be a boxcar full of girls—maybe with their heads shaven—I haven't thought it through yet but will fill it in later stop."

Executive criticism is traditionally blunt, violent and indirect. Darryl to Dick to me—with Dick generally voicing the criticisms as if they were his own, softening or intensifying the blow as seemed necessary.

The indirectness continues down the chain of command. When a picture is shooting and They are frothing over rising costs, lousy dailies, delays or an ill-fitting bra on the girl, the producer is called on the carpet, screamed at, threatened and instructed.

"You go down there"—the set, the location—"and tell that cocksucker"—the director—"that he better stop playing with himself and make up those days! Got me?"

There's a good reason for indirection. The instruction is meaningless because there's never an "or else" attached. Every director worth his salt assumes that They are his enemy and the enemy of Art and Reputation. He also assumes that the producer is the running dog of Front Office Imperialism and he (director) will not be moved.

"I *told* the illiterate bastard that it was going to take sixty-five days. I *told* him you can cut all the time you want on the schedule but I think it's gonna take sixty-five days! So don't come sucking around me."

"But he says you *promised.* . . ."

"Promised!? They cut the damn schedule on me and I said, 'I'll try.' So I tried."

"But isn't there some—"

"Excuse me, willya—I think he's lit"—meaning the cameraman. "Don't want to waste time, do we?" Calling to the set: "Ready? Come on, people . . . places."

So the front office rages at the producer and New York rages at the front office and it is said that the banks rage at New York. *They.*

What became painfully clear was that *Von Ryan's Express* interested Darryl Zanuck, the man who gave you *The Longest Day* and a long series of war pictures before it. Colonel Zanuck.

David Westheimer stopped laughing. What Colonel Zanuck wanted was a much harsher, far more traditional war adventure. David remembered the Italian POW camps with mixed emotions—his Italians were gentle, quirky and no fans of the Germans. Colonel Zanuck wanted them mean as hell, cowardly and low-comic, except for the one good guy, of course, small differences of attitude adding up to a large difference about the tone of the movie and remembered truth. Colonel Zanuck objected to a line in which one of the POWs, just after a brush with Ryan the martinet, smarted off to a friend: "Bird colonel—you bet he is—chicken!" Colonel Zanuck said that no enlisted man would have said that, pointing out that he was a colonel and therefore *knew.* David had been a lieutenant while I rose to buck sergeant in that same war —and we thought we knew too. Wrong.

Behind the scene, something else was working. The novel had become a best seller. Management thinking about the size and scope of the film was being revised with the sales figures. A project which had begun as a nice little WWII adventure was becoming a Big Picture. And somehow that Big Picture had been placed in the hands of Little People, David and me.

The very weakness of my position protected me, I suppose. It was not necessary to fire me in order to make a Big Picture. The studio which had made a producer of prizefighter Fidel LaBarba could accommodate another coffee carrier. But Westheimer had to go.

When I was employed in my first studio job at Columbia, I saw the principle demonstrated. Producer William Goetz, one of the great names of Old Hollywood, was at Columbia, preparing to make a film from one of the later novels of Erich Maria Remarque—a Class A project all the way.

At one of those executive meetings in Sam Briskin's office the production was discussed.

"Who's Goetz want for screenplay?"

Story editor Fadiman said, "We've been talking to Presnell—Goetz likes him and he seems to have a lot of good ideas."

"Who?"

"Bob Presnell—Robert Presnell, you know? He did—"

"I never heard of him," Briskin said. "What does he get?"

Fadiman looked at his notes. "He got thirty-five on his last credit— I think we can get him for under forty for this one."

Sam shook his head. Some people never learn. "Forty thousand for a Bill Goetz picture? You can't do that. For Goetz you gotta get somebody better—like for sixty, seventy-five thousand."

Years later I told the story to Bob Presnell, who said only, "I knew we weren't asking enough."

When this happens the writer is said to have "written himself out" —a phrase which every WGA member translates as "the son of a bitch didn't know what he wanted so he sold me out." Often true, but not always. So Darryl instructed Dick and Dick told me and I told David Westheimer he was off the picture—that another writer was being sought. "Who?" David asked.

And I, like a famous Tammany mayor of New York, said, "They haven't told me yet."

Then David said the first of two bitter things I ever heard from him. "You stayin'?"

I don't remember what I answered, if I did.

So David Westheimer left the *Express*, having created the whole thing, shown courage and loyalty and humor and having written a screenplay which was enthusiastically approved by the man supposedly in charge—until suddenly he was "written out."

Months later when I showed him the accepted new screenplay with an Italian prison camp full of desperate, starving, maltreated POWs, David made his other bitter remark. "What you gonna call it?" he asked gently. *"Bridge on the River Po?"*

10

The Screenwriter as Pinch Hitter

NEXT UP WAS Wendell Mayes, who arrived late one morning, looking like a man kidnapped off a yacht.

Screenwriters come in many styles, but even the ones who affect mousiness have some way of letting the disdain seep through the tatters when they're called in to fix a script. A producer interviewing a second writer is, after all, a man who has shamelessly cast off the tired old first wife who stood by him when things were tough. . . .

Maybe he wasn't wearing a blue blazer, white slacks and an ascot at the throat, but I'm positive he smoked a cigarette in a holder—something I associate with Dutchess County, New York—and I seem to remember his saying something about not really knowing much about these army things because he was a navy man himself. Phillip Reed, remember him? He played lovers and weak older brothers. Wore an ascot, and sometimes a fine wool turtleneck, way back then in black and white.

Mayes had been working on and for a Big One. *In Harm's Way* was to be a naval epic of WWII for Otto Preminger, but work had been suspended and Mayes given a sort of furlough with the understanding that he'd be recalled to sea duty later on.

Mayes was not my selection to follow Westheimer. In fact, I had learned of his impending arrival only on the morning of the day we met.

"I gave the stuff to Wendell Mayes," Dick Zanuck said. "He *loves* it. He'll be terrific, don't you think?"

I said to Mayes, "Dick Zanuck says you love the novel."

He laughed. "I think it can work."

A really competent and experienced screenwriter does not minimize the task at hand. Given the Bible with the original cast, a screenwriter will sigh, smile bravely and say, "I think I can *lick* it"—an expression which is not misleading. *They* were dehumanizing the enemy long before helicopters were invented. We don't talk about novels and short stories—we buy *best sellers* from *synopses* and then read *the full material,* which is then given a *treatment* or maybe a *step-outline with cutoffs* before going into screenplay. So first you figure out how to *lick* it.

Mayes didn't think *Von Ryan's Express* was all that much. A war adventure yarn, useful, not great.

"I guess They want an action picture," he said. Then he added, "It would help if I could have some of your ideas—after all, it's your picture. What did They *say* They wanted?"

Careful now.

I said, "Westheimer and I did a screenplay—did you get a chance to look at it?"

"Oh?" His manner changed. "Did you work on it? I didn't see your name."

"Yeah, well . . ."

"I'm sorry," Wendell said. "Sure, I read the screenplay. As a matter of fact I asked Zanuck why don't they just shoot it? I can't do any better."

I knew enough to wait.

"But he wants it *different,* doesn't he? Darryl Zanuck? More action, more adventure—more of that crap, right?"

"He thinks the right script can attract a major star."

"I doubt it," Wendell said. "But I'll come in tomorrow and we'll try. Okay?"

Some writers pour out pages and then throw them away. Some want to tell everything before putting it on paper; some write in longhand on lined yellow pads and some scrawl and rescrawl at angles over and over on the same pages, joining paragraphs with arrows which loop around the margins and between cramped lines. Some want to show you every line, others hide as long as possible and hate to show anything less than a retyped, bound and titled work.

Mayes, a thorough professional, would show pages every few days and consult on problems. What interested me was his vision of what the problems were. I began to realize I was lucky.

In the bitterly conflicting claims of screenwriters vs. directors, I lean reluctantly toward the writers. Maybe some directors have transformed stupid screenplays into brilliant films—but I have not seen them. Most directors like to rewrite, but very few can.

What Wendell did was examine every scene and sequence not only in terms of story content but also and especially as a visual experience.

"How can we make the escape more interesting?"

In the novel, the prisoners, penned in locked boxcars, grab one of the German guards when he comes to feed them, pull him into the car, get his gun and uniform and so on.

He fretted. "What else can we do with that?"

I grew impatient. What was wrong with the way the book worked? Surely that's about how it *would* happen.

"Yes. But it's dull."

He called for research on WWII Italian railroad boxcars.

The air vents? Too small. The windows would be noticed. The roof?

"You know what would be great?" Wendell said. "If they could *dig* their way out. That would be different."

"Why not?" I said. "The floors are wooden."

And so they were. Out of that grew one of the film's major sequences —a long, tense build from despair to hope to action to a great stunt, as the prisoners pry up the floor timbers in the swaying boxcar and, one by one, drop to the roadbed, slide and roll free, missing the wheels by fractions! *Heart-stopping suspense! Electrifying action! Don't miss it!*

The months passed. Both Zanucks liked it now, and I got no more Penteled cables. Talk turned to actors—the regular shuffle of bankable names. Burt Lancaster is doing *The Train* what about Paul Newman his deal is out of sight Bill Holden can't work in this country for tax reasons and we want to make part of it here Kirk Douglas is doing something besides who wants and there are those guys like Steve McQueen and James Coburn but how can you take a chance on new . . .

Richard Burton, Jack Hawkins, Trevor Howard—we talked about them all. But idly, just warming up. When you are serious about one of Them, you send the best and most finished screenplay and a firm offer. Many stars and their agents simply refuse to read a screenplay unaccompanied by a firm offer.

Wendell admitted that the project was looking impressive. It was still one of *those* pictures, as far as he was concerned—but "if They give you enough money you might get *something* out of it." And in his elegantly casual way he added, "We're having some people over Friday night. Think you can make it?"

It was an address in Bel-Air. Like everyone else, Wendell had a little map imprinted on the invitation which arrived the next day.

Bel-Air is probably the most elegant of the bedroom subdivisions of Los Angeles. It is an immense area of green canyons, curving roads and scenic vistas in which mansions stand, some as isolated and splendid as Italian hill towns, others tantalizingly seen as a flash of stone and white pillars behind walls and gates and rhododendrons as you drive by. Glimpses of statuary, fountains and slated mansard roofs seen through foliage which drops off suddenly to sweeping green hillsides, empty but cared for. Bel-Air is roughly rectangular, stretching westward from Beverly Hills toward the sea, rising from Sunset Boulevard, which wanders along the base of the Santa Monica range, to the top of the mountains which divide the "City" from "the Valley." Whereas in Beverly Hills multimillion-dollar homes shoulder each other—all plainly visible from the street, all set back the same distance—Bel-Air estates hide from the tourist and the sightseeing buses. In Beverly Hills there are sidewalks and kids playing in their Little League uniforms, riding around the block on shining French ten-speeds, past driveways clotted with Corvettes, Mercedeses and Cadillacs. But in the *real* Bel-Air there are no sidewalks and no sight or sound of children; the car behind you, urging you not to dawdle, is either a delivery van or a Rolls with tinted windshield or one of the cars of the Bel-Air Patrol, a private police force which is a lot more in evidence than the West Los Angeles police who are supposed to "protect and serve" Bel-Air.

Real Bel-Air (which residents call "Old Bel-Air") is rimmed, at the very crest of the mountains, by a much newer section which comprises nine-tenths of the Bel-Air population in perhaps one-tenth of the acreage. There the subdivider's aesthetic is plain—the variations on "California Ranch Style" line the curving streets and tricycles are seen in driveways. There's a shopping center and a hospital and a real-estate office—"Bel-Air address, 3 BR w pool & view, a steal at 485M."

The Mayes' house was one of those, a California ranch house set close to the road. Like many houses out here, the front was essentially blind. These houses face their backyards, pools, patios, barbecues and views. It was a big party, cars lined the street—and the front door opened to that gust of party sound and that special mixture of Mexican canapés, expensive cigars and heavy perfume which is as native to Hollywood parties as parking attendants. Wendell made the introductions, leading me from room to room, past sofas and card-table groups; the usual blur of faces and names and grazing smiles. There were perhaps thirty or forty people, none of whom I recalled having met before but all of whom seemed to have known each other since childhood. A lot of familiar names, some famous. I remember only Billy Wilder, hunched over a card table, playing and talking with great animation. He acknowledged the introduction with a jerk of his chin and without missing a beat of the story he was telling.

When in doubt, smile, nod and eat the guacamole dip. Hot, isn't it? What? Uh—hot . . . the dip. Oh . . . Edge into a conversation, miss the point, try another group, sit on the arm of a sofa, have another drink. What time is it getting to be?

Then my host reappeared, leading a lion. "I think you know Mr. Preminger," Wendell said.

I had met Otto Preminger once before. Bantam Books had just published the paperback edition of *Exodus* with gratifying success—books melting off the racks, sales department beaming and reorders pouring in.

It had not been a successful meeting. What Preminger had in mind was that Bantam should change the cover of its edition to tie in with his advertising campaign. To facilitate matters, he had prepared the whole cover—a stunning symbolic design by Saul Bass with bold lettering which said, "Otto Preminger's *EXODUS.*" Somewhere below it added, "Novel by Leon Uris."

When I explained that our cover was already a success and that we would change neither the art nor the authorship, I got a glimpse of the Preminger temper. He told his portfolio carrier there was no point in discussing with fools, suggested that he would take the matter higher and left. Bantam continued to publish with the same front cover, although I think notice was taken of the Preminger film in some other way.

Now Preminger remembered me and said something graceful, and we shook hands, standing. Next thing I knew he was making an announcement.

"Mr. David has generously released our host to me so Wendell Mayes can return to the screenplay of *In Harm's Way*"—something like that, oddly phrased, I remember.

In the small silence I blurted, "Hell I have!"

He had already turned away; now he pivoted, massively, like a bronze door.

"You refuse?" He could hardly believe his ears.

"I'm sorry," I said, "but we're not quite—"

"You are not quite—to me?"

He was bellowing and, as I remember it, advancing. Maybe not, but I do remember his voice continuing after me as I tried to get out of range, tacking from room to room, looking for my date and the doorway. As I got there Preminger rounded the living-room corner, still shouting. Behind him a glimpse of Wendell Mayes, choking on suppressed laughter. He waved, I waved, and out.

I was summoned to Zanuck's office next morning. He was on the phone as I entered, his hand over the mouthpiece.

"Get on the extension," he whispered.

It was Otto Preminger, explaining forcefully and in detail how rude I had been, how inconsiderate, profane and stupid. "You know, Richard —I met this fellow once before in New York. He was a shit then and he is still a shit, you see?"

Dick nodded happily. "I know what you mean, Otto," he said. "The guy's impossible. Everybody says so."

Preminger calmed down. "Of course he is only a beginner. No doubt he will learn."

"No doubt," Dick said, strangling, "if he lasts that long."

Preminger grew kindly. "I don't mean to do him harm—just tell him Wendell Mayes is leaving at once and it will be enough."

"Gee," Dick said, "I wish I could, Otto—but I can't."

"What? You won't let Mayes go?"

"Not until he's finished—another few weeks."

"Another few weeks!?"

"Afraid so, Otto."

"You dare—" I could hear him inhale. *"You are a shit too."*

Slam.

Dick put down the phone and grinned at me. "Can you be done in another couple of weeks?"

"Sure," I said. "I guess so. Why? What'll he do?"

"He could sue us," Dick said. "He's right, you know. I did tell him he could have Mayes back when he needed him. Didn't you know that?"

I didn't. I was filled with admiration.

"Dick," I said, "you really are a shit too."

"Sure," Dick Zanuck said. "We all are."

11

Enter the Star:
The One and Only
Sinatra

A COUPLE OF weeks later the draft was done and Wendell Mayes left *Von Ryan's Express* for *In Harm's Way.* This new draft was duly mimeographed and bound, and production estimators and department heads began breaking the pages down into sets and props and travel costs. We creative people began principal casting.

At a studio, principal casting is not done by the casting department. Like war, it's too important to be left to professionals. And too much fun.

The Sunday paper says that fewer than two percent of Americans earn more than fifty thousand dollars a year. But if you are a "major" creator at a studio, it is quite possible never to meet anyone who doesn't make at least that. This is more a result of defensiveness than snobbishness, since it gets harder and harder to play the egalitarian game with people who hate your imagined success as much as they long for their own. It gets very mean at some of those parties. After a while it's easier to stay home and be comfortable among mirrors.

All of which makes for devastating social currents and undertows. Beverly Hills, the best-protected community on the planet, probably houses more vocal cop haters than Harlem. Those kids who drive foreign cars and Corvettes to the immense parking lots at Beverly High are mostly dressed like mendicant friars—barefooted, afro-topped, beaded, frayed, tasseled and smelling of Brut and pot. Beverly Hills took a referendum on the Vietnam War and opted out by a good margin. Like Lenin's Russia, Beverly Hills left the war early, on moral grounds.

They boycott lettuce and eschew table grapes and are convinced that Richard Nixon is a closet anti-Semite—a powerful gut reaction stemming from a wincing Yiddishness which they do not concede except perhaps to the shoals of doctors, lawyers and psychiatrists whose offices line the cross streets. *Sorry. We do not validate.*

The community surely supports more furriers per capita than New York, despite the climate. And police or no police, it magnetizes burglars. Ringed by Chinese restaurants and belted by branches of the great department stores along Wilshire, Beverly Hills may have fifty percent of that two percent.

But if everyone is rich or talented or generous or democratic or sick? It's tough to feel it when all about you is the evidence that God is post-Freudian and that comfort heals only one generation. Watch a Beverly Hills matron pulling her long car out from the curb. An imperial wave of the hand and zoom! "You saw me put out my hand, mistter!" These ladies cannot be intimidated except by their decorators, their hairdressers and, of course, their children.

For these fierce, proud, cultivated and nervous humanitarians, the motion-picture industry is Kipling's Great Game—they die in its service and the rewards are medals. Their pleasure comes down to manipulation—finally, nothing else engorges the ego.

So casting, "putting it together," is one of the real uses of power—a process that brings out the Byzantine richness of the Industry, user and used, one flesh. Since I was the producer, I was full of constructive ideas. The flaw in my thinking, of course, was that it proceeded from the outsider's view; I was trying to find actors who seemed to embody the people on the pages. The Ryan of the book and of the script was one of those Nordic lion tamers—Hitler's own vision but on Our Side. Burt Lancaster, Kirk Douglas, Brando dyed yellow for *The Young Lions.* What about one of the rising people—McQueen, Coburn? The same names as before. When casting, you say the same things about the same people over and over again, hoping for incandescence.

Late one morning, Celia, my secretary, picked up the phone, said, "I'll tell him," and called around the corner to me.

"He wants to see you."

Zanuck got up, came around the desk and stuck out his hand as I entered.

"Congratulations," he said. "You've got Von Ryan."

Frank Sinatra.

Frank Sinatra?

"This guy is supposed to be a West Pointer, all spit and polish, Dick. He has to talk like those guys. Precise . . . grammar . . . I mean, it's none of that 'Hey, baby, how's your bird.' The character won't work unless . . ." And a lot more until I ran down.

"He'll be terrific," Dick said. "We'll just get someone to polish the dialogue."

———

"Oh, Mr. David," said Celia, my secretary. "Oh, please. No. It's *wrong.*"

Appalled by her outburst, she turned red, stammered, "Excuse me," and ran to the ladies'. My middle-aged maiden lady secretary Celia, who never rapped anyone, never complained about staying late and spoke of *Von Ryan's Express* to her friends as "our picture," came back after lunch slightly crocked.

"I have nothing against Mr. Sinatra, Mr. David. It's just—he's so Eye-*tal*ian. . . ."

The phone rang and rang. . . .

"Jesus! Whose idea was that?"

"Sammy Davis plays the German officer and they all escape in a Dual Ghia."

"Terrific. Italian ham on Ryan."

"You'll never finish it."

Those were the days of the Rat Pack and all those stories of who was in, who out and who in limbo. I didn't really think of Sinatra as an actor —his adventures were in a part of the newspaper I didn't read. *Man with a Golden Arm? From Here to Eternity?* Sure. But *Robin and the Seven Hoods, Ocean's Eleven, Sergeants Three* . . .

I sniveled, "I thought the studio was suing him about walking off *Carousel.*"

"Maybe," Dick said. "But I think that's all settled."

"Everybody says he's nothing but trouble."

"He'll be great in it," Dick said. "Just gotta find a director who can handle him."

. . . and rang.

"So he grabbed the script and he tore out four pages. 'There,' he says, 'now you're not behind anymore.' "

"I know all those stories," Dick said.

"They're true, aren't they?"

"You bet your ass they are," Dick said cheerfully. "He's supposed to be some kind of fucking monster."

"So?"

"So he's going to be your star. You'd better figure out how to love him."

Afterward Zanuck told me that Frank Sinatra had just phoned him out of the blue and announced that he was going to play Ryan.

I said, "What do you mean, 'announced'?"

"Wait," Dick said. "You'll see."

It was something like a treaty. There were lawyers and helpers, spokesmen on mysterious errands which probably involved the location of his parking spaces, offices—who knows? Big, affable Howard Koch, Sinatra's general factotum, showed up one day for what seemed to be a briefing session. "Let me tell you what he's like. . . . "

The man himself was at Warner Bros. finishing up *None but the Brave,* a war adventure which he directed and starred in. According to Koch, Sinatra's legendary impatience was so great that during the filming he threatened to walk off "if that fucking director doesn't get moving." I assumed the story was apocryphal but the point valid.

"When he's ready," Koch said, "you better be ready too, baby."

I was trying. With Sinatra as Von Ryan, the screenplay needed to be rewritten once again, this time voiced and made credible for the star. I proposed and was allowed to hire Joseph Landon, an old friend, a novelist of some quality and a man whose ear was tuned to Sinatra's Hoboken streets by birth. Moreover, Landon's war had been fought in Italy, where he had been a navigator on B-24s out of Cherignola. He brought to the piece what Mayes could not—a specific, gritty knowledge of the ground. Again I was lucky.

What to do with Sinatra/Ryan? I improvised. We would take him out of West Point, make him a ninety-day wonder—a guy who thought of himself as an airplane driver and a professional survivor.

"That's a terrific idea," Zanuck said. "When will you guys be ready?"

To Them, there's no problem in changing a character in a script. Alter the dialogue, change a few stage directions, and that's it. In fact, if the script is worth a damn, one profound change in the nature and quality of the hero means a pretty complete rewrite. The motives change and so do the responses. What one man might do, another wouldn't imagine, and so on throughout the whole interlock.

But everything in *Von Ryan's Express* turned on the character of the man. In Westheimer's best-selling vision, it was a kind of triumph of the

Leader, that cold-seeming, misunderstood martinet isolated by the Loneliness of Command, driving and dominating the disheartened rabble of prisoners for their own ultimate good and his own final triumph —understanding. At the end of the novel, the rescued men look at Ryan and they know at last that he loved them all along.

Screenwriter and novelist Joseph Landon took it in stride and turned for help to Joe Levine from the streets of Brownsville—not Texas.

"It's easy," he said. "We play him like a hood."

"A hood from West Point?"

"There ain't that much difference," Landon said. "Only difference is language. One guy calls it authority, the other guy pisses on authority but he wants power. What's the difference—it's just style. They're both loners, both wrong-bettors—right? One goes hundred percent by the book, the other goes hundred percent against. Comes out the same— you'll see."

I was dazzled, and began to see.

Once before this same Joe Landon had opened a view for me. I a New York editor, he a writer from Hollywood, we were lunching or having a drink or whatever in one of those private clubs on the Upper East Side —one of those places in a converted mansion off the park. Walk downstairs, give your name quietly and be shown to a table by a bent, white-haired waiter in a red jacket. Soundless carpets, wooden walls, teakwood toothpicks.

Landon fairly snarled his discomfort at the place—stared around at the evidences of empire and offered sardonic, class-oriented comments on the canapés and the drinks. He had to admit the crystal was first-rate. It was one of those scenes where John Garfield comes to the girl's house and it turns out she's the daughter of a millionaire. "Hey, kid—you really live here?"

Finally we ascended into the street—squinting against the sun, walking west toward the park. Landon was silent for a minute or so. Then:

"You a member of that club?"

"No. I used someone else's card."

"Why?"

"Why not?" I began looking for taxis at the corner.

But he was serious. "No kidding," Joe said. "You expect to *become* a member of that club?"

"Sure, maybe," I said. "A lot of publishing people go there. I suppose someday—"

"Jesus!"

"Why, what's the matter with it?"

Joe stopped and looked at me intently. "I like you," he said. "But a place like that—you know, I'd rather see you hustling broads at Palm Springs."

I laughed and a taxi came.

But I thought about it. And I thought about it when an offer came and I decided to leave publishing for the movies. But I have not made it to Palm Springs.

When you're producing a movie you make decisions. Men whose wives wouldn't trust them to pick out the wallpaper for the upstairs toilet freely make decisions about remote and exotic locations, sets for jungles and palaces, wardrobes for duchesses and carhops. It is intoxicating—and probably contributes to the lifespan of Industry marriages.

Not that there was that much to decide about *Von Ryan's Express.* Zanuck had ruled that the picture would be in Italy—as much as possible on the actual ground of the story. Only the prison camp and a certain number of interiors were to be constructed at the studio—at enormous expense.

"Two reasons," Dick Zanuck said. "One, it's going to be a long, tough picture out in the Italian boondocks—and Sinatra *hates* long locations.

"The other reason is because we gotta get some production going on this lot—we're paying the bastards anyhow."

"But doesn't it cost a *hell* of a lot more? I mean, we're going to build something that we can probably find standing in Italy. And we're figuring maybe five hundred extras a day in the prison-camp sequences—won't that run the cost up?"

"Double. At least," Dick said. "Maybe more. But it'll bring this place to life again—the town'll know we're here."

I didn't understand studio bookkeeping in those days, so I thought I was listening to a patriotic speech from a young industry statesman—and, allowing for the vinegar of the years, maybe I was.

You'd suppose that the wardrobe in a war film is a matter of research, not haute couture—but there's more to it than that. The point is choice, of course. What time of year was fighter pilot Ryan shot down? What uniform would he have been wearing? Yes, but *could* he have been wearing something else? Call the Air Force liaison man, Colonel Whatsis. (The armed services maintain officers out here whose main function is to advise on the details of war movies. Only on details, though. All large matters and screenplays that need approval and cooperation must be submitted to the Pentagon, whence return letters full of technical points which are often helpful and dramatic points which are sometimes hilarious.)

Both Westheimer and Landon, experts by virtue of having been and done it, agreed that Colonel Ryan would undoubtedly be wearing flight coveralls. That's what everybody wore, they said. But the experienced veterans of wardrobe-department campaigns urged caution, and I phoned the Air Force man to ask the question.

He said flight coveralls—no doubt about it. But I pressed on: Would such a colonel have a choice?

A beat, as we say. Then, "Sir, a field-grade officer has quite a lot of latitude, you know. . . ."

So it turned out that Colonel Ryan could be wearing damn near anything from a Class A uniform to flight coveralls to a ballet tutu.

Wardrobe merely grunted at the news and whipped out sketches and swatches. They didn't have to wait for the information. They knew.

"Now, if we can get approvals on them, we can start on Mr. Sinatra's wardrobe ahead of time and when he comes on the lot we'll be able to get the final fittings."

"No problem," I said.

With an armload of sketches and a lot of cloth samples, I phoned Howard Koch, who said, "Gotcha, baby. I'll be right over."

In less than an hour he was in my office, beaming, offhand and very efficient.

"He ain't gonna like these things, baby."

"But he *has* to like them. He can choose the pink elastiques or the khakis or the coveralls or the leather jacket or the flight boots or the G.I. shoes or the service oxfords or—but it has to be something the character would have worn, right?"

Koch beamed out loud. *"Has* to? Frank?"

I said, "But aren't you guys just finishing up a war movie over at Warners? He ought to be used to the wardrobe by now."

"Sure," Koch said. "That's the trouble. I think he's tired of it."

"Come on—aren't you exaggerating?"

Koch shrugged. "You asked me."

"Well, show it to him anyway. We have to get the stuff started."

"Uh-uh," Koch said. "Not me, Saul baby. You want him to look at these things now, *you* go over and show 'em to him."

I phoned downstairs. "Sure, go ahead," Zanuck said. "Give you a chance to get acquainted." Then he laughed. "Have Howie at least phone ahead and tell him you're coming."

Howie obliged instantly. "Frank was on the set, but the girl says to come ahead over." He clapped me on the back. "Tell you what. I'll drive you over and back. Have to be back here later anyhow."

I can't remember what kind of car it was—but it was not one of the Dual Ghias driven by Sinatra and his friends at that time. It was some kind of big convertible, I think. What I remember for sure is that it was equipped with a telephone. And as we pulled out of the lot onto Pico Boulevard, Howard Koch picked up the phone and called in.

"Hi, honey, leaving Fox right now. Taking the freeway to the valley. ETA twenty minutes."

I looked my astonishment, and he shrugged.

"He just likes to know where everyone is."

The Sinatra company was working on a sound stage filled with jungle —a quite elaborate set clad in trees and vines, rising at the side to a hillside which featured a small, muddy stream dropping into a jungle pool. It was slippery, and a lot of people said, "Watch your step."

Koch led me through the dripping greenery until we came in sight of a couple of portable dressing rooms backed against a stage wall.

"He's in the one at the left. I'd better go see what they got done today." He disappeared into the philodendrons.

The door was ajar, but I knocked anyway.

"Come," said the famous voice.

I grew up an inattentive member of the Sinatra generation. I had never bought or owned one of his records or attended one of his concerts or dated one of his bobby-sox millions. The first time I was really exposed to what everyone else grew up on was during WWII—when circumstances forced me to listen to "Nancy with the Laughing Face" a dozen times in a row. By the third time, it had gotten through to me and I said, "Hey, that's kind of nice—what is it?"

Which was, of course, greeted as an attempt at wit.

I suppose I was expecting that thin, hollow-cheeked guy in a sailor suit—Gene Kelly's sidekick. I guess I was expecting swarthy ("He's so Eye-*tal*ian") or rude ("He's not gonna like it")—anything but the restrained and pleasant man who got up to greet me.

"You must be my producer," Sinatra said. "Please sit down. It was nice of you to come all the way over here."

The other day I asked a beautiful girl who'd had one date with Frank Sinatra to flash on one word to describe him.

"Courtly," she said.

Frank Sinatra doesn't inspire neutrality. But for all the torrents of words, most people meeting him for the first time are surprised. Like Paul Newman, Sinatra is one of those insistently blue-eyed people. Face to face, you are very aware of his high color—a bright ruddy complexion and startlingly blue eyes. Like other great celebrities, his smile has the turned-on power of total assurance; not many of us *confer* benevolence and welcome as naturally as the Pope stretches out his ring hand. If that charm was self-conscious once, it is not now—nor is it condescending.

We talked about *Von Ryan's Express.* He was very familiar with the novel and aware of all the departures we had made from the text. Some he questioned. I explained the character change we were constructing —without Landon's metaphor—and his comments were objective both as to the character and his own imprint. Like most big stars, Sinatra has a remarkably clear image of himself as seen from the outside. All stars have to have it if they want to be stars—as distinct perhaps from Great Actors. To the extent that an actor realizes a part, he loses his own candlepower. In making the character more real than himself he delights critics and wins the respect of his peers. But the star system is a brand-name system, and a star who constantly surprises his fans loses them.

Sinatra is an exception in a way—his Maggio in *From Here to Eternity* was a piece of total immersion, as was his work in *The Man with the Golden Arm.* But *Four for Texas* and all those other Clanpix?

"Let me tell you how I happened to read the book. You know Harry Kurnitz?"

I did. Harry Kurnitz, who died in 1968, was a playwright, novelist and international wit who wrote—among other things—*How to Steal a Million, One Touch of Venus,* and *Tonight We Sing.*

"Right. That's Harry. Love him. Anyway, we were driving down to the Springs after the preview of *Robin and the Seven Hoods* and we're driving and Harry is quiet. I mean, he doesn't say a *damn thing* for fifty miles! So finally I blow my cool and I say, 'Okay, Harry—so you hated it—right?' And he turns to me and he says, 'You know what, pal? You gotta stop making these home movies.' "

He laughed, tilting back in the chair and then leaning forward, pointing.

"So I said, 'Bullshit, Harry—there's nothing great around.' And he says, 'Hell there ain't, you can go into any bookstore and find better stuff than that!' So I said, 'Okay, bigmouth, name one book you think I ought to buy.' And you know what he said? 'I got one in my hotel room right now—a war story, *Von Ryan's Express.* That's the kind of picture you ought to be doing.' "

He tilted back, shaking his head with the memory. I had a feeling the apex of the meeting had passed.

"Let's see what you brought," Sinatra said.

I brought out the wardrobe sketches and the cloth swatches. He riffled through professionally, asking questions about which scene was being suggested, approving a few things, and finally he shrugged.

"I don't much like this stuff," he said. "Let's see what else they can come up with—especially for the opening."

He handed it all back and waited for me to leave. I didn't.

"Excuse me, Mr. Sinatra," I said. "Let me explain the problem."

A long look. "Go ahead. Explain."

So I went into a lengthy, perfectly obvious and passionately logical explanation of the wardrobe—the various possibilities, the allowable combinations, the whole works. I dwelt on the need for an "authentic look," invoked Westheimer, Landon and my own stretch in North Africa at about that time. He heard me out right to the end.

Then he said, "Friend, are you telling me I *have* to wear this stuff?"

Back to the wall. Thermopylae for kids. I clutched my swatches.

Somebody said, "This is the wardrobe, Mr. Sinatra."

Now he really looked at me. A small smile.

"Why argue?" he said. "Who's your boss over there?"

"Dick Zanuck."

"Dick. And who's *his* boss?"

"His father, I suppose—Darryl Zanuck. But—"

He leaned back, reached behind him and got a telephone, keeping me impaled with the look as he spoke.

"Hi. Get me Darryl Zanuck. No, I don't know where—somewhere in Europe, I suppose. Rome, maybe. . . . I'll hold."

Outrage! "Put down that phone!" It was my voice—a little treble.

He blinked. The chair came down as he straightened. "Why?"

"Goddammit, Mr. Sinatra," I said, "this is my first picture—and you're going to ruin the whole damn thing for me. Now cut it out!"

I can still hear him laughing, while I stood there like a statue of Civic Virtue, complete with sketches and swatches. The commotion brought people to the door, but Sinatra waved them off.

"Ready in a minute," he said. "Let me just finish with my producer." Then he got up and tapped me lightly on the arm. "How about the leather jacket with the ODs for the opening sequence?"

12

Positioning Yourself
in the Deal

T HE DAYS BEGAN to flash by. Once Sinatra turned up
uninvited. The door opened, I heard my secretary gasp and a
stingy-brimmed hat sailed into my office followed by Frank Sinatra, who
had read the new pages and loved them.

"It's gonna be a hell of a show," he said. "Coming to the meeting?"

It turned out there was a meeting to iron out contractual details—
studio lawyers, Sinatra's attorney Milton Rudin, his man Howard Koch
and assorted general's aides—in the office of Owen McLean, 20th's
genial, back-slapping Executive Head of Talent (a studio title used for
uncovering a multitude of contract players).

I had not been invited, of course, but I wasn't going to admit it to
Frank Sinatra—and when we entered the office together I could see
McLean's antennae shiver. Respect.

The meeting dealt with a number of matters of expense and prerogative. It was conducted in a tone of brutal factuality, polite but naked of
euphemism, as befits talk about real money. Sinatra's expense allowance was negotiated without difficulty in spite of the size of the chunk;
the studio view was simple: Give him what he wants as long as it's a flat

sum—he'll spend twice as much anyhow. Questions of billing—Sinatra's company to be involved in the production, of course—and where does that credit go? No problem. Now, as to the star's billing?

Name above the title, first, worldwide and in all advertising. Maybe a problem there—what if we get Richard Burton for co-star, won't there be a conflicting demand?

Back and forth, the studio people infinitely flexible, every sentence too long, curved and humble. Other lawyers paraphrasing each other while Rudin waited and Sinatra drummed his fingers. Then Rudin, restating the issue in short sentences and shorter words, until Sinatra interrupted.

"Tell you what," he said. "I'll make it easy for you. No billing clause."

"Frank—" Rudin started, but Sinatra waved him off.

Eyes were flashing, those little chin and wrist movements, as lawyer half turned to lawyer and got no answer: What's the son of a bitch up to?

Sinatra stood. "No billing clause," he said. Turning to Rudin: "Look, Mickey—if the guys out there don't want to put my name first the clause don't help. If they do, what the hell does it matter?"

Later on I asked a passing guru, who laughed. "That must have scared the shit out of them."

Sometime during those days They made a deal with Mark Robson to direct *Von Ryan's Express.* I learned the fact when Harris the Agent phoned to congratulate me.

"You're on your way," he said. "You didn't—? Uh-huh, uh-huh. Yes, sure. Well, you know how busy Dick is. Of course. Just an oversight. You'll love him."

It never occurred to me to ask about Robson's deal with the studio. He was going to direct the picture, right? Right, said Harris the Agent, adding again, "You're on your way."

I had no reason to doubt the selection. Robson was a man of considerable reputation with a long record of solidly made, often successful pictures, beginning with the great hit *Champion.*

He was pleased to meet me. Delighted, in fact—a middle-sized man with a round face, steel-rimmed glasses and a radiant smile.

His speech was rapid, almost stammering, warm and energetic. He rocked on the balls of his feet when he spoke.

"It's going to be a great experience for you," he said.

Like many another Great Man, Robson was finicky about his professional surroundings. A couple of days were spent decorating his offices across the hall from mine. His secretary drove back and forth to his home in Brentwood, lugging paintings and art objects to see how they looked. Mark had a small, pertinent anecdote about each piece.

"Luristan—you know? We had to smuggle them out one at a time. In the brute cases. Twenty years if they catch you taking it out of the country. Like it?"

One piece gave trouble. It was a large relief of some sort—a heavy piece of terra-cotta with bits of stuff embedded, the whole thing encased in a wood frame. The girl had apparently hung it wrong side up —I say "apparently" because the work was relentlessly nonobjective. Robson looked, and his face clouded. He called her into the office.

"Take a good look," he said. "See anything wrong in here?"

The girl looked blankly at him and around the room.

"Take your time," Robson said. "Look carefully."

Assuming lightheartedness, I started to say something, but he gestured sharply, not fooling. "No. Let *her* find it."

She didn't, of course, and he finally lost interest, went to the wall, turned the thing right side up.

"Doesn't that look better?"

"Yes sir," she said.

We are mostly competitive by nature and totally so by trade. To watch a pretty girl watching pretty girls on a sound stage or in a commissary is to see natural selection operate with the speed and passion of breeding fruit flies.

Robson spoke once of his early struggles.

"Believe me, it used to be tough," he said. "We had to fight for everything. You new people are lucky." He squinted sharply, made a birdlike bob of his head. "You know, if I hadn't fought like hell to get my name up there *nobody* would have known I made *Champion.* Believe me."

I'm habitually early to office—the hour or so before the phones start is a useful time to me. When I heard Robson's voice in the corridor hush next morning, I was pleased. Coffee cup in hand, I went to greet a fellow morning type. The hall door was open and his office door ajar. As I crossed the carpet I realized he was on the phone and paused. His voice was very clear, with the remembered enthusiastic warmth.

"That's right, Hedda. You're absolutely—thank you. I sure do. Who? No. No, just one of their staff people. Of course my company is producing it—that's right. You too, dear . . ."

I backed out. A few minutes later he was in my office.

"Good morning, good morning, partner," he said.

Next day Hedda Hopper ran the story, crediting Robson as producer and director. I wrote her a note, saying there must have been some misunderstanding. Miss Hopper did not answer, and in her column Mark Robson continued to be credited as producer.

I whimpered to Harris the Agent, who reminded me what a break I was getting on my first picture and assured me that They would know the real story.

Energy was a Robson trademark—a slogan too, as I would learn. But now he plunged into the complicated preparation with an infectious sense of excitement and importance. He studied the screenplay, asked questions, made some minor requests for changes—almost always aiming at movement in a scene, something bold, something graphic.

"I don't understand this scene. Explain it to me."

I would explain, feeling foolish.

"I still don't get it—can't it be simpler than that?"

Sometimes it could, and he would beam.

"Isn't that better?"

Because Sinatra was still finishing his own film, the star and the director didn't meet immediately—although they had each approved the other. Robson had heard all of the Frank-the-Tiger stories, of course, but he was not intimidated.

"I've studied the way he works," Robson said. "I've talked with people who've worked with him, and I know we'll get along."

Surprisingly, considering the stories, Sinatra's major demand was simply that he be kept busy. When the three of us finally met and talked, he made the point repeatedly.

"Just so I don't have to sit on my ass half the time," he said. "Believe me, I'm always going to be ready—and when I'm on the set, I expect to *work.*"

"Mark better be careful," said Howard Koch. "You better tell him Frank means everything he says. Everything. No matter how he says it, you have to understand one thing—he's not exaggerating."

"So what?" I said. "The only thing he wants is to keep busy. What's the matter with that?"

"Is that *exactly* what the man said?"

"I can't remember his exact words, but it was something like that. He said he wanted all his work to be scheduled together so he can be working all the time."

"Well," Koch said, "you gonna do that?"

"Why not?"

He shook his head. "Baby, I forgot this is your first picture. Let me tell you how it works. . . ."

How it works is this: If the scene being shot involves a conversation between two people, the traditional and safe "coverage" of the scene would demand a "master"—a filming of the whole scene in such a way that all its elements are visible, including its geography; "individuals" —each participant in the conversation seen by himself through the whole scene; "close angles"—perhaps both together but favoring first one, then the other; and probably "close-ups" for emphasis. These and more are the stuff of the director's choices, and the amount of "coverage"—the number of angles filmed—is normally the director's sole prerogative.

After you shoot one of the principals, you must then relight and shoot the others *in the same scene.* This means the one who has been shot now has to sit around and wait—often for hours and hours. It is expected that such a person will not leave the set so he can make the proper responses to the other actors who are *now* being shot. It is tedious as all hell and Sinatra hated it. It is also unavoidable if scenes and sequences and locations are to be completed. And Sinatra's demand was so extraordinary that I suppose no one took it seriously. Only he did.

"What the man means," Koch said, "is just what he says. You shoot all of his stuff, then you move on."

"You mean you just *leave* the other people till later?"

"Unless he's in it, you leave it."

"But what if you have to move—"

"Listen, baby," Koch said, "this story runs up Italy, right? Well, you just might make all the stuff facing north until you get to the Swiss border—then go back and shoot everything facing south."

"Very funny," I said.

"You think so?" said Koch cheerfully. "He thinks that's what you agreed to do."

"Jesus," I said. "We did."

Finally we had another draft screenplay, voiced for Sinatra, incorporating Robson's contributions and Darryl Zanuck's injunctions. Always heightening the conflicts, exaggerating the miseries of the prison camp, the confrontation between Sinatra/Ryan and the British POWs, we had taken a major liberty with the text. The Italian prison camp, instead of Westheimer's feckless menagerie, had become mean, starving, desperate and cruel. It was unquestionably more dramatic than the novel, even if it was flagrantly unfair to the Italians. ("What you gonna call it—*Bridge on the River Po?*")

The reference to getting Richard Burton to co-star with Sinatra had not been idle. It was Sinatra's idea and one the rest of us applauded. As

I understood it, the strategy was to allow Sinatra to make the approach.

"Why don't you just ask him?" I said to Zanuck.

"You don't understand these things," Zanuck said. "Actors can talk to actors better than people can."

"Did he read the script yet?"

"How the hell do I know?" He buzzed the intercom. "Did we send Burton a copy of *Von Ryan?* A week ago? Okay."

To me he said, "Too early for an answer."

"Robson likes Peter Finch. Should we send him a copy?"

"No. I'd rather have Burton," Dick said. "Besides, we have to let Frank play it out."

Maybe days passed. But I recall that it was in the hot middle of the afternoon that my phone rang and I heard Celia's voice quaver.

"It's Mr. Sinatra." She sounded frightened.

When I picked up the phone he began in the middle of the sentence. " . . . goddammit, why didn't you tell me you dumb bastards were suing the Burtons for fifty million dollars? Here I been waiting on the guy, sending him candy and flowers, romancing the shit out of him, and all the time—goddammit—making a fool out of me—"

When I got a chance I said, "Frank, I don't know anything about this. Are you sure—"

"*Sure* I'm sure, for chrissake. Don't you know what's going on in that place? Does anybody?"

"Frank," I said, "just hang on, will you? Let me get Dick on the other line and ask him. Okay?"

Putting him on hold, I rang through frantically to Dick Zanuck. I was badly shaken as I told him what was going on—the enraged Sinatra waiting behind my hold button.

"Where'd he hear that?" Dick asked.

"How do I know? Jeezus—is it true?"

"Damned if I know," Dick said. "Hang on while I call legal—just stay right there."

The line remained open and I could hear him calling the legal department on the interphone.

"Hello? Yeah. Listen—are we suing the Burtons for fifty million dollars?" Pause. "No shit. Fifty million? Okay. Thank you."

He turned back to me. "You hear that?"

"I sure did," I said. Then, "Listen, Dick—Sinatra's still waiting. What should I tell him?"

Richard Zanuck, son of Darryl, said, "Damned if I know." Then suddenly he broke into high-pitched laughter. "Whatever you say, don't knock it. We might win."

13

Some Major Casting, Some Minor Groveling

"**Y**OU PEOPLE bring it on yourselves. You knew the son of a bitch was a drunk [or lecher, thief, child molester or other variety of nogoodnik] before you hired him, didn't you? Look at what he did on *Mutiny on the Streetcar*—damn near put the studio out of business. But you hired him again anyhow, for chrissake—so you only got yourselves . . . "

They are not doomed to repeat history because *They* refuse to learn. *They* know, but are in the grip of a couple of immutable laws.

"Downside risk" is the term that floats the loan and sinks the ship at one and the same time. It means: We know the bastard costs four times as much as he's worth and that he brings his unsanitary private habits and his revolting friends along with him but unless we have a Name to make the exhibitors buy the goddam thing in advance, we are exposed to the possibility that the finished picture *might not get a single booking! With* him we get five thousand Fourth of July advance bookings before anyone knows how bad it might be. So pay the money and try to set it up so's we don't get wiped out if the thing's a bomb.

"The floor" is the TV-sale money. Even a little picture shops for an actor who is merchandisable to the networks. There's a list.

Ecology buffs may ponder the fact that what's called the divorcement
—that antitrust action which forced the studios to sell their theater
chains, and ended block booking and other monopolistic sins, also gave
birth to downside-risk thinking, riveted outrageous star costs into place
and generally reduced the Industry's ability to experiment, maintain
plant facilities and contract player rosters.

And the critics help.

When it took four days to get across the country and Hollywood was
as far from New York as the founding moguls from their origins, hardly
anyone out here really cared what critics said. The pose is still maintained, but in fact, critical assaults wound as deeply as the critic hopes
—the new moguls read all the reviews, watch all the grimacing TV
culture-tasters and wince. Not only all the way to the bank either, but
also on the long ride back. Critics adore actors and directors (when they
adore anything), and whatever else that adoration breeds, one of its
flowers is fiscal irresponsibility and contempt for the game itself. So the
actor who may be a guarantee against downside risk won't play in your
piece of simpleminded entertainment. He wants to read how his por-
trayal of "the agony of our guilty time is reflected in Richard C. Bankable's unforgettable portrait of the syphilitic colonel, trying to impose his
sterile lust on the folksinger who wandered into his tent seeking her
father." As a result, they won't take the jobs unless you clobber them
with money or grease them with meaning—or both. From all of this
streams a flow of movies which reflect in whole or in part the deepthink-
ing of stars and the people who write about them—none of whom ever
get the blame for the turkey they stuffed.

"Goddammit—we got no product after April! Nothing! So let's take
the Rick Bankable package. See if we can get him to take out that
syphilitic-colonel scene—or at least soften it to clap. . . . See if you can
get the goddam budget down two-fifty—okay, so take it out of
days. . . . "

In other words, find some way to shorten the remaining production
schedule and cut back on daily expenses, thus eventually reducing the
total movie budget.

It's a dream. Bankable and his favorite director may agree to the
terms—even in writing—but they're going to shoot the scene anyhow
and will fight like tigers to keep it in the finished film. It may increase
the budget past the red line; it may diminish the bookings by ten
percent out there where they *hate* that kind of thing, but Bankable and
D.W. Auteur couldn't care less. And the critics will publish Bankable's
complaint that his film was gutted.

They have come to expect and tolerate behavior by stars and auteurs which would make a gargoyle weep, let alone an accountant. When one of these folks does behave moderately well, They turn to jelly. It is an industry where statues are raised to enormously paid people who work a few days out of each year and spray contempt like musk—if they just do what they're paid for. ("We're in the monster-making business.")

So, with Richard Burton unavailable because of a fifty-million-dollar lawsuit, Trevor Howard was hired to play opposite Sinatra in the plum role of Colonel Fincham, half mad, half messiah—ranking officer in the prison camp until Ryan/Sinatra shows up. He read the script and cabled his delighted acceptance, and everyone was pleased. Howard Koch, speaking for Sinatra, said, "Hell of an actor. We love him for Fincham."

Robson only nodded, coldly, as I remember.

After the Burton embarrassment, Frank Sinatra was not difficult or demanding about casting. He was kept informed of the major choices and agreed with all except one. The part in question was that of the ranking American enlisted man in the prison camp full of British POWs. In the picture, the sergeant becomes devoted to Ryan/Sinatra and dies in his colonel's defense. Sinatra rejected our candidate, and his objection was a brief flare of overkill.

"I don't want the fag bastard."

The actor Sinatra wanted and got was his (then) close friend and shadow, Brad Dexter.

Robson shrugged. He had liked the other actor better, but he readily conceded Dexter's adequacy and Sinatra's *droit de seigneur.* When I noted that we were going to be carrying a lot of the star's personal quadrilla—a couple of stunt men, Howard Koch, his household staffers, an actor pal named Richard Bakalayan and Sinatra's favorite cinematographer, William Daniels—Robson shrugged.

"The actors are okay and Bill Daniels is one of the best in the business," he said. "Besides, I'll get my own gang, don't you worry."

I took it in. "That's a pretty tough way to do it, isn't it?"

"What?"

"I mean you don't have to call a guy a fag bastard just to get someone else in the job."

Robson peered over his glasses at me. "You know whatsisname?"

"No. Just I've seen him, of course."

Robson beamed. "Well, don't jump to conclusions."

No one else was surprised. "He *had* to find a spot for Dexter," Hough said. "The guy saved his life, pal."

It was a well-known story to Sinatra watchers. During the filming of *None But the Brave* in Hawaii, Sinatra had nearly drowned—swept out to sea in a powerful current, rescued by Brad Dexter. They were now inseparable.

It made sense to me, and I said as much to Koch, who shrugged and muttered something about an old man with a surfboard.

"Wait a minute," I said. "You mean it wasn't really Brad?"

Koch flipped his hands. "What's the diff? It's what the man thinks that counts."

Casting the rest of the parts wasn't hard. A best-selling book full of action and color, Frank Sinatra, Trevor Howard, Mark Robson . . . it all had that rich and juicy smack, and everyone wanted in. Big Picture. Italy in summer. Rome to the Alps, hundreds of extras, stunt men, special-effects wizards—the whole grand works.

Trailing along behind Robson, I attended budget meetings with various departments, as each scene in the script was analyzed and its requirements noted. At a major studio, staff departments function like automatons. If the screenplay says the hero wanders into a museum and destroys a dozen priceless Rembrandts, someone in the properties department will calculate that twelve Rembrandts averaging $300,000 apiece will cost $3,600,000 and the props estimate will show that figure. At the ensuing meeting the head of the department will say to the producer or director, "Say, you wouldn't mind if we use fakes for those pictures, would you? Or are you planning to shoot the scene close-up?"

If you look astonished, he'll shrug. They are not naive—they've been clobbered too many times to question even the most imbecilic demand. If the script calls for it, they'll do their best to supply it. If the producer or director is lazy, or assumes too much, he may find himself watching an actor destroy a real Rembrandt someday.

On one point Robson was insistent. The important German and Italian parts had to be played by real Germans and real Italians.

"All the Hollywood Italians are caricatures by now," Robson said. "They've been imitating themselves for years and by now they're not a damn bit like real Italians. Believe me, we'll do better casting them in Rome."

But the studio wanted the main parts cast before anyone went to Rome, so the matter was compromised by hiring a couple of "real" Italians who had worked for Robson before, Sergio Fantoni and Adolfo Celi, respectively the "good" junior officer and the "bad" commandant of the prison camp. There was one more important Italian part, that of the train's engineer. In envisioning the film, Robson dwelt on the importance of that man's Italian face.

"He's kind of a key. Every time the train moves we'll see him—we'll cut to him looking back like they do. It's very important that we cast it over there."

As it turned out, we did. Once the company had moved there, Vito Scotti, a Hollywood actor of Italian extraction, was hired and sent to Rome, where he spoke broken English and charmed everyone and got the job.

So, in the end, the picture was cast in the traditional way from traditional sources. The only major part cast in Rome was the part of the girl —the Italian mistress of the German train commander.

Flashback.

Sometime during my first week in Hollywood, I entered the Columbia dining room as a new screenplay was being discussed. Someone at the head of the table was having it out with someone eight or nine chairs down—so it was loud. The man at the head was interrupting the other man's answer with the impatient sound of a man determined to get at the main facts.

"Okay, okay—we know all that," he said. "What I'm asking you is, what page does the cunt come in?"

There was no girl in Westheimer's book, but from the first day we never doubted there would be one in the film. In fact, the girl in the film may well have been Westheimer's invention, right at the beginning of the effort.

No one took literally Darryl Zanuck's cabled suggestion that we attach to the train a boxcar full of girls, maybe with their heads shaved, but one girl—*sí.* Movie time. I don't remember the page number of her entrance, but it was early enough.

As noted, that part was finally cast in Rome after I joined the company there. We had not intended to cast it there. In fact, I had been interviewing girls at the studio when I was suddenly summoned to Italy. There I interviewed some twenty or thirty Italian girls before settling (with Robson's approval) on Raffaella Carra, who did her best with the undistinguished invention. When I began the interviews at Cinecittà, I got a phone call from Darryl Zanuck, in residence at the Excelsior. I had never met Zanuck Senior and was not going to argue with anything he said, but I was surprised all the same.

Was it true that I was interviewing girls for *Von Ryan*? How many was I going to see? Well, there would be a car waiting outside the studio office, and each interviewee was to be driven from the studio to the Excelsior—"whenever you're done."

This was explained to each of the girls in turn. None of them seemed especially surprised.

14

The Von Ryan
Advance Party
Beachheads in Rome

*I*F WESTHEIMER'S story was a dream, still it was a dream with footnotes. The imaginary train that was seized, diverted and finally crashed across the Swiss border into freedom traveled on real Italian railroad lines. Every mile and station was documented with timetables and railroad maps and letters from Italian railroad officials. Maybe it didn't really happen, but it should have, and the author went to a lot of trouble to prove (to himself) that it could have.

But cameras can't photograph what might have been—and twenty years later there was no way to recreate that reality. The route had been electrified, trellised with high-voltage transmission lines which made scenes atop the boxcars impossible, so stretches of nonelectrified railroad line had to be found. And everywhere in Europe, skylines bristle with postwar buildings which would have screamed anachronism in the background of the movie. Careful as we were, there's a scene in Anzio wherein the occupying Germans race down the boulevard against a background topped with TV antennas. ("Screw it—if anybody asks, say it was a clothesline.")

Location scouting had begun as soon as there was a screenplay marked "final." Art director Hilyard Brown had been shipped off to find and photograph locations which would fit the landscape of Westheimer's novel as redreamed by Wendell Mayes and Joe Landon, neither of whom had seen the terrain. Brown was an old Italian hand, having spent a year building Cleopatra's galleys in the seacoast town of Anzio where he was regarded as a public benefactor—having spent more money locally than anyone since Nero.

They are not as stupid as *Cleopatra* argues. *They* try like hell to avoid commitment to the big sums until they're sure, but it's a battle They often lose because the Enemies—agents, actors, directors and producers—are relentless in their efforts to get the money out where they can grab it.

David Brown, a 20th Fox executive who survived all the civil wars but the last one, once told me that the way to a successful career was through the deal, not the picture. "Only one thing counts," he said. "Get Them in over their heads."

Now he is partnered with Dick Zanuck in the very successful Zanuck/Brown company—but even allowing for satire, they proved the point when *Jaws* went far over budget but was finished without stinting and went on to shatter all box-office records. *They* were clearly in over their heads—and a good thing too.

They know the enemy's mind, of course, and they fight back when possible—often clobbering the easy marks with frustrations generated by the hard ones. If your arm twists it will be twisted.

"He wants *what?* Fire the son of a bitch!"

But if the son of a bitch is the star whose presence made the picture go and it's already half finished . . .

Directors and leading actors are expensive, their time computed on the Big Clock, so economy dictates they be hired last and for the shortest time possible. As a result, many of these talented people are accustomed to seizing authority and forcing often spasmodic insights onto the film at the last moment, frothing at the least demur and constantly wielding the ultimate threat of commencement without preparation. Who would start pouring out millions of dollars in a few frenzied weeks with an unfinished screenplay, sets and locations uncertain and a leading lady in the process of changing husbands? Nobody in his right mind would, but They have and will again—faced with a shortage of product, a pay-or-play contract with Rick Bankable who won't be available after such and such a date so you just better start on time, baby. They know and They do it—screaming.

Hilyard Brown traveled from Spain to Yugoslavia and up and down the Italian peninsula and returned with a lot of photographs and a few unsolved location problems. Now the Big Clock was ticking audibly—start dates had been set—so after a series of hasty meetings, back he went, this time with an assistant, various production men and Mark Robson himself.

"See you in the fall," Robson said to me. "Take care of the store." Then he added, "You've been a real help. Don't worry about a thing."

In the remaining weeks before shooting was to start in Rome, Robson, Brown and Co. were to recheck all the locations Brown had endorsed and, they hoped, find some he had missed.

The missing pieces were all in the ending. The screenplay called for some hair-raising stuff with a bridge and a tunnel mouth, skirmishes on sheer cliffs and a final, spectacular bursting of barriers as Ryan and what was left of the men made it into Switzerland. Then, after a moment, the sentimental tag: Ryan, surveying the litter, the burning boxcars, the broken, exhausted, but wildly happy men, calls for attention and directs them to start cleaning up the mess. Only now he's smiling. And the men cheer.

But the staging had not been found. There were plenty of alpine tunnels on the road to Cortina D'Ampezzo, but they just didn't offer what Robson had in mind's eye. The photographs looked spectacular enough to me—a single-track railroad snaking along the shoulders of the needle-pointed Dolomites, looking up to perpetual snow, straight down to pine tops and raging streams.

I asked the obvious question.

"Why don't we just rewrite the ending to fit the terrain that's available?"

And got the obvious answer. "Mark likes it this way. He *sees* this ending and he wants to find it."

Landon's view of the problem was equally foreshortened. "The bastards just hate to send a writer on a location trip," he said.

Zanuck advised me not to rock the goddam boat and Harris the Agent suggested I get going on something else—start lining up my next picture.

"But they haven't started shooting this one yet."

"Sure," said Harris reasonably, "but there's nothing more you can do. Are they going to be shipping the dailies home?"

I didn't know.

"Well, if they do, you can keep up with it that way," said my guide and mentor.

Back to Zanuck. "We'll be looking at everything—just Robson's deal is we can't put it together until he gets back." Then he added, "Don't worry—you'll see a lot of it. After all, we're doing the prison camp right here on the lot."

The prison camp and breakout—perhaps twenty-five percent of the movie—would employ hundreds of extras and require a lot of heavy set construction. In the budget discussions it had been estimated that doing it at the studio would increase the film's cost by anywhere from $300,000 to $700,000.

So plans were drawn and construction began on a magnificent prisoner-of-war compound—posts, barbed wire, guard towers and huts for the prisoners. Sound stages and studio maintenance buildings were false-fronted into two- and three-story stone and masonry Renaissance buildings complete with towers and parapets. The sight lines were carefully figured so the wide lens of the camera would not look past Calabria and see Beverly Hills. It was a marvel—approximately $100,000 worth of marvel which might have been rented for a fraction of the amount in Italy—but without contributing to statesmanship, of course.

That set stood, almost intact, for several years. Contrary to accepted wisdom, most outdoor sets are strongly constructed. Set-striking (tear-down) costs being what they are, such grand sets very often outlast the companies and managements which built them.

I busied myself with odds and ends. Privately, I was trying to come to terms with arrival, looking into other people's faces for permission to feel like a success.

"You got it made, baby."

Once upon a time the golden plateau was to be "grown-up." "Take it easy, kid . . . wait'll you grow up. . . . There'll be time enough." But the announcement never came, the elevator never stopped at that floor, and one day some kid exactly my age called me "sir" and I realized that the only shock of recognition is memory.

Success? I had a new house, a new car, a new career and a new wife (new for me, at least) and I *bought* a dress suit "for Industry functions." But it takes longer than that. Several years later, with my name on a couple of hit movies, I attended an informal party at a little house in the hills above Sunset Strip. Wandering out onto the porch after dinner to look at the lights, I became aware of someone staring at me in the dim light—a youngish, baldish man named Rubin something, a friend of someone's friend, something in commercials. Glaring.

"Hi . . . Rubin. Nice view, isn't it?"

He was drunk, I thought, as he came toward me. But what he said was clear enough.

"Fuck the view. You goddam bastard. You really think you're something, don't you?" Now he was yelling. "Well, let me tell you—you stink and your goddam pictures stink too. Shit. *Shit!*" Then he threw the drink.

I had arrived.

In an industry where even the popcorn sellers get a piece of the action, I was a salaried employee with roughly the same rights as a grape picker before Chavez . . . but with a hell of a lot more money than I had ever seen before.

From my office windows I couldn't quite see the Italian prison camp rising day by day, but I could hear it. Power saws and hammers, the shouts of workmen and the rumbling of the trucks. At noon, on the way to the commissary, I would check the progress of construction, wondering if anyone watching knew whose . . . "See that guy over there? He's the producer."

Robson's progress was reported in a series of cables to the production department, and I formed the habit of dropping in there at the end of a day to find out what was happening with my movie. Tentative locations had been found, but, "Mark's not completely happy with them and they're going to keep looking. . . ."

Weeks passed. Still the word was, "Haven't found it yet."

Stan Hough, head of physical production, summoned me to a meeting in Zanuck's office. "He wants to talk about the ending."

Hough was pacing the carpet when I arrived. "I dunno," he said. "Here's the latest. Robson's got some place in Spain he's all hot about. He wants to send a survey party over there . . . inland from Málaga someplace. Christ!"

"I didn't know we'd been looking in the south of Spain."

"We weren't. It's someplace Mark remembers from some other picture, I think. He says it's terrific, just what we need, but . . ."

"But what?"

"What?" He shoved the budget at me. "A move to Spain at the end of the picture? The whole fucking company? You know what kind of money you're talking about?"

"Couple of hundred thousand, anyway."

"Why the hell can't the ending be shot right there in the Alps?" Zanuck came out from behind the desk and marched off into the next room where I could hear him wrenching open the refrigerator door. He would be getting a Coke. Angry.

"You want one?"

"No," I said. "I don't see any reason why the ending won't work right up there near Cortina. No thanks. . . ."

"What does Hilyard Brown think?"

I shrugged. "He says the Spanish thing sounds great, but . . . "

Dick Zanuck sat down and sucked at the Coke. "I'm telling you," he said, "if the survey goes to Spain, that's where the goddam scenes will be shot. It's always like that. The thing to do is to head it off."

He stabbed at the intercom, and I heard Stan Hough.

"Yeah, Rich?"

He hesitated and looked up at me, and I left. That evening I dropped in on Hough.

"I understand Dick killed that Spanish junket," I said, with the off-handedness of an insider.

"Hell no," Stan said. "They're going." He took in my surprise. "What the hell—nothing's easy."

A week later we looked at photographs of a spectacular sheer cliff, a tunnel and a railroad bridge—all blazing hot yellow stone, dry and leafless. El Chorro, fifty or sixty miles inland from Málaga.

Terrific. No doubt about it.

"All the same," I said, "isn't it going to look funny? The train tearing along in the high Alps, grey stone, waterfalls, pine trees, snow caps—and then suddenly all this desert color? It's supposed to be the Swiss border."

"We can fix it in the lab," somebody said.

Zanuck looked uncomfortable. "Did you ever discuss this stuff with Sinatra? Good. Let's let it ride for a couple of days. I'll talk to Mark about it when he calls."

It hadn't occurred to me to discuss such a question with Sinatra, but in any case he wasn't around. Koch told me he had gone to London, that he would fly either from there or from someplace in France to Rome in time to begin filming. Koch himself was leaving the next day to prepare for the advent.

"You know about the villa? The guys found this terrific villa outside the city—some Roman senator rented it to us for a couple of months. I'm going to check it out, you know? Make sure everything works—change the shower heads, that kind of stuff."

"What's the matter with the shower heads?"

"I don't know—nothing, probably." His eyebrows lifted. "What's the matter, baby—you think it's a big thing to go to Rome just to check the shower heads?" He clapped me on the back. "Relax. Ruthie and I are going over for a couple of weeks just to get things started right. What do you care? It's on Frank's tab." ("Just give him whatever he wants as long as it's a flat deal.")

Howard Koch cheerfully agreed that the studio had made a good deal. Then he looked at me narrowly.

"You ever been to Italy?"

"No."

"That's what I thought. No plans for you to go, huh?"

"I'm watching the store."

Koch grinned his sidesaddle grin. "Relax, baby. They'll be crying for you over there. I don't think Mark understands the man."

With less than a week to go before what film contracts call "commencement of principal photography," I got a phone call from Zanuck.

"Pack a bag for a couple of days. You and Stan and I are going to go over to give *Von Ryan* a sendoff. Okay?"

Zanuck and Hough were already in the limousine when it arrived. There in the driveway of my new home ("It'll look terrific when those bushes get bigger") I kissed the children and the new wife goodbye, climbed in and sat on the jump seat, waving as the long black Cadillac backed down the driveway. The little dogs barked and scratched against the windows.

I think there was light rain falling when we landed in Rome—at least, what I remember is that kind of blankness. Maybe it was the disappointment of all that green glass and tile and steel angles. I had been reading about Rome since I was a kid. Caesar's *Commentaries* and DeMille's movies—*I, Claudius* and *Decline and Fall*—had left me unprepared for an airport called Leonardo da Vinci but looking like Des Moines. I didn't exactly expect togas—but *something*. . . .

There were cars and people to meet us; the wonderful, heady "I'll take care of your stuff through customs, sir—you just wait over there" of traveling for a studio. Then we got into several small cars and set out for the city. A few minutes down the narrow, tree-lined road there was a break and a view. I saw flat-topped pines, a ruined aqueduct and the city spread across the famous hills. The dome of St. Peter's was clear, telescopically sharp.

Then we were in the city, rattling along avenues of raw-looking, yellow brick apartment houses.

"There's the Colosseum."

"Where?"

"There. No, quick, the *other* side."

Too late. We swept into the city in a throng of small cars and motor scooters, honking, screeching, revving blue smoke, swerving sharply in and out, bowling grandly around huge six-lane circles and suddenly into one-way alleys. Short streets, cobbled, leading always to fountains, mostly dry. . . .

"Jesus—does he have to go that fast?"

The Grand Hotel is an ark from another time—a peeling stone whale, beached and disconsolate, about half a mile from the jazzy action of the Via Veneto. It is furnished with operetta props, chandeliers in every room, even the bathroom—but hanging not quite straight and with gaps in the rows of crystals.

Drinks in the lobby. Dinner. A walk on Via Veneto, where the ranks of sidewalk chairs were jammed in front of one awning, inexplicably vacant under the next one. We were tired.

The *Von Ryan's Express* production offices filled a long, narrow brick building bisected by a corridor, with perhaps a dozen rooms opening on either side. The floors were tiled, the walls concrete, the ceilings very high. Footsteps echoed and reechoed in the hall, conversations blurred and the tapping of typewriters amplified. To compensate, everyone yelled. The light was dim against the summer heat and glistening in the dampness of those sweating walls. I hesitated to use the one tiny toilet at the end of the hall—it stood in a pungent slick, sodden with newspapers and hopeless paper towels.

"Use mine," Robson said. "It opens from my office." He beamed. "Besides, it's something to see—it's famous."

Robson's office was at one end of the building. It was decently furnished—with some attention to comfort—and it had sound-deadening stuff on the walls. You could feel your muscles ease as the racket outside shut away. There was a door on the far wall which he opened with a flourish.

The bathroom was blue and gold and brilliant green. Tilework as fanciful as a Chinese New Year swirled across the floor and up the walls. Glass and marble and carved gold spouts—the works.

"This was all Liz Taylor's dressing room for *Cleopatra*," Robson said. "They put in this bathroom especially for her." He looked owlish over his glasses. "Think I can cope with it?"

The other rooms were not so much functionally bare as barely functional—unpainted wooden tables, folding metal chairs, sagging file cabinets and stacked cardboard boxes labeled in crayon—IN, OUT, MAIL, VOUCHERS, TRANSPORT, etc. The telephones rang constantly and were answered by anyone. The accepted technique was to snatch up the phone with one hand, put the free hand over the other ear and yell, *"Pronto!"*

"You think this is a mess?" Robson shouted happily, nudging me. "Wait'll we get going."

Zanuck and Hough just nodded at everything, smiled and kept moving, Zanuck glancing at his watch from time to time as we shook hands with our Italian functionaries and the foreign production manager, a tieless, shirt-sleeved, three-day-bearded, typical Sicilian bandit who turned out to be an Israeli by the name of Sam Gorodisky.

Back into the little cars and away to meet Howard and Ruth Koch and inspect the Sinatra villa. It was a long ride, far out on the road called Annulare which rings the city. As we drove along past farms and fields we were waved at by attractive girls sitting in twos in the shade every mile or so. Since they made no effort to stand, but just smiled and waved, I thought it an especially lethargic style of hitchhiking and said so. The driver turned his head and laughed. They are not hitchhikers, signore, they are prostitutes—mostly patronized by truckdrivers and such. Where? In the fields, where else? The boss drops them off in the morning, picks them up at sunset. Why not?

From the road all you could see of the villa was a high masonry wall tipped with spikes and wire, a pair of dense, wrought-iron gates with a sentry box inside and lots of tall trees, which became famous one night later when paparazzi dropped from them like acorns.

The villa itself was beautiful, a two-story stone building standing in a kind of park at the head of a long loop of driveway. Flower beds and statues, a swimming pool, arbors. Off to one side I saw laborers dismantling a tennis court, uprooting the posts and carting off the screens and benches.

Howard Koch gestured. "Works out just right for the chopper pad, doesn't it? Look at that—a clear approach almost all the way around, if we take down a couple of those trees. Terrific?"

There had been quite a lot of talk about Sinatra's use of helicopters, but I hadn't taken it all in.

"It saves time," Koch said. "Besides, he doesn't intend to go into the city."

"But he'll be shooting right in the middle of Rome—San Pietro railroad station."

"No sweat," Koch said. "We already cleared it. The chopper can land right alongside the station—he does his day's work and up, up and away. . . ."

"That's the deal, all right," Hough said. "Everywhere by chopper. Everywhere."

We watched the men roll the net away.

"He's mad at the city." Koch shrugged. "They gave him a hell of a bad time a few years ago—1953, was it? Don't know exactly when, but I guess he was kind of on his ass and doing a concert tour. Anyway, something went wrong and they booed him—*booed* him. Someone said they were yelling, 'Send out your wife'—Ava, you know, then. . . .

Anyway he walked off and I guess he's been sore ever since."

"I think Rome's getting off easy, don't you?"

After another one of those long, multi-course dinners on another one of those outdoor terraces ("What's that wine you ordered last time—Valpolicella? That's it, waiter, Valpolicella") the visit was over.

"Let's all go down to Gucci's," Zanuck said. "Pick up gifts for the wives on the way to the airport."

It seems to me that it was a Sunday—I remember being surprised that the shop was open. The cars waited at the foot of the Spanish Steps while we all bought handbags of colored leathers. "Put 'em all in one bag," Zanuck said. "I'll take 'em through."

He and Hough kept exchanging looks and suppressing snickers. What?

"Nothing," Zanuck said. "Just it seems funny to be going home without that old guilty feeling." It had been too brief a trip for that.

We were in the little TWA private lounge when the plane was called. A uniformed girl opened the door, smiled and beckoned. Zanuck and Hough stood. Both turned to me and stuck out their hands.

"Goodbye." Dick Zanuck broke into his high-pitched laugh, Stan Hough nodded and shrugged, grinning.

"Goodbye?"

"Your stuff is back at the Grand waiting for you. Don't worry, I'll deliver the pocketbook."

I was trotting along behind them on the way to the gate.

"Your wife packed enough stuff for a couple of months."

"Say hello to Frank."

"Keep them cards and letters coming."

At the gate Hough paused. "Take it easy. Don't let 'em get you. And have a good time."

I watched them go through the gate—standing there in the middle of Italy holding my two-suiter. Someone tapped me on the shoulder. It was the driver of the car. He smiled broadly and reached for my suitcase.

"We go back to Grand Hotel, signore?" He didn't wait for confirmation but moved off toward the car. I followed.

15

$
Seduced, Abandoned,
and in Charge of
Production

STUDIO HEAD TO PRODUCER:
"Get your ass down to the stage and tell that son-of-a-bitching genius that he makes up those three days this week or we pull the fucking plug!"

PRODUCER TO DIRECTOR:
"Just came down to see how you're doing, bubbe. . . . Yesterday's stuff was great, just dynamite. . . . R. J. loved it, told me to tell you. . . . Oh yes, R. J. was asking about how you figure to pick up the time . . . ?"

The director may say many different things, rude or polite, but he will include the phrase "I know it's your job to ask these stupid questions," and go on to explain that a bad script, inadequate preparation time, etc., have resulted in the problems he predicted. Still, he hopes to pick up time in the next sequence. . . .

If the crisis is really dire—"New York is screaming"—the studio head himself will go to the set. There he and the director will embrace, joke with the actors and exchange endearments. Everyone on the picture will understand that management is enraged and that threats are being made.

STUDIO HEAD TO NEW YORK:

"Auteur's down another half day. I told him he has to make it up or we replace him." New York knows the threat is idle—replacement cost will be worse than the lagging schedule, but They are comforted by the show of belligerence.

In the steamroom conversations the whole process is called "blowing smoke up their asses."

Who cared? I was in Italy, living on per diem, producer of a major American film. I prepared to step into the cab of *Von Ryan's Express.*

At Cinecittà, a cheerful, busy Mark Robson told me how pleased he was that I would be along. "Stick with me, kid . . . I know you'll be a great help." Then he was off. Robson had representatives in Rome and there were meetings and interviews to attend. Every day or so his picture would appear in an Italian paper or magazine; his name, followed by a string of credits, followed by the name Sinatra.

I went to Harry the Production Manager to see about an office. In the field, the production manager of a motion-picture company is chief of staff to the director's commanding general, but with one important difference. In making a film, shooting starts only *after* victory.

The production manager's job is exacting. Long before people are hired, the script has been broken down into its minutest components, hardware, bodies and time. Each component is hired for the shortest time possible—travel time is figured, the number of meals to be consumed, hotel accommodations (divided into classes) and per-diem allowances where necessary. The actual filming is calculated the same way, and careful estimates are made as to how many pages of the script will be shot on a given day, at a given place. Thus movies are mostly shot out of sequence—scenes unconnected to each other by any consideration except economy. If the first and last scenes in a film take place at the same location, they will be shot at the same time. If there are crowds at different points of the story, every effort will be made to group those massive expenses as much as possible. If an actor appears at intervals in the film, every effort will be made to "get rid of him all at once" and avoid "a long carry." Naturally, all these requirements may conflict and a bit player may find himself "carried" for many weeks because grouping his scenes together would inflict some far greater expense. Production men reconcile these conflicts and come up with the shortest, cheapest schedules consonant with union rules and the demands of directors and stars. One odd result of the system is that there are often short-term people working in a film who have only the sketchiest idea of what it's about. When those people are actors, it sometimes results in some pretty strange interviews, and it always results in bizarre gossip.

There are some directors, chiefly men from the theater, who insist on shooting in sequence. Actors adore them as much as production men despise them. An old-time production man working for one of those directors feels himself shamed by the contact. He will drink bourbon at lunch and mutter darkly, "Look at him. The cocksucker's *lost.*"

To these janissaries, a green producer is only a millstone. Harry the Production Manager, a short, angry man with a flashing smile under a perpetual frown and a phlegmy habit of throat clearing that made secretaries flinch, looked pained at my request for space.

"I'll have to look around," he said. "We're kind of cramped here."

At that time at least three of the rooms were absolutely empty. I pointed it out, but my uncertainty showed. "They're allotted," Harry said briskly. He turned away, a man with things to do. "Don't worry, I'll find you something. . . ."

It didn't work out that way. While the company was in Rome I wandered around in the rising uproar, reading the incredibly long and weirdly misspelled cables from the studio, dictating soothing and optimistic answers and occasionally rewriting a page or two at the director's request.

"You know that scene on page twenty-four where they climb out of the boxcars and walk up an embankment? Right. Well, this place we're going to shoot hasn't got an embankment. Flat. So here's what I'm going to do. I'm going to have the men exit and then just crowd up against the boxcars while they wait for orders. See?"

What il Signor Regista wanted from me in each such case was a rewritten page to conform with the action which had altered by circumstance. There was no one else to do it, and I didn't know that it needn't be done, that the script clerk would incorporate all such changes into the shooting scenario as filming took place. So I waited for one of the bilingual secretaries to go to the can, dropped onto her folding chair and typed the altered pages, new scene numbers and all, then took them across the reeking hallway to the publicity department, which had a hand-cranked duplicating machine, and hey presto. Copies for everyone and duplicates shipped to the studio. It was not my idea of David O. Selznick's role on *Gone with the Wind,* but someone had to do it.

I was fascinated by the technique of phoning in the cables with which we reported everything, every day. The girls would first take dictation, pages of it, then phone the cable office and proceed to first say, then spell each word to someone on the other end who presumably understood no English but had a good ear. In spelling the English words, each letter was verified with an Italian place name—Roma, Milano, Bologna, etc. Our two English-born secretaries, Judy and Jennifer, sat at adjoining card tables amid piles of boxes and files, typing and screaming out the cables while people tumbled in and out of the steaming, clattering rooms—shouting questions, demanding signatures, pawing through papers, looking for matches (scarce and unstable in Italy), for information about hotels, dates, transportation, vouchers and authorizations—in English and Italian and (after a bit) German. Blond Judy and dark-haired Jennifer, both exceptionally pretty, highly paid, wire-nerved and perspiring in the heat, pointed, shrugged, smiled and shrilled endlessly into the rotten Italian phones. I remember that the illustrative word for the letter *d* is the town Domodossala, and I can still hear the clear English sound of exasperation rising above the hubbub. "No, no. *Domodossala,* you bloody idiot."

Filming began with bits and pieces—the train loaded with German soldiers crossing an intersection; the same train, but now with POWs all over the rooftops. Angles on crossing guards. Saluting, not saluting, holding back civilian or military traffic, checking papers—all those incidental bits of tissue which give a film atmosphere.

Everyone who makes movies has a secret hyphen, and maybe a public one too. Either way, the secret one colors his approach to his work.

Robson was a publicly esteemed director-producer, but his private hyphen was director-editor. As one who got his training in the cutting room, his direction never forgot that he was accumulating coverage for editing. To this kind of director the control of that first assembly is vital, of course, and Robson's contract guaranteed him that nobody would put the film together until he did—an assurance instantly and callously violated without a qualm by management. It's easy enough; the studio instructs the lab to knock off an extra print of each selected take, then some trusted studio editor assembles and edits the film as it comes in —all secretly, of course. When the director finds out, his screams are heard and lawsuits are threatened. To imagine a studio with millions of dollars at stake so placid and trusting that it will wait for months and months, hoping the director had covered every contingency, is a bit much. But directors demand and get such hollow promises and the people who write about auteurs seem to believe that a film can and ought to be made as a poet makes a sonnet or a blacksmith a horseshoe.

So Robson directed the early bits and pieces, and I got a chance to watch those small choices being made. Should a crossing guard be smoking a cigarette as the motorcycle and sidecar approach the barrier? Should the officer in the sidecar gesture a demand that the guard get rid of the offending cigarette, and should the flustered guard, trying to salute and obey at the same time, maybe drop his weapon? "Great. A character bit. Memorable. Do it. No, it's too much—vaudeville. Never mind the cigarette. Hey, you in back there—could you just lean on the wheelbarrow while this all happens? Not a member of the company? Shit. Well, ask him if he wants to make a couple of lira. Hurry up, for chrissake. What about the train? Is it ready? What's the matter with those walkie-talkies? They are? Okay. *Action.*"

We attended the dailies in groups. Robson's group was a family unit, his wife and daughter and private secretary. It was intimidating; no discussion was possible and there was none—only polite smiles on entering and leaving. It was immediately clear that Robson was not interested in the old give and take about the day's work. I was not exactly learning how to make a picture, but I was learning my place.

I had better luck with the art director and his assistant.

On a location picture like *Von Ryan,* the art director's job becomes very broad indeed. He finds locations for the various scenes, and he must rebuild and dress them to conform not only with the time and the place of the particular scene, but also with the mood and point. He must guard against anachronisms which might show up in the lens—TV antennas, license plates, cars of the wrong vintage, details of costume, signs, and whatnot. He must also make positive contributions—repaint for freshness if the scene wants it, age and weather if it leans the other way. He may be called upon to invent and scrawl graffiti, kill a shining surface or varnish a dull one which won't otherwise be visible on the film. He may be found spraying brown leaves green or green ones brown, manufacturing and placing phony boulders, pillars or street lamps and a great deal more. Not all art directors are so versatile, of course, and many a brilliant interior set designer is lost out of doors, and vice versa. On *Von Ryan,* Hilyard Brown and his assistant Ed Graves were tireless, cheerful and endlessly inventive—never calling for a carpenter if a hammer was handy, never without an alternative, always ahead of the production's needs.

My first contributions to the film itself were marginal. In checking upcoming locations with Hilyard or Ed, I stumbled upon one of those mysterious truths—art directors can't spell. So I corrected signs and dredged from memory some of Mussolini's slogans to be scrawled on walls past which the movie's trucks would roll. When these were accepted without demur I grew braver.

I had not been in the Industry long enough to learn to equate film quality with squalor; to me *Von Ryan* was a romantic adventure story, a masculine fairy tale to be dressed as a fairy tale is dressed, vividly, in rags or robes. So whenever possible, I would nag for a more picturesque corner, for a glimpse of a postcard vista, a fountain, a broken pediment. I was a tourist who had spent years in a history-of-art class long ago studying and copying (charcoal and wash, heightened with poster white) all the landmarks and artbook examples. Westheimer's novel had little of such stuff—his memory was too drably accurate for that. The screenplay followed the novel, and since the actual railroad line through Rome passed through industrial outskirts, we might as well have been in Newark.

Go through Rome and not glimpse St. Peter's or the Forum or the Colosseum? To hell with that.

"No problem. We'll put a camera on a truck and shoot moving points of view of all that stuff, okay?"

"Do it."

So it was done and shipped off to the studio. And much, much later —in defiance of truth and those somber standards most directors honor —those glimpses were cut into the film. Every time the POWs stole a look out of the prison boxcars they saw something that said "Rome, Italy, folks."

Once Brown and Graves got the idea, there was no holding them. Colonel Ryan's plane was supposed to crash in a field near an olive grove. They found a grove on one of those incredible terraced hillsides, crowned with a walled town, approached through an avenue of cypress and oleander.

As principal photography day approached we began worrying about extras. The problem was simply that we needed lots of German soldiers —the reality of occupied Italy, guards for the POWs, squads of pursuing troops, the works. We had uniforms, but the Italians waiting in long lines at the employment offices of the studio looked like—Italians. Sam the Foreign Production Manager told Harry the overall Production Manager that it was a cinch, don't worry. But I worried—and when I mentioned it to Robson he frowned, summoned Harry and gave orders. Harry went off, returned and informed me there would be an extra call —German-type extras only—on the following day.

"Mark says you can handle it."

In Hollywood, only secretaries and agents take leisurely lunches; if you're working on a picture it's usually quick and sometimes on the fly. Not so in Cinecittà, Rome. The Italian custom was a heavy lunch, wine and the works, then a siesta and finally back to work as the shadows lengthened. We Americans never really formed the siesta habit, but lunches grew long and social, gabbing away for drowsy hours while the sensible Italians slept or made love and slept. For us the reward was a building pleasantly silent, the smells of sweat and urine absent for a while, telephones and chairs available; the American hour.

Not that day. Harry the Production Manager met us on the terrace outside Cinecittà's studio restaurant.

"Looking all over for you, David," he said, hawking and leering amiably at Judy and Jennifer, who winced at the sound. "Your extras are waiting for you. On the far side of the building."

He grinned. "Better get over there," he said and trotted off.

Nearing our building, there was a sound like Saturday at the zoo—many voices all talking at once, some shouting.

As we came around the corner the sight was remarkable. There were perhaps two hundred men, mostly young but some teenagers and some grandpas, all crowding up to one of the side doors, waving their fists and conversing heatedly with one of our Italian assistants, who stood on a bench, pressed against the door, looking desperate. Every once in a while he would yell something, but the yell would be instantly drowned by the response. We stopped, and as we did, the assistant saw us and pointed. The whole crowd fell silent, turned as one and swept off caps and hats.

They were all blond. All of them—ranging in color from platinum to a kind of circus-wagon orange, through every shade of yellow in between. Swarthy faces, dark eyes and eyebrows—but hair all blazing yellow in the sunlight.

Now they surged toward us, and the girls ran.

Even in Hollywood, using professional extras, the mass "cattle call" is no fun, but this one was the worst. Trying to ignore the alternately pleading or threatening looks on those desperate and grotesque faces, I somehow picked half and dismissed the others. When I turned to go they all followed me. I stopped and turned back to them. They stopped too—the chosen half smiling broadly, the others looking like murder. Fortunately the Italian assistant began yelling at them, and at his voice they wheeled on him and a shouting, pushing fight broke out. I didn't wait, but turned and dodged into the building. The girls were inside, watching from an office window.

"Poor bloody bahstards," Jennifer said, in her genteel accent. "Somebody went round to the unemployment and put up notices saying we needed German soldiers for a film, so they all went out and dyed their hair. Christ!"

"Awful. But what are they fighting about?"

"They're not really fighting," Judy said. "They're trying to make deals with the assistant. They know damn well you'll never remember one of them from another, so they're trying to make deals for the jobs."

"The assistant will get bloody fat on this one," said Jennifer.

16

§

We
Commence Shooting
in Rome

*L*ET THERE BE MONEY. Let the great hose from the bank, strained and tumid with gelt, gush greenly forth on the weary who have believed . . . and let the cooing of agents be heard.

Every week the trade papers are full of production announcements; producers, directors, stars and start dates are confidently stated. But every Friday the log of films actually being shot tells the drab truth. A hundred brave announcements may yield one produced film. The rest are hope, puffery or agents and managers chumming the water.

"Is it really going to go?"

The person asking knows the respondent doesn't know and the respondent knows the questioner knows. . . .

"Absolutely. *They*'ve got it almost all put together."

If the answer means anything, it means They have consulted Them and jointly decided the project might be worth four million eight all in but exclusive of overhead . . . if. If one of five young men, one of three young women and a director acceptable to both stars and to management can be brought together at the price and during the time period in which the film should be shot to make the release date wanted for it.

That decision makes it a "go" project.

To achieve principal photography is a sort of miracle now—even then it was a triumph against odds. But there we were. During all those weeks the army had been assembling in Rome, the arrivals ranging from unobtrusive to noticeable to performances on a par with Garbo's entrance in *Grand Hotel.* But regardless, each reported at once to the production offices, drew his hotel assignment and per-diem money and disappeared. Except for fanatics, rehearsals are unknown. *They* hate to spend money not immediately visible on the screen. Of course, a strong director will get his rehearsals before the camera. "Let's try it again, please," when each repetition costs a hell of a lot more than rehearsal time.

Howard Koch said, "Tomorrow's the day. You come with Ruthie and me to welcome Frank. Your star. Right?"

"Right."

"Besides, I bet you never saw anything like it."

"I'm sure," I said. "Should I order a limo?"

"Hell no. Ride with us."

"I meant for Sinatra."

"Hey," Howard said, "you forgot. With Frank you have to remember these things."

I remembered. Sinatra was not going to set foot in the unmannerly city of the Caesars.

" . . . plane will taxi to the end of the last runway and the chopper will land right next to it. He gets out of one and into the other and that's it."

"You mean they let him off first?"

Koch stared and laughed. "You think Frank flies commercial? It's a charter, baby. He's only coming from Nice."

Only a few of us insiders were supposed to know the day and hour of Sinatra's arrival, but the airport was full of people clustered around the last gate, waiting, pointing, looking at us with that look they have when awaiting the start of major sporting events or the sight of Sinatra.

Years later I watched as a late-hour room at the Fontainebleau filled with people who were there because they knew Sinatra came there for late supper after his show. The star and his friends always sat along one wall at rectangular tables; the rest of the room was filled with round ones. As the customers filed in, they seated themselves with the men together, backs to the Sinatra wall, and the ladies squeezed close across from them, facing it. It was a kind of *sol y sombra* seating, almost as if the chairs with a view of Sinatra cost more. And throughout that evening, other guests would stop in the doorway and peer through the haze with that look. Seeing him, the women would say something, the escorts would shrug and in they'd come, each couple picking its way through the tables with the man leading, guiding and muttering, "Oops, excuse," while towing the lady, whose eyes never left Sinatra. One loop of the room and out. Sometimes an especially bold couple would take a route which brought them really close, and sometimes a glassy-smiling lady would say something—usually just the name. When that happened, Sinatra would always hear it and he would glance up and brighten minutely before turning back to the always busy and laughing conversation at the long table.

The airport crowd was looking at us with some of that intensity as we *scusi*'d our way out and took our station at the foot of the last ramp. Behind us the crowd pressed noses and palms against the aquarium-tinted plate windows, craning past exit guards.

I heard a helicopter thrashing, and one appeared from behind the terminal, hovered and settled about fifty feet away. The rotor blades continued to swish idly as the pilot opened the door and waved.

Koch waved back. "Don, Frank's pilot. He can fly anything. You wait —you'll see him put that thing down on a tablecloth."

I had not met the pilot or realized one would accompany the star's group. "Where's he been all this time?"

"Been? He's been busy as hell, getting to know every place he might have to fly into—getting permits and all that. Pretty tough, too. They take a dim view of Frank's chopper coming down on the platform of a railroad station."

"I should think so." A railroad station? I began visualizing where a helicopter might land in some of the narrow corners planned for shooting.

"Confidentially," Koch said, "we'll have to play it by ear in a couple of spots where they just wouldn't budge. One place they said there's a secret army installation and they just won't let anyone overfly. . . ."

The plane was about ten minutes late. It was not announced, but suddenly everyone was pointing at a giant DC-7 which taxied off the runway and made its way over to the helicopter. We went down the landing ramp and waited at the bottom.

I don't remember how many were on the plane, but I do recall that Sinatra's man George came down the ramp first, shook hands with all of us, whispered something to Howard and trotted off to the helicopter. Sinatra came briskly down the stairs, saying "Hi hello howareya" without warmth. To me he said, "Everything all right?" and without waiting for an answer took Koch's arm and moved off a few steps. I couldn't hear what he said—Howard seemed to be trying to explain, but Sinatra wouldn't have it. He shook his head, walked off a few feet toward the helicopter, then turned. This time I could hear the words.

"Did I *ask* you how much it cost?" With that, he went to the helicopter and got in. Instantly the machine revved, flexed itself and began to move.

As we watched it go, I looked my question.

"What was that about?"

"The goddam plane. Can you imagine? 'I told you to charter a jet!' he says."

"So why didn't you?"

"I *told* him," Koch said. "There just wasn't anything available for charter. Nothing. Christ. I even tried to buy one, figuring I'd sell it back home. But the modifications you have to make cost a fortune—we'd never have got it back."

Howard was cheerful again by the time we threaded our way through the crowd, which was starting to break up now. Now we were really stared at—pointed out with those expressive chin gestures and knowing squints. Obviously we glowed from Sinatra's light, an afterglow like luminous paint. It was my first taste of henchhood. . . .

Long afterward, when Howard was the big man at Paramount, I asked him whether Sinatra's remark was serious.

"He didn't really want you to buy a jet airplane for that flight, did he?"

Howard shook his head. "I don't think so," he said, "but you couldn't be sure. With Frank, you couldn't be sure about things like that."

We began shooting *Von Ryan's Express* on the following Monday morning at one of Rome's railroad stations, with a major dramatic scene out of the middle of the picture.

A movie company on location moves in like the circus, by night. When I arrived, about eight-thirty in the morning, we were in business —our tents and elephants in place. It was impressive. Trucks, generators, sound equipment, camera equipment and portable toilets. Dressing-room trailers, first aid and breakfast—the ubiquitous coffee urn flanked by the pastries and the crude sign suggesting you leave some money. There were places for cast and crew to park and arrowed signs indicating which way to go for what. Great parallel ropes of cable were everywhere. Rows of lights and light stands, ladders and stacks of the green wooden cubes called apple boxes. Crewmen trotted back and forth carrying things, responding to instructions in two languages— neither understandable to me nor to the nodding, smiling, black-suited Italian functionaries who stood by watching it all.

At the center of it all was Bill Daniels, white-haired, pink-cheeked and quick-tempered, one of the legendary lighting cameramen from the great days of MGM. Garbo's cameraman.

The people who visit movie sets—fans, executives or critics—see the whole effort being made at the service of the actors and the director. Really, the entire undertaking, from machines to people, is in the service of the camera, and its needs determine all the possibilities. When Daniels said to Robson, "I think you'll have to play it over here, Mark —I can't light that setup," there was no contest.

Robson's willingness to begin with a difficult, major scene employing all the principals was bold and typically canny. If there was going to be *that* kind of problem, he wanted to know right out front—before people got to know each other and the inevitable cliques and rooting sections were formed. He was establishing a command presence on the set, a presence he would need. And if the film shot was anything but disastrously bad, it would be heady stuff in the dailies, which They would see three days later. All the same, it was a gamble.

Robson had worked with some of the actors before, but not with the major principals. Few of the actors had even met before that morning, and none of the British or Germans had worked with Sinatra before. After introductions were made, the people who knew each other drew off into groups, chatting, smoking, drinking tea and coffee and eyeing Sinatra, who sat waiting in a canvas chair propped against a pillar, surrounded by his friends. In front of the group, quartering back and forth like a sheepdog, kneeling, rising, now on a ladder, now on his back looking up, our unit special photographer, Dave Sutton, snapping, snapping, snapping . . . "Could you just look up a second, Frank?"

Trevor Howard, Edward Mulhare and the others watched. I saw Robson, busy getting the setup, glance that way and shake his head. After a half hour of this I took the unit publicist aside and suggested he tell the photographer that there were other worthwhile subjects around. The publicist, a sardonic young man, flickered a smile at me and strolled down the platform to talk to the photographer, who reacted like a kid being asked to get off a merry go-round while it was moving. But finally he turned and began nodding his head as other pictures were suggested. Just then there was a loud staccato squawking sound. Bill Daniels, squeezing the rubber-bulbed old-time car horn he had strapped to the camera.

"Let's *go,* everybody. Ready on the set."

Sinatra was already trotting up the platform, taking a last drag on a cigarette as he went.

Rehearsal. Pretty good. Adjustments—would Sinatra move in tighter, please? "Dispatcher, you don't know who to be more scared of. That's it. Right. You just grip the guns and try *not* to look back. Cut your eyes a couple—right. That looks pretty good. One more, please."

Bill Daniels turned to me. "Like to look through the camera?"

Thrilled. I watched through the camera as Mulhare led the others into the office, took a deep breath and advanced on the dispatcher, slapping one glove into his palm as he spoke. I watched as the dispatcher hesitated, saw Sinatra and Howard tighten as the door to the office opened and the two raincoats came in, peered and sat.

"Okay," Robson said. "Let's make one."

I turned to him. "Can I talk to you a second?"

He was impatient. "What?"

As privately as possible I said, "Those two Gestapo agents are covered when they sit down—I don't know if you noticed. . . . "

"So?"

"So since the suspense sort of depends on our seeing the threat in the background . . ." He was staring at me. I shut up.

He turned back to the camera. "Okay, let's try it," he said. "Quiet, everyone . . . places."

And while the assistants were echoing the call for quiet and the camera was getting ready to roll, he glanced back at me.

"We'll get them in the individuals," he said. "Now why don't you find a chair someplace."

Action . . .

17

§

Two Weeks in–
and in Trouble

"**D**ON'T WORRY about buttoning up the contract. I've been doing this a long time, and believe me, the picture will be out in the drive-ins before the paperwork is finished."

Your lawyer tells you that with a smile and the obvious sense that he's said something reassuring.

You make all the promises, many of them impossible and a few humiliating. The boilerplate in those contracts has piled up for a half century, and the small type may obligate you to deliver something obsolete since sound. But the clauses stay in, and so do all the penalties—what They can do to you if you should fall short somewhere. They promise only "best efforts" and "consent not to be unreasonably withheld." A Moslem marriage contract favors the wife more.

Moreover, both sides understand that if things go wrong, the studio will simply refuse to honor the contract. You will then meet in the office of an honors graduate of some illustrious law school who will say, "Fuck you, sue us."

If you are one of the very few—actor, director or producer—who come to wield great power in the Industry, you may very well become "difficult" when you get the chance to screw Them in turn. The problem, of course, is that it's almost impossible to injure Them without mowing down lots of innocents too. The problem of the clean shot.

We were less than two weeks in when it became apparent that we were in trouble. True to tradition, we had promised more than we could deliver. And as Koch had said, Sinatra demanded exactly what had been promised. On the set, he never stopped insisting the deal be followed to the letter. And, of course, he was within his right.

"I have to keep working," Sinatra had said, over and over again. "I mean, I won't sit around on the set and wait. Now can you do that?"

"No sweat." I still remembered the meetings in Zanuck's office—Zanuck looking to Robson, who beamed reassurance. And other meetings without Sinatra present—talk about schedules and moves and putting things "back to back to keep going" and "throwing the reverses off till later" and other arcane bits which meant very little to me at the time.

Now they meant trouble. Harry the Production Manager spent every spare moment bent angrily over the production board, and there were many sudden, frowning consultations with Robson—even on the set. The shooting schedule was being revised every day, as it became ferociously clear that Sinatra would settle for nothing less than the outrageous letter of the understanding.

"But Frank, if we stay with your stuff and leave the others until you're done, we blow the light and it won't match. You can see that, can't you?"

"Absolutely. So what're you gonna do?"

And he would stalk off while Robson, face working, sent someone to find Harry. And the schedule would be twisted again while Robson tried desperately to work out some way to give him the full coverage he was used to while keeping the star working. Given his style of careful, methodical coverage, it must have been torture.

I got an odd illumination on the point. Late one afternoon I had been called back to Cinecittà to verify something or other. Finishing too late to return to location, I went to the screening room and asked to see the dailies, film shot three or four days earlier and just returned to the company for viewing. The projectionist was willing, and I took a seat and signaled him to roll, but just as the light dimmed, the door opened and a small man entered, walked to the end of my row and sat in the aisle seat. We watched in silence.

When it was finished and the lights on, I saw the other man was a neat, grayish fellow with glasses, a toothbrush mustache and a pursed upper lip.

"How'd you like the stuff?" he said.

I was noncommittal but he bored in. "Just so-so, you think?"

I shrugged.

He got up. "That's Robson for you," he said. "One, two, three, kick. One, two, three, kick." Then, just as abruptly, he wheeled and left the room.

I watched him through the door, then signaled the projectionist. "Hey—who was that?"

The squawk box blurted, then: "Are you kidding? Darryl Zanuck."

And there was no shortage of people making things worse. If there had ever been a chance of an understanding between Robson and Sinatra, it evaporated after a couple of nose-to-nose confrontations out on the set for all our small and jealous world to see and hear. Always behind Sinatra were his friends, quick with the meaningful and contemptuous asides, murderous with the nudges—"You gonna let him get away with that, Frank?" For them, Sinatra seemed a kind of loaded gun which they would point at the director's head. Often I saw Sinatra grow impatient with the game—almost as if he was waiting for a different gambit. But he would not back down, and Robson couldn't. He had no grace to offer, only pride, and there was nowhere for him to back.

Naturally, rumors of trouble reached the studio at once, and I spent long, long hours on the telephone with Dick Zanuck. "Now here's what I want you to say when you see Frank getting pissed off . . . you got that?" Since the connections were often terrible, my rehearsals didn't accomplish much more than let Dick Zanuck, half a world away, feel he was controlling the situation. But even if I had been a letter-perfect tiger, it wouldn't have helped much.

To make matters worse, I was quickly compromised—at least in Robson's eyes. In those on-the-set eruptions, Sinatra rarely relied on any strength but his own. He *told* you how it was and disdained any offers of proof. "I'm warning you" and "You hear!?" was about as close as he came to explaining his reasons. But once, in response to some rejoinder about the difficulty and extravagance of that way of working, he said, unexpectedly mildly, "Look, Mark. I *know* all that. I didn't tell you how to schedule the picture. I just told you what I wanted, and you told me, *in front of witnesses,* that you could do it. That was the deal." Suddenly hard again. "So now *do* it! You hear?" He turned away and noticed me nearby. He turned back. "There's one of the witnesses!" He pointed. "Your producer."

Everybody waited. "Well?"

Whatever I said was full of "buts"—but it slammed the door as far as Mark Robson was concerned, and confirmed my isolation. Now Robson stopped talking to me except for necessary business exchanges. The production staff, headed by Harry the Production Manager, who expected to do Robson's next picture as well, treated me correctly, but made it a point not to volunteer anything. "Oh, yes, Mr. David, there *was* a cable for you. Maybe they sent it to your hotel." I was never an intimate of Sinatra's. He was unfailingly cordial and polite to me, but our talk was always business and I was not invited to the villa.

And the next time I tried to use the Gorgeous Elizabeth john, it was locked. It got to be wading time down the hall among the Italian graffiti. The toilet paper down there gleamed a mottled pinkish-gray in the light of the single bulb. It had a smooth, hard, chinalike surface and made a crisp sound when folded. Tossed onto the reeking wet floor to act as a blotter, it floated.

All the same it was Italy and it was summer. The weather held brilliant and clear, and Robson had agreed to shoot the recapture sequence in Hadrian's Villa—a meaningful score for my campaign of nagging him into using as many beautiful and unique locations as possible instead of the nondescript reality called for in the script. He had balked at first, complained that it wasn't the look he had imagined—but in the end he was as knocked out as the rest of us with the splendor of it, astonished at how easy it was to get permission to film in one of the great monuments of ancient Rome.

To this day I have no idea why. We moved into the enormous, partly reconstructed ruins of Emperor Hadrian's summer palace as if it were our own backlot. We weren't guarded or watched or warned, although everywhere we looked there were neatly stacked chunks of statuary— limbs, pillars, pediments, tessera, some vivid fragments of mosaic, just lying around for anyone to cart away. Incredible. We told each other that you'd be jailed for life if someone caught you, but no one went to jail. I pocketed a handful of tiny marble floor tiles. Hadrian's cufflinks now.

The art directors were ecstatic. And Bill Daniels looked and looked again and grumped his pleasure at the avenue of thickly laced trees which could be used for a day-for-night sequence. He nodded approval at the splendid ruined arches piled on each other. "Do the high fall over there," he said. Robson peered through a rectangle made of his fingers and nodded.

The stunt men were already gathered in a little group, pointing, gesturing, figuring out the fall. "You can hide the boxes there but he's got to arch his back, this way. I think he ought to go sideways and shove off—to clear that piece, see?"

In the film sequence, the escaped POWs have hidden overnight in

the ruins, expecting to be led to safety in the morning. Instead, they are
betrayed to the Germans, recaptured and put aboard the train whose
trip furnishes the story.

The enemy is first seen by a sentry perched high on a ruined tower.
Crying alarm, he is shot and he topples. It was not a terribly high fall
—maybe twenty-five feet—but the ancient, jagged outcroppings made
it tricky. Around the camera there was a lot of pointing and head-
shaking. Then I noticed cameraman Bill Daniels deep in conversation
with one of the stunt men, who was clearly demonstrating not only how
the fall could be done, but how the shot should be made. And surprisingly, Bill Daniels was nodding his shaggy white head in vigorous approval.

Bill Daniels, kindly and endlessly helpful to me, was one of the legendary autocrats of the camera, intolerant of sloppy work and contemptuous of the game of Me Too.

Actor to cinematographer: "What kind of lens you using for this one,
pal—a forty? Oh, a fifty—yeah, yeah, of course"—a quick gesture—"you
gotta get all this . . . sure, right, right, right . . ."

Bill Daniels did not put up with this kind of harmless ruboff. Instead
of making the helpful reply, he would wait for the full stop. Then
crisply, blue eyes magnified enormously by the oversized pilot-style
glasses he wore, he'd say, "I just don't know, Marlon. What lens would
you suggest?"

This terrible old man protected his pink-and-white complexion by
wearing a floppy-brimmed hat with a large handkerchief tucked in
behind like a foreign-legion kepi. To see that handkerchief waving
agreement to a stunt man's ideas about where to put the camera was
striking. I walked over, listened, asked a few questions and fell into
conversation with a slim, flat, sad-eyed, broken-nosed fellow with a
hip-shot stance and a sudden, wide smile. Buzz. Robert "Buzz" Henry.

Some years and several movies later, I saw his name on the credits
of one of those old black-and-white movies you see on the higher chan-
nels on Saturday mornings. He was called Robert "Buzzy" Henry then
—a child co-star in a story about bluegrass, mint juleps and a race to be
won, a picture starring Stu Erwin. I watched, and saw a deer-eyed kid
who seemed always to be grinning shyly down from a large horse.

"Let me ride him, Pete. I just know I can win that race if you can get
the Colonel to let me. . . . "

When I learned all that, I marveled. Buzz had been a child star of
some candlepower way back then, but he never mentioned it until I
brought it up myself. He was not shy—rather it was part of the grace

of a man whose surprises were always pleasant and whose friendship was full of unexpected bonuses.

Buzz was not gaffing the stunts on the show, but his sense of just where the camera should be to see a piece of action was already notable. I asked the innocent's regular question. "Will you rehearse it?"

They laughed and Buzz said, "Not unless we miss the first time."

Foolish question, ritual answer. Then he realized that I really didn't know and said, "Want to help us set it up?"

I did, and he led me over to the group of stunt men who were already helping to stack the cardboard boxes—squinting from time to time at the pinnacle from which the fall would go, making short arcs with their forearms to suggest the angle.

Like everyone else, I had assumed that falls were made into mattresses and was fascinated to learn that such pads were only used for short falls. High ones were then made into piles of cardboard boxes. "Got just the right amount of give to slow you up." Nowadays they do use mattresses filled with air, with special valves to let the air rush out at the moment of impact.

Buzz explained with that offhand manner stunt men affect, complicated, in his case, by a whimsical cowboy style and an unexpected giggle. Just when I needed one, I made a friend.

Here in Oz, everyone wants something—a heart, a brain, courage. Is it different where you are? There was a time when it was important to be athletic. There were fist fights in night clubs, agents talked about "punching the son of a bitch out," trainers made housecalls in Beverly Hills and many an All-American jock became a movie maker.

Of course, such a jock-mogul could not pretend to keep his innocence, but he remembered it. Moviemaking is brutally physical even now—far more than the young men with criteria can imagine.

So the Industry's plebeian jocks, the stunt men, have always seemed special and pure—a kind of gentle warrior caste like Kurosawa's samurais, menacing, high-principled and comfortingly for sale. Stars and executives who will rage if you speak disparagingly about Hottentots will talk about stunt men as if they were Arabian horses.

Von Ryan's Express rolled onward like a Panzer division, bypassing strong points, leaving behind pockets of resistance. Every day the helicopter arrived just as everything was ready, and Sinatra would jump out, fully dressed, made up and ready to go. Still crouching away from the rotor blades, he'd wave at the pilot and the machine would snarl, lurch forward and rise, the noise deafening, propwash tearing at everything. And when his work was done (one of the Companions having radioed from the set) the chopper would be right there and he'd vault in, wave and disappear over the rooftops and into the setting sun.

It was enough to drive a co-star to drink. Too late, I hired the longest, shiniest Lincoln Continental-with-driver in Rome for Trevor Howard, who was effusively grateful—but the haunted look was in his eye for the run of the picture. Since Howard was a gentleman, unfailingly civil, there was unhappiness but no great fuss. And only once did the director's simmering rage and frustration surface.

A huge night scene—hundreds of men scrambling pell-mell from the train into the darkness, only to have that darkness erupt into blinding, earth-shaking explosions, as the ammo dump nearby went up. Spectacular stuff, dangerous and difficult and very expensive. We had a large audience, too, come for fireworks.

The scene starts softly, all stealth, everyone holding his breath. The train grinds to a halt in the darkness. The pretend-Nazi guards climb down, look around, and we focus on our two leading men. The decision is made—"We get out here!" And now the British commander moves to the first boxcar, slaps the door smartly with the flat of his hand and calls in an urgent whisper, "End of the line, lads. Everyone out!" And that starts it.

But it had been a wet evening. What happened was this: The train stopped, for once wondrously accurate. The guards piled off the top. The camera moved in, and now it was Fincham/Howard's moment. He hitched his belt, scuttled over to the leading boxcar, paused, swung—and missed. Down he went, rolling in the cinders. Hysterical whoops of laughter from cast, crew and the watching hundreds. And over it all I could hear Robson's voice, cutting like wire. "Keep cranking! Stay on him! Keep cranking!"

That was a late night.

Rome was aware of *Von Ryan's Express.* Sinatra's decision to live "quietly" without coming into the city only set fire to the imagination of the press—and everyone was agog with stories of wild doings behind the villa's walls, stories that seemed to have been updated from the ripe stuff about Nero's Golden House and Tiberius' island. Much as we enjoyed the stories and natural as it was to want to believe, the sight of Sinatra on the set bright and early, snapping his fingers, impatient to get going, suggested strongly to the contrary. As he once told a reporter who questioned him about such yarns, "If I did half of what they say, I wouldn't be here—I'd be in a bottle at Harvard."

Still, the Companions told of a steady flow of visitors from all over—

and sure enough, people like Mike Romanoff would show up on the sets, be around for a while and disappear.

We heard Ava Gardner was visiting and waited in vain for her to appear. It was disappointing to Sinatra-watchers and especially to the growing retinue of little men festooned with cameras who now followed us everywhere, looking for Frank. They kept up a round-the-clock surveillance at the villa, and by climbing trees and telephone poles, using long lenses and possibly hot-air balloons, managed to snap occasional blurred and hurried photographs which appeared all over the press, accompanied by lurid captions. If a photographer was lucky, he would be seen by Sinatra just at the moment—then he'd have one of those treasures, the man shaking his fist at the camera. SINATRA BLAZES DEFIANCE AT THOSE WHO CRITICIZE HIS INCREDIBLE WAY OF LIFE!

A once-qualified Sinatra-watcher, I have often been asked—or rather told—that the man courts publicity. If so, I didn't see it. The view that if he just minded his own business the press would let him alone seems to me obviously silly. In fact, he does mind his own business. But he insists on anybody's right to privacy in public—which is not only impossible, it's really what stirs everyone up. I never saw him do any of the things other celebrities do routinely to make sure they're bothered. Maybe if he'd allow his enemies to pick his friends they might dull his finish—but I doubt it.

While working in a steep railroad cut which bisected a dusty little village twenty miles from Rome, we had visitors. From my perch on a slope above and behind the camera, I saw a long, black car crammed with people pull up at the barricades on the far side of the cut. A uniformed chauffeur got out and began an animated discussion with one of our guards, posted there to keep innocent villagers from wandering into WWII. Many glances toward the set, followed by shrugs and that eloquent, palms-up "Don't ask *me*" sign. Finally our guard gestured to the chauffeur to wait while he went to the set to inquire. As he left I could see many faces inside the limousine, all turned whitely toward the set.

After a while our guard trotted back up the hillside to the waiting car. His gesture was clear—"No way!" There was a sputter of argument which ended when our man simply turned his back and walked away, stopped and stood firm, ignoring the car. The chauffeur spoke to the passengers, waved his helplessness, shrugged and got back into the driver's seat. After a moment the car backed up and turned around, inching back into position. Then it rolled off in a cloud of pinkish dust.

I had forgotten the incident when, some days later, I came upon Judy and Jennifer reading one of the local papers, both of them with that look that meant another juicy Sinatra item. When they saw me they both said, "Why didn't you tell us?"

"Tell you what?"

According to the paper, the "Sinatra Company" had been visited by a group of Sinatra's relatives from somewhere in the south. These poor people had supposedly scraped up their pennies, sold their dry farms and mortgaged the cows in order to rent an automobile so they could visit their famous relative. And when they got there, armed men had ordered them off at gunpoint while Sinatra stood behind them and watched. Something like that—very colorful.

"What was it like?"

"Did he really call them 'dirty beggars'?"

I told them what I had seen, spoiling a good story. "But who were they?"

At the first opportunity I asked Brad Dexter, companion number one. Were they relatives?

He looked around and lowered his voice confidentially. "Damned if I know," he said. "Frank just said, 'No—no visitors.' "

18

§

The Guy Who Can Handle Sinatra

IN THE FINALE of *Von Ryan's Express*, the burning train crashes through into Switzerland and freedom. By that time only one or two boxcars are still attached. The others have been thrown across the path of the oncoming German wolves.

By the end of the third shooting week, we were doing just that to the schedule. In my copy of the screenplay, the crossed-out pages, indicating scenes shot, were sprinkled with shots and angles left behind in the headlong rush to keep the star busy.

Robson was trying to gain time. He crammed and squeezed, held down retakes and pared off marginal locations. So we never made the grand helicopter shot planned for Florence or watched our train slide by Pisa's tower, left to right. But those were frosting. We gambled with the cake itself by not going to Milan—scene of the most important action in the escape, the desperate attempt to get the train through an immense urban rail complex unseen by the Germans until too late. To elect to fake the whole thing—to make it up out of bits and pieces shot here and there over many months—was calculated recklessness but we were desperate. A section of a Roman freight terminal was festooned with lighted signs saying MILANO. Sight lines were blocked with travel posters, and we shot the scene at night, kept the camera close and moved fast. If it had not worked, we wouldn't have found out until months after shooting was finished, actors gone away and crew dispersed. To have gone back to Italy then would have been staggeringly expensive. For a director as careful and methodical as Robson to take such a gamble must have been very hard. And we had not solved the problem of the omitted shots, made frightening by our commitment to move to Cortina. There we would film the action sequences leading up to the ending itself, which was to be shot in Spain unless I could persuade Robson to shoot it in Cortina. Then, with the ending done, we would return to Hollywood to film the prison camp, the escape and a number of difficult stunts in addition to inserts, process shots, matching close-ups and so on—the normal end-of-shooting debris. In all of this, the one rigid date was for our move to Cortina, the schedule for working there comparably tight. After all, we were straddling a nation's railroads at the height of summer tourist season. Bad enough in and around Rome, where shoals of black-suited RR officials attended our every move, winced at our delays, smiled painfully and answered politely, always glancing at those gold pocket watches. But around Rome there were lots of tracks available. We caused confusions and delays, but no major stoppage. In the Alps it was a different story. We were using the only line there was—the major artery from the mountain cities to the plains which fed them. Once we moved to Cortina, the die was cast and if those omitted shots had not been made, they might never be. So Robson tried to gain time any way he could.

We consulted railroad maps and nagged officials for information about spur lines, dead ends, sections where few trains ran. Then one day —triumph! Someone had found a completely abandoned spur line not twenty miles from Rome—complete with double tracks, sidings, switches and an abandoned station. The promised land.

Next morning the art directors and I set out in a small, trolleylike rail car, gasoline powered. We chugged along the right-of-way, turned off onto sidings from time to time to let the important stuff go by, and finally came to the place. Sure enough—an overgrown switch, obviously unused, and four streaks of rust bending off to the right, to disappear into a thicket of overhanging branches.

We gawked enthusiastically. Our guide was pleased that we were pleased, signori. We urged him on. He smiled, took off his black coat, folded it over his seat back, got out and went to the switch. The key finally went into the slot and the track mechanism groaned as he strained at the handle. Then the rusty steel parallelogram turned and clicked into place. Back he came, beaming, put on the black jacket, started the motor. Slowly we bumped across the joined rails and into the hanging branches. He stopped the car again, got out and turned the switch back into position, more easily now.

It was marvelous. Clear of the branches, we entered a shallow valley. The countryside was nondescript—no place, anyplace. There were trees, distant hills, cutbanks and a small station complete with outbuildings. Ten miles of railroad where we could work day or night without interruption!

We were wildly excited, kept yelling to the driver to stop, clambering out to peer through our fingers. "Hey—you know that scene where they have to stop to get water? Look this way . . . "

Our guide caught our excitement, and the little car began accelerating like a sports car, with us cheering and exclaiming over the chugging of the motor. We sped onward through Canaan.

Screeching. Ripping and tearing—the car suddenly jolting wildly, floorboards breaking upward. The little car had left the rails. We went banging and crashing along the ties for some fifty feet—then slowly, slowly, over and down in a storm of broken glass. Finally, silence and the smell of gasoline.

No matter how remote or inaccessible the movie location, when you're shooting there are always spectators. They materialize from sheer rock faces and empty hillsides, out of jungle thickets and swamps. You know they're there when the camera turns and the cameraman screams, "*Cut!* There's somebody moving in the background," and the director turns on the first assistant. . . .

The crashing car must have made a noise like artillery in that valley of small farms. But in the quiet after the car stopped, only birds and the distant barking of a dog. Like in the movies.

We picked ourselves up carefully, checking. Lots of small cuts, ripped clothing and bruises—nothing broken. The official stared at his badly torn black jacket and, staring, wept. Hilyard Brown shook himself like a wet dog, then suddenly shoved the upended door open and dropped to the ground. "Come on," he yelled. "Give us a hand." And scuttled off.

We climbed out, puzzled. By then Hilyard was back with a long timber—like a two-by-four—from somewhere. He jabbed it fiercely under the car and began to heave on it. "Come on. Find something and help!" At that point the timber snapped and he sprawled on his face on the sandy ties. When he sat up he was sane again.

There was nothing to do but walk back down the track, hoping to spot a house with a telephone. It was hard to get the official to leave his wrecked car. He kept sticking his fingers through the holes in his jacket, shaking his head and muttering in Italian. It was even harder to persuade him to use his English again.

A short distance down the track we saw what had happened. There, where a narrow country road crossed the rails, sand had filled the tracks to the brim. The car had rolled up the packed sand and off. We switched to the road, plodded around a bend and in the distance saw a house which looked prosperous enough to have a telephone. We felt better. As we approached the house it began to rain lightly.

The spur line was a great timesaver, however. We approached the end of the Rome-based pages with over a week to spare. Except for the bypassed shots, of course.

The dilemma was solved as movie dilemmas are always solved—with the laying on of money. Lawyers had conferred, friends had been consulted, Dick had talked to Darryl, and Sinatra had agreed. A hiatus. A vacation with pay for the star while Robson tidied up the loose ends. And what a nice vacation. A yacht had been rented—a big one, big enough for Sinatra and his house guests and then some.

"That's right. They'll sail around the goddam Mediterranean for a goddam week. When you guys are ready for him in Cortina, he gets off the thing in Genoa and flies up to meet you. Okay?"

"It's no crazier than anything else," I said.

Suddenly Zanuck ordered me home. "For discussions. Get on the next plane."

A day later, dizzy and anxious, I showed up in his office.

"Here's the problem," he said. "Robson wants your ass fired off the picture. Phil"—Robson's agent—"is on the phone every day about it. What do you think?"

"What do I think about what?" I was still woozy from the long flight, disoriented by the change. Fuck it. Easy come, easy go.

"Can you stick it out with him?"

Stan Hough, sitting at the side in a back-tilted chair, let the front legs down. He was grinning. "Take it easy, Rich," he said. "He thought you were firing him."

Zanuck relaxed, peering at me. "You did, didn't you?"

"Sure."

"You sore?" Having someone on the defensive always made him gleeful and generous. "Don't worry. You're not leaving. Stan told me about the way you handled Sinatra."

"That's right," Stan said. "Day I was there."

I remembered. We had been going to shoot a little scene in a small dispatch tower which stood among the rails off the end of the platform on one of the Rome stations. The stairway up the tower was narrow, the office at the top cramped. Knowing I would be in the way, I had remained on the platform while Robson and Sinatra and the key people went to look. In a few minutes they were back, everybody scowling. Sinatra went past me down the platform and dropped into a chair. Robson stalked up and announced that we were not making the shot.

"He doesn't like the setup. He says we can pick it up at the studio when we get back. Got that?" He was talking to Harry the Production manager and Hilyard Brown. But loudly.

It made no sense to me. "What can we do today if we don't do this stuff?"

Robson shrugged. "He says a train scene."

"No way," said Harry the Production Manager. "By the time we get the train into position, we lose the whole day."

"Well, producer," Robson said, "you want to talk to him about it? He's *your* friend."

I turned to Hilyard. "What will it cost us to build the set at home?"

"About fifteen thousand dollars," Hilyard said, "counting everything —not just construction."

I walked down the platform to Sinatra, sitting among the Companions. "Frank—can I talk to you about this?"

"Why not?" He gestured to the others. "Give us some room?"

I don't remember the conversation except that it was brief and perfectly reasonable. Sinatra had felt that the cramped area made a decent shot impossible, but when he learned there was no alternative for the day and the cost of building it at home, he readily agreed. "Makes sense. Tell Mark I'm ready whenever he is."

I told Robson that Sinatra had changed his mind. Robson shrugged again and moved off toward the tower. I remained where I was.

"You were terrific, Sauleroo. Terrific."

Stan Hough.

I goggled at him. "What're you doing here?"

"Well . . . we heard things were getting pretty rough, so Dick thought I ought to come over quietly and take a look. I just got here." He clapped me on the shoulder. "Is this a sample?"

I described the skirmish. Stan listened quietly, nodding a couple of times. When I finished he said, "Okay. He likes you." He smiled broadly. "I won't even unpack. I'll tell Dick it's all under control." He turned. "Walk me out to the front, will you? I'll get a taxi from there."

"Where are you staying?" We walked across the tracks to the street of the station. "You can use one of the production cars."

Stan laughed. "You think I was kidding? I'm turning around and going home." He looked at his watch. "I can just make the polar flight. *Ciao* for now."

By the time I saw Zanuck again the story had been inflated enormously with that passion for mythmaking we all share. The version I now heard recounted sounded as if I had gone down the platform with a whip and a kitchen chair and brought off a triumph.

That's why I wasn't being fired. I had become the Guy Who Can Handle Sinatra.

"Jeezus, Dick," I said. "You're going to get me killed. I didn't *handle* Sinatra. He just changed his mind after I explained the situation."

"What's the difference?" Dick said. "He believed you, didn't he? He made the shot, didn't he? You're one of his pals now."

That's what he wanted to believe, and I couldn't change it. The point was academic to everyone but me—and my disclaimers were taken for Hollywood Humility. I shut up, hoping only that no one would tell Sinatra that I claimed intimacy.

"Anyway, that's not what we wanted to talk to you about," Dick said. "We want to talk about Spain. Mark is absolutely set on it. He says he can't shoot this ending in Italy."

"Well," I said, "that's probably true. The pages in the screenplay were written to fit that Spanish location, remember?"

"Why don't you cut the crap?" Dick said. "Does it *have* to be in Spain?"

"No. There's plenty of spectacular stuff around where we shoot in Italy. It just means restructuring the action to fit what's there."

"Can you do it?"

"Look, Dick," I said, "I can write it that way and find the locations and do everything but one thing. I can't make Mark do it if he won't."

Stan Hough threw up his hands. "Goddamm it—we're talking about a couple of hundred thousand dollars!"

"That's right, goddammit," Zanuck said. Both of them were looking slit-eyed at me.

Now the bell was on my neck. I asked the only question. "If he insists, will you replace him?"

Dick stood up. Meeting ended. "Look," he said, "work out the Italian ending, show it to Mark—try to make him buy it. Maybe get Frank to help you."

"I'll give it a try."

Before I went back to Italy and our second front, Hough told me there had been serious discussion about the risk of replacing the director. "But when I saw how you got along with Sinatra, I told Dick to forget it—the picture'll get done."

Back to Italy with my job clarified. Armed with the jawbone of an ass.

19

"You Germans! Back in the Tunnel!"

M EDIA BUNTHORNES and Berensons get a lot of mileage out of the idea that movies are the mirror of cultural change, announcing the hot moment like those little pop-ups that tell you when the turkey's done. Maybe. But the Late Late Show is also a museum of cultural fossils made in a Hollywood at flood tide—and we're stuck with them too.

Poor Stepin Fetchit and Butterfly McQueen lived to see their marvelous vaudeville turns condemned by black Cromwells. Wonderful Henry Armetta, flapping one arm with mock ferocity at the red-faced Irish cop who swiped a banana from the fruit stall, fell to the new sensibility like all the Smith and Dale tribesmen. But the root image doesn't die—those American caricatures born with the movies just change the trimmings, and Redd Foxx shuffles on, grinning and shrewd and mean; Flip Wilson bobs for laughter; while Moms Mabley gums her way through routines that used to feature a dipper of snuff in the bad old days. We have been saved only from minstrel shows.

The movies erased a lot too. The dour Celt became the laughing Irishman; Kublai Khan and the Dowager Empress split into Fu Manchu and your laundryman, while France and the French disappeared for decades into a froth of oo-la-la, Maurice Chevalier and bearded heel clickers with a passion for kissing men on both cheeks. Balzac's world vanished into the library stacks. Rudolf Our Arab rode like the hot wind through dreams of sand dunes and oases, founding a dynasty of Baghdad movies—fountains and palm trees and archways and dancing girls, tits and scimitars and romance. The other day I watched an Arab politician complain bitterly about the "bad image" his world gets in our media. What an insult to Jon Hall, Maria Montez, Jeff Chandler and Co., not to mention legions of makeup men. And just why does he think Frederick's of Hollywood features harem pants in those "turn him on" catalogs?

As for Henry Armetta and the bananas, only the bananas went. The fruit stand became a restaurant and the restaurant's back room became a headquarters and the cops became doormen. Henry rose to power. And when that rise was canonized in *The Godfather,* actor Marlon Brando paid his respects to history with a difficult facial makeup that jutted his jaw and muzzle. He hunched his shoulders and lo—Henry Armetta.

North of Rome is an Italy never seen in American movies. And from rainy Venice north into the Dolomite Alps the change is drastic. As the land rises into mountains, you pass through towns with streets swept clean by wind. The sharp sunlight bounces off flat-shining wooden buildings, and restaurant windows advertise those pale, plump, herb-smelling sausages served with boiled potatoes. The heraldic plaques of beer makers hang over doorways, and there's not a banana in sight.

I had been in Cortina D'Ampezzo once before, looking at the locations with Robson. Cortina is a famous ski-resort village—the site of the 1956 winter Olympics and a well-known winter playground for the international rich. Steep, narrow streets, cobbled squares and fountains; high-gabled wooden buildings overhanging the sidewalks; clean, quaint, expensive—cuckoo-clock charming. The hotel rooms were a kind of luxury I had not seen. Flowered wallpaper; great, shining light-wood wardrobes and dressers; high, soft beds—everything smooth and polished and smelling sweetly of wax. Wonderfully worked and inlaid wood was everywhere—the wardrobe doors bellied outward and closed into delicate moldings which hid the joinings in sweeping rococo curves. Bedposts were massive knobs and pineapples and rosettes. The bathrooms were big and white, the china heavy and solid. Sumptuous.

The company was in residence when I got to Cortina. Now the alpine railroad chase got under way. This whole section of the movie is action —the fleeing POW train pursued by a German troop train, strafed by

ME-109s, dodging in and out of tunnels, tearing up track and fighting rearguard actions with oncoming waves of the enemy while clearing rubble off the tracks ahead. All of this was shot outdoors, on the narrow railroad line chiseled out of the shoulder of the mountains, in tunnels where there are icicles in summer, along a right-of-way where you look over the edge and see the tops of pine trees hundreds of feet below. To get to the locations we went first to the nearest tiny railroad depot. From there we walked the tracks or were ferried to the day's action by handcar.

Except the star, of course. He continued to use his helicopter. But operating a helicopter at high altitudes, in narrow canyons full of unexpected gusts of wind, was dangerous. And sometimes there was just no place to land. One morning the bird arrived and circled and hovered, approached and backed off from the narrow porch where we waited. Finally it gave up and descended to the canyon far below. We lined the bank and watched as Sinatra got out, made up and in costume, and struggled up the steep mountainside, grabbing at bushes, sliding and scrambling till he got to outstretched hands. He was still puffing and red, legs shaking, when he made it to the setup.

"Okay, what the hell we waiting for?"

Relations between star and director had not improved. In these action sequences Sinatra's impatience and demands for precision were constantly in conflict with Robson's desire for lots of coverage, his film editor's knowledge that the more he shot now, the better his range of choices later.

"What the hell do you need that for?"

"I need it, that's all."

"Well, I'm telling you you'll never use it."

Once, after a brief and bitter challenge over some bit of business, Sinatra paused and called to the script clerk, "Now I want *you* to make a *special note* of *this* scene, you hear?"

He turned to the rest of us. "I want to see that piece of film and I want to keep track of it." His voice rose, clear and crisp. "And if that piece isn't in the final cut, I'm going to shove one end of it up that guy's ass, wrap him in the rest of it and set fire to the whole thing!"

There was uneasy laughter. Regardless of sympathies, all of us were a long way from home and hoping for the best.

Every day the question of the Spanish ending grew larger and more inflamed. It was already too late to cancel without penalty—provisional deals had been made, hotel space and location crews engaged. All the same, a hell of a lot of money would be saved if the move was canceled, even after paying penalties.

I had promised, and I tried. I studied the winding alpine rail line in the Cortina area and eventually worked out an ending full of wild risks, staged where narrow iron bridges crossed stone crevasses that dropped away for thousands of feet, where icy waterfalls sprang out from the rock face and blew away into white plumes in the constant updrafts. Spectacular, I thought.

I put it on paper, then tried it out on Buzz, who went out to the locations I had picked and shook his head admiringly.

"Sure's hell kill somebody here," he said.

"Can it be done?"

"Yeah," Buzz said, eyes measuring the tricky places. "Want me to figure it out?"

"After I show it to Mark."

But first I telephoned Zanuck and told him what I had in mind. He shouted approval on the transatlantic telephone and urged me to get Robson's approval at once. "Show him the saving. Tell him his profit participation might depend on it!"

And Stan Hough on the extension: "Get your pal Sinatra to back you up. It's his dough too."

But the realities were different. When I finally persuaded Robson to hear me out, he did so without reacting. Then he said, "I don't understand it. Write it."

I wrote it in screenplay pages, gave it to him.

He handed the pages back. "I'm sorry. It won't work."

He turned away, but I persisted, "Why not?"

He stopped. When he turned it was in a yelling rage. "Because it *won't*, goddammit! Now get off my back!"

When I looked to see who had heard, everyone was busy doing something.

In Rome there had been friends to see in the evenings and sightseeing on Sundays. But Howard Koch was gone, suddenly appointed head of production of Paramount. And here in Cortina I was stuck. I would go to the location in the morning, return at the end of the day's work, watch the dailies, eat in the dining room, go upstairs and wait for Zanuck's call. Sundays were the worst.

A film company on location is unnerved by the presence of the Front Office—and a producer on the set blurs the lines of command for a lot of people. If he is strong his presence undermines the director's authority. Like it or not, a lot of people will check his expression every time the director gives an order—and they'll gossip about replacement every time he says something they can't hear. If he's weak he's worse than useless; any gopher can run errands better and without embarrassment. Old hands are accustomed to seeing the director challenged by the star. They know it will work itself out—bend, break or work in a crouch— but the producer is They to them. So what was I doing there? Why had I been summoned home suddenly and unexpectedly returned? Everyone knew about the argument over Spain; Robson's rejection of my alternative had been very public. So why was I back again?

Isolated and lonely, I was very aware of the speculation and the sidewise glances, and I responded like a trained dog. I began suggesting to Zanuck that it might be a good idea if I came home and got started on something else. He suggested with greater force that I stay put and make sure the Spanish shooting went right. Since I hadn't been able to cancel it, it was my responsibility. . . .

I slid into that frame of mind where I was sure people stopped talking when I approached. And it doesn't take much of that to make it true —as the joke says, even paranoiacs have enemies. I kept to myself as much as possible and counted pages left to go.

I didn't know how tight my wire was until one evening when I came down the main staircase into the lobby on my way to see the dailies. That staircase is a Tyrolean chalet version of a grand ballroom entrance. Shiny wooden treads, end-grained like butcher block, float down from two sides to meet at a landing which descends broadly into the lobby. From that landing you can make an entrance seen by everyone in the bar.

As I started down somebody called out, "Hey, producer—how did you like the dailies?"

It turned out that Robson had run the film early, and for some reason or no reason I had not been told. Ha ha.

As practical jokes go it was mild. Even assuming malice, it was minor. But for some reason I took it like a beheading. There they all were, and I knew I should shrug and keep moving, but I could not. Instead I turned and started back up the stairs.

"Hey—where you going? I've been waiting half an hour for you." Sinatra calling out to me from the bar. As I turned, he waved. "Over here in the corner."

I made my way through the crowd, the Companions elbowing room for me. As I got there he said loudly, "You bring the script with you? Good. I wanted to talk about tomorrow's stuff."

He turned to some scene, tried to read and gave up. "Too noisy here. We can go over it later. What're you drinking—ever drink Jack Daniel's?"

It turned into an evening. It was somebody's birthday, and Mr. Sinatra's party had engaged a room in an elegant local restaurant—a room with a huge, square table and comfortable chairs and a fireplace. There was a birthday cake, brought in by two men—king-sized, puffy with icing, tier on tier like a wedding cake. It caused one of those uproars —voices shouting "Speech," flashbulbs popping, "Stand over here," "Look this way, Frank," "Watch it for chrissake you spilled my drink," until Buzz lifted little David Sutton, the photographer, and sat him squarely into the birthday cake—which splashed white icing like milk in slow motion. Sutton wiped off the sticky stuff and laughed. The music got louder. Sinatra, who always makes the seating arrangements, insisted I sit by him, and somehow, through the noise and the hilarity, we talked about the script. Finally it was very late—the fire had burned down and you could hear the popping of the embers. Someone was sleeping under the table. Sinatra stood up and we all rose. Then he said quietly to me, "Feel better?"

I nodded.

"Okay," he said. "Let's go. Morning comes early."

With Spain set, time was once again the enemy. Again there were dates to be met—hotels, local crews, clearances and transport arrangements.

Action!

"Let's do it again. Once more! All the Germans back in the tunnel— Ryan and the others behind that big rock. *Germans! When the shooting starts I don't want to see anyone laughing, goddammit.*"

Day after day the enemy charged and fell. Day after day Sinatra and his men cut them down in windrows, rat-tat-tat-tat with the gag tommyguns which seemed always to jam at a crucial moment. Young James Brolin, a studio contract player with a small part in the movie, was particularly jinxed that way; somewhere there are miles of film of a fiercely scowling Jim Brolin charging over a hilltop, firing, then suddenly stopping, staring disgustedly at the gun and mouthing the perfectly clear and heartfelt comment, "Oh, shit."

German soldiers toppled in sheaves. Buzz and the others slid down hillsides, plopped off tunnel faces, crumpled behind rocks. Stunt men began snickering. Still the Nazis fell. I worried. I began to imagine hoots of laughter in theaters.

When we broke for lunch one day Sinatra made his way over to my rock and squatted beside me.

"What do you think?"

I said, "I think they're going to run out of Germans before VE-Day."

"Yeah." He was very serious. "Listen—what would you think if he gets killed? Ryan."

Mostly we are accused of destroying Art, which is to say misery, in favor of that Hollywood Happy Ending. Not this time. We talked about it, and I was instantly convinced that it was right for the movie. Try as I might, I could only imagine howls and jeers at the overblown heroics we were filming. I remembered a near riot in a theater full of British soldiers watching Errol Flynn single-handedly reconquer Burma. . . .

I said, "You know it's going to raise hell . . ."

"Sure," Sinatra said. "You think it's right, though, don't you?"

I did. But I was cautious. I worked it all out on paper. Clean, simple, startling. It would come at the very end—in Spain. Ryan and the last of his men fighting a desperate holding action—keeping the Germans off while the tracks are cleared for the last dash—a tunnel, a few hundred feet—into Switzerland and safety.

The tracks are cleared, the men scramble aboard, the train begins to labor heavily into that tunnel. "Come on, Ryan!"

He and the others glance back, see the train moving. Last chance. They turn and run, dodging from side to side. One after another scrambles aboard as the train picks up speed. Ryan is the last to run. "Come on, Ryan!" Now he turns and starts loping up the tracks. Behind him we see the Germans appear, out in the open now, firing methodically. The train is moving faster, but Ryan is gaining. From the retreating platform we reach out to him. His hands are outstretched. Another few steps and—CUT to the German officer who kneels, takes careful aim and fires. Almost at our fingertips Ryan falters and falls. We stand paralyzed as his figure recedes down the tracks. Something like that.

Zanuck loved the idea. "You sure Sinatra wants to do it?"

"It was his idea."

"What about Mark?"

He hated the idea. It violated the book, the spirit of the film, the rhythm of the scenes, the author's sacred trust and the Screen Directors Guild agreement. Telephone calls, cables: WILL NOT BE RESPONSIBLE FOR DESTRUCTION OF THIS FILM.

Zanuck on the phone. "Listen—I think you guys are right, but I'm getting a lot of flak about this. How about you shoot the ending both ways?"

It seemed reasonable enough to me. Robson shrugged. Having exploded, he was icy calm now. "Why not?" Hang yourself, he meant.

When I brought Sinatra the good news he just said, "No."

"No? No what?"

"No alternate endings."

I thought this was unnecessary roughness, and I said so. Sinatra took me by the upper arm and looked intent.

"Now listen to me," he said. "I've been in this business a long time, and I'm gonna tell you. Never give Them a choice. Know why? Because they'll always choose wrong."

More phone calls, cables, suggestions, protests. Finally capitulation.

"It'll be great," Sinatra said.

"Put it in writing," said Robson.

20

§

Von Ryan's Train
Arrives in Spain

WHAT HAPPENED in Spain probably couldn't have been
predicted or avoided. In that elegiac classic *The Gunfighter,*
we know the hero will be challenged from the moment he rides in; he's
what's described by our own bards as an example of the "attractive
nuisance" principle of law. If you have a sandpile in your yard and some
kid scales your fence, plays in the sandpile and breaks his neck, it's your
fault. You maintained an irresistible temptation. God maintains an "attractive nuisance" in Mt. Everest, of course, but He has a good press.

While still in Rome, Sinatra's effort to maintain privacy by living out
of town had driven the press mad. The furor grew loud enough to be
the subject of serious discussion. Treaties were suggested. At one point
the papers were full of stuff about a deal being made with "the King
of the Paparazzi"—only it turned out he was self-crowned. Characteristically, Sinatra reacted in his own way. One day he decided that either
he or Rome had been punished enough—and that night he appeared
on Via Veneto just like the other strollers.

The strategy was to let them take a lot of pictures, wave, smile and
wait it out. They'd go away, once glutted.

Wrong. They didn't want easy, waving, smiling pictures. They took a lot of those and fell back. The party moved on up the street. Then, cannonading out of the shadows, a disheveled blonde came barreling straight into Sinatra. Bang! Now the flashbulbs really popped as he clawed her off. SINATRA APPEARS, ATTACKS ROMAN VIRGIN ON THE STREET! BRAZEN ASSAULT BY AMERICAN SINGER-GANGSTER! In the ensuing activities somebody's arm was broken, and Rome rejoiced in the scandal.

But Spain was sedate, controlled, quiet—a police state. We expected a couple of weeks of hard work and quiet nights.

Since housing arrangements had been made late, the company was split into two groups—one staying in Málaga, in the hotel which served as headquarters for us, the other in the nearby resort town of Torremolinos, at a modern hotel called Pez Espada. Robson was in Málaga, Sinatra in Torremolinos. The location itself was sixty-odd miles inland, in a baking-hot yellow gorge called El Chorro. There the railroad passed between steep, dry cliffs, immediately onto a spidery and spectacular railroad bridge over a great, steep crevasse, and instantly into a tunnel bored through a tawny mountain. From the tunnel mouth, a kind of balcony footbridge had been hung onto the sheer face of the mountain. It edged around for a couple of hundred feet and finally disappeared into a narrow slit in the rock. It was used by pedestrians, I was told. Since the hills around were absolutely barren and the nearest road a half mile away, I wondered why anyone would want to climb to that scary ledge. Later I saw that the empty hillsides were pocked with caves and the caves held people. The ledge was for them—a shortcut through the mountain to a nearby village. It was going to be a tough location. Two hours travel each way—water to be brought along. But Torremolinos, where I was assigned, was a bright, hot and noisy contrast to out-of-season Cortina. It was little-Miami-Beach style—not grand and sober like Málaga—but I liked it.

"Best restaurant? Right here in Pez Espada, señor."

In the bar that evening the hotel manager bowed in a well-dressed youngish American accompanied by two women. I noticed because while he seated them he politely pointed me out, and the man came over and introduced himself—the American consul. Offices in Málaga, of course, but he'd heard we were here and wanted to know if there was anything he could do for us, just anything at all. The women with him were his wife and his mother, who happened to be visiting.

I said thank you and I'd be sure to introduce them all to Mr. Sinatra when he came downstairs. The consul signaled, the ladies joined us, and we chatted the evening away. I think Sinatra and the Companions finally showed up and made everyone happy.

Next day was Sunday, and the company explored the town, went sightseeing in old Málaga, enjoyed the hot sunlight and the beach sand. Umbrellas, girls and hot-dog stands. Every now and then, standing in a shadow, the men with the patent-leather hats and uniforms—the Guardia Civil. When you looked at one of them he usually smiled.

Sometime during the afternoon I joined Sinatra and the Companions lounging in the lobby, drinking tall drinks, idling in the heat, looking at the people who were looking at us.

A girl strolled by in a sort of costume—an abbreviated paraphrase of a suit of lights. She was wearing one of those flat black hats, she was good-looking, and her walk said "Pay attention." We all did, and as she passed us, she turned and smiled over her shoulder. The whole thing was a kind of burlesque of a pickup, disarmingly obvious.

One of the Companions jumped up. "Want me to get it, Frank?"

He laughed. "Sure. Buy her a drink."

She had a little English and a bright smile, and she was nervous. The reason turned out to be a photographer, whom we finally spotted peeking out from behind pillars, snapping with a long lens. He had even less English and was even more nervous; he'd probably been reading those Rome-based stories about paparazzi torn limb from limb, cameras smashed and all that. He clung to his cameras, shielded his face and kept his knees together. The boyfriend.

Sinatra told the girl to tell her friend that he could take all the pictures he wanted if he would clear with the unit publicist. The two of them just stared at him while he explained, and it had to be recited several times before they nodded.

"Capish?"

They laughed delightedly, stammered in Spanish and backed away.

"Not bad for the afternoon show," said Sinatra, rising. He and intimates were off somewhere—a cocktail party on a yacht, I think. "See you around dinnertime."

In Spain, that's nine or ten o'clock at night, often in an outdoor courtyard hung with lanterns. Pez Espada's is one of those—a kind of sunken garden overhung by big old trees. At one side there is a kind of pavilion-bar flanked by the bandstand where a guitarist throbbed steadily.

To get to the courtyard, you walk through the hotel, out onto a terrace and down a few stairs. Before I got outside I could hear the commotion, and as I stepped out a group of people shoved past me, snarling and spitting angry Spanish. Behind them came the manager, shaking his fist.

Sinatra and the Companions were at the bar, talking excitedly, Frank with a handkerchief pressed to his face.

"What happened?"

I think it was Dexter who explained. The afternoon girl in the flat hat had joined them at the bar just a moment before. She threw her arms around Sinatra. He pushed her away, flashbulbs popped, she slapped him with a glass, which broke, he slapped her back. She screamed, her photographer friend rushed to the rescue, the Companions held him down and the management broke up the whole thing. It was them being hustled out of the hotel as I emerged. Not exactly routine, but nothing much by Via Veneto standards.

We talked a while, had a few drinks, and that was that. Morning would be very early—ready in the lobby by six A.M., "having had."

Next morning the night lights were still on—the cast and crew milling around in the shadowy lobby, everybody looking bewildered and nervous. At my question someone pointed to the exits. Each one was guarded by one of those Guardia Civil men—armed and unsmiling. Outside in the gray light, I could see a couple of military jeeps and a sort of command car.

"What the hell's up?"

"They won't let us go—they shoved us back into the lobby."

There was a knot of people gathered to one side, talking loudly, gesturing. The hotel manager, badly rattled, flanked by a couple of soldiers and John Delgado—Sinatra's double. They were talking to a smallish man in a gray suit. Delgado waved me over.

"This is the inspector—Torremolinos. He doesn't speak any English."

I shook hands with the inspector as Delgado explained to me. He nodded, bent slightly at the waist and spoke to me in Spanish. I understood "Señor Sinatra" and nothing else.

Delgado looked unhappy. "He says Señor Sinatra must come with him to the police station to explain some charges that have been made against him and two or three other people."

"What kind of charges?"

The inspector shrugged. I noticed that he looked tired—as if he had been up all night and had not shaved since yesterday. His necktie knot was very tiny and pulled to one side. He wore black-and-white perforated shoes. I thought of Thomas Gomez.

Meanwhile the lobby was filling up. Each time the elevator door opened, some smiling cast or crew members would step out, look around and stop dead, staring at the armed guards. Then each one would sidle over to the corner where our people stood and start asking *sotto voce* questions which got no answers.

Through Johnny Delgado I tried repeatedly to get some idea of what was up. No response, just the polite shrugs, small smiles and the request for Señor Sinatra.

I said, "Tell the inspector I will see whether Mr. Sinatra is still here."

He translated, and the inspector looked at me sadly and shook his head. I made a smile, called one of the stunt men over and said, "Go up to Sinatra's room, tell him about the cops and tell him not to leave the room no matter what, until I say it's okay."

He nodded, popped into the elevator.

I found the manager. He was badly shaken and didn't make much sense. It was all something to do with the girl of last night, señor. But he didn't want to talk about it—he wanted to be somewhere else.

"Wait," I said. "What happens if Mr. Sinatra doesn't come down? Will they go up after him?"

"No." There was apparently a law which forbade the police to do that —something about the lack of magnitude of the crime.

"What crime, for chrissake?"

He excused himself and disappeared. Suddenly I remembered. The American consul in Málaga! I had his card.

I tried to phone him, but the Spanish telephone system resisted. Then I saw the number-one Companion, Big Brad. Drawing on henchhood, I signaled him to join me around a corner of the lobby. There I asked him to sneak out the side door, take one of our production cars and go like hell to Málaga for the American consulate and rescue. He shook my hand and went out the side door. I heard the car start up and move off.

Back to the main lobby just in time to see one of our assistants, a huge, somewhat shy young man named Richard Lang, collared by the guards, shoved outside and into one of those cars. At that, Companion number two, agreeable, flat-nosed, spaniel-eyed Richard Bakalayan, had had enough. He jumped up.

"Is this a free country or isn't it?"

The question, delivered with a kind of New York cabbie intensity, was instantly answered. The inspector nodded, and Dick Bakalayan was thrown into the car with Dick Lang. The vehicle drove off.

Delgado, looking sadder than ever, explained that they had mistaken young Lang for Brad Dexter—now on his way to Málaga. They had been looking for Sinatra's two "associates," he said—and they had grabbed two men who fit the vague descriptions. By accident, they got one right.

The sun was well up by now. Suddenly I remembered the director and realized that he knew nothing of all this. By now he and a lot of the cast and crew would be well on the way to the location. Command decision? Picture first, if possible. With Delgado interpreting, I asked the inspector's permission to send the rest of the people to work. After all, he had the two "associates" and Mr. Sinatra would no doubt be down soon to answer his questions. As a servant of his government, he understood that my responsibility was to continue this very expensive and serious undertaking for which arrangements had been made by negotiation between his government and mine in the name of international cooperation, etc., etc. I kept up this flanneling until his eyes began to glaze, and he finally sighed and nodded. I pumped his hand and told Delgado to take a car and driver and get out to the location as fast as possible, explain the problem to Robson and urge him to improvise—to shoot anything and everything he could, using Delgado for Sinatra. Although the years had changed Sinatra's face, filling those hollow cheeks, Delgado, once a striking double for the star, was still a ringer for him in some angles.

He took off. The sun was up and the heat was rising.

21

§

The Girl, the Slap,
and the Guardia Civil

A T INTERVALS I placed phone calls—to the consul in
Málaga, to the embassy in Madrid, to the studio in Hollywood.
I posted myself where I could hear if the phone rang, watch the elevators and keep an eye on the Enemy, who had settled himself in a lobby
chair with a view of the elevators. Each time I made a call or pleaded
with the hotel operator to try harder, he watched with sympathy, offering a small, tired smile and shrug at each obvious failure.

Sometime before noon the phone rang for me. It was Dexter, calling
from Málaga. He had had a hard time finding our eager-to-help consul,
and . . . "Well, here he is, *you* talk to him."

"You understand," the consul said, "this is strictly a local Spanish
matter and there really isn't very much we—"

I screamed, threatened, pleaded. He regretted the difficulty, of
course, but wouldn't it be simpler all around if Mr. Sinatra would just
do as they asked and go to the police station and answer a few questions?

"But—what if they just throw him in jail? Look what they did to Lang
and Bakalayan!"

"Lang and Bakalayan?"

I explained what had happened, demanded he at least get them out right now.

"Well . . . I don't know. That *is* more serious, of course," he said. "What are the charges against them?"

I nearly bit the receiver.

"I don't know! They won't tell us!"

He thought that over. "I see. That does make a problem, doesn't it? Tell you what," he said. "I've got to go out of town for a few days, but I'll try to cut it short and be back before the weekend. If this doesn't get straightened out by then, don't hesitate to phone me."

"But . . . wait . . ."

Then I was talking to Dexter again. "That chicken bastard is running out the door right now," Dexter said. "He's scared. He said that broad is related to somebody important and she can make a lot of trouble. Did you try calling the embassy in Madrid? Good. That was his idea too." He hesitated. "You think Frank needs me?"

"Not as much as I need to have someone the cops can't get their hands on," I said. "You stay close to the production office there—see if you can get through to the studio, and if Robson calls in, call me here."

"Check. Oh, hey, listen—did I hear they grabbed Bakalayan and *Dick Lang?* Yeah? What did they want Lang for? He wasn't with us."

"They thought he was you."

"They thought . . . *you're kidding!*" He sounded offended. "Who in hell could mistake Dick Lang for me?"

There was another call for me. One of the wire services wanting to know what was going on—a rumor Sinatra was in jail for attacking some girl in a hotel? I denied knowing anything, told him the picture was filming that very minute out in El Chorro and pointed out that the star was in every shot.

"He hasn't been arrested?"

"Absolutely not."

"Oh. Well, call us collect in Madrid if anything happens, will you?"

"Absolutely."

When the inspector went to the men's room, I rode upstairs to see how Sinatra was holding up. He was not exactly joyful, full of glum speculation as to what this was all about. I told him what little I knew about the girl, but he thought there had to be more.

"When I was here in that Kramer thing I sounded off a lot about Franco," he said. "They've probably been laying for me ever since."

The idea was more satisfying and a hell of a lot scarier. Money might solve the one—but what would solve the other? I stretched the truth about official U.S. help and tried to sound confident.

"Meanwhile just stay here—have stuff sent up—and I'll let you know the minute we get it squared."

In the lobby again. The phone call was for me—and a tinny, distant voice announced that I was talking to the embassy in Madrid. Whoever I spoke with was reassuring. "Yes, we heard about it and we've been working on it all day. It takes time, you know, everything goes through Madrid first and then it goes out down the line step by step. And sometimes people down the line want to check back, you know, and it just takes—"

I said, "But is it all settled at *your* end?"

"Yes, absolutely. Your inspector will be told the whole thing has been settled. Maybe another three or four hours."

I thanked him and was told to phone back tomorrow "if there's any hitch. But there won't be. And give my best to Mr. Sinatra."

I phoned upstairs with the good news. "He says it'll be all over by tonight."

"That's good," Sinatra said. "I want to be out of this country tomorrow!"

I pleaded. "All right," he said, "what's the least we can get away with?"

"We need a day," I said. "The angle from the train. The full-face stuff at the death. No way to fake it, no way to double it."

"Okay. One day. But you tell Robson—no extra shots."

I promised.

The inspector was back in his chair, looking attentive. I found someone who could translate a little and went to him. He rose, weary, stubbled but polite. I tried to convey the information. He nodded, questioned the translator, who questioned me, and we struggled toward an understanding. At length the obvious was clear. He would be happy to see it ended, but he simply had to await official information.

I said, "You look tired. Perhaps you would join me for some coffee?"

The translator extended the invitation. Like everything in Spanish, it sounded better. The inspector made a little bow, a grimace. Then he prodded himself tenderly in the stomach and said something that sounded rueful. The translator said, "The inspector regrets, but his profession makes an uneasy stomach and he does not drink coffee." He brightened. "He says, how about some Coca-Cola?"

We had Cokes and smiled at each other. It was well into the afternoon.

The siege was lifted quite casually about an hour later. There was a phone call for the inspector. He listened, nodded, hung up and left, waving to me as he went. The guards and the jeeps all went with him. And half an hour later a car pulled up and out came Bakalayan and Lang, rumpled and heroic and ready to tell all. And by then some of our people were back from the location, anxious to hear, excited at the melodrama. Sinatra and the others came downstairs, and the hubbub lasted well into the night.

Next day we went to the gorge and worked while the production office phoned frantically for planes, trains, taxis to Gibraltar; any ticket in any direction as long as it led out of Spain. Somehow it was accomplished. Everyone would be out of Torremolinos and Málaga within forty-eight hours, and most of us would be out of the country. Marty, the publicity man, and I were booked on a late-afternoon flight to Madrid, a connection to the U.S. on the following afternoon.

We filmed prodigiously that day. I don't know how many setups Robson shot, but it never went so fast before. And the look of strain and tension on the actors' faces was most convincing. We got back after dark, exhausted—but with the work done. Everybody packed that night; the bar was deserted.

In the morning I went to Málaga to help close the production office. By the time I got to the hotel there was a phone call from Marty.

"Listen, chief," he said. "They came and got Sinatra. He's at the police station in Málaga now with a bunch of the guys."

I found a driver and tore off to the Málaga police headquarters. There a polite and smiling cop informed me that Señor Sinatra and his friends had already left. They had just about enough time to catch the plane.

Marty filled in the details. Just after I had left that morning the police showed up again. Same routine—sober, blank, persistent. Señor Sinatra was required to sign a few documents for the Málaga police. Yes, they were aware that the whole matter had been settled with the Torremolinos police, but of course that was another matter. They were from Málaga and Señor Sinatra was required to sign a few documents. . . .

Hopeless. Sinatra was called. Having been assured that he would make his plane, he agreed to go—and a whole troupe went with him. There was a brief formality at the police station, a document admitting some sort of guilt. The translator assured Sinatra that only a fine was involved, and he signed. The fine required everyone to empty his wallet to make it. And that was that.

In New York, the newspapers had lots of stories of the whole incident, mostly incorrect. There was an interview with Brad Dexter—who told the whole story in the first person.

22

§

The Wrap, the Premiere, and the Hit

*I*T'S EASIER here to believe in unicorns than in virgins, maybe because there's no market for unicorns. All the same, everyone who works in films has felt the new-snow magic about a movie set before it's been used and seen that magic gone after the lights went off. When you leave a set, even after the briefest use, it's old.

Our prison camp was one of the grand sets, a massive outdoor construction in the heart of the 20th Fox lot. The visitor, turning in from Pico Boulevard, drove along the imposing white administration building, nested among hydrangeas, oleanders, grass and sharply edged flower beds, paused for the gate cop, turned sharp left (SPEED 8 MPH) and confronted Campo Concentramento Prigioneri di Guerra 202.

Behind barbed-wire fences and massive gates, rimmed with those wooden guard towers, more than half an acre of stony-dry parade ground. Almost in the center was the punishment cell, a corrugated metal truck body half sunk into the ground. On a slope to the right were the rows of prisoner huts, and rising behind it all on three sides, a massive peeling stone fortress, ancient, shabby and fierce—guard quarters, the home of the commandant and the soldiers. Once inside the gates you were in southern Italy. Turn in any direction but straight back, and it was perfect, one of those marvels for which Hollywood was once famous, truer than the truth, magical in its falseness.

Big Picture. The studio bulged with *Von Ryan's Express.* Sound stages filled with constructions—cutaway tunnels, a prison infirmary, real Italian boxcars (some charred), a piece of a Spanish tunnel mouth and a wonderful, elaborate reconstruction of the train commander's private car, authentic to the curtain rods over the windows and designed to be pulled apart like a Chinese puzzle for the camera's sake.

Big Picture. Torrents of extras filled the commissary day after day and milled around the dusty parade ground to the hoarse shouts of third assistants—"Background people this way. No no, look at me. When I raise my hand this group goes that way while the rest of you . . ."

Sinatra. The trade papers and the movie columns filled with us, and a man from *Time* or *Newsweek* interviewed me for an Industry Revival story which turned out to be a hymn to Darryl the Father, Dick the Son.

If it was an investment in drumbeating, it paid. The "packaging agents," the great white sharks of the Industry, began to eye the studio with grinning interest again.

And enough to go around, too. Having little left to do, I would hang around the set at peak traffic times, being recognized. And if I wasn't there, why, there stood the canvas folding chair with my name stenciled across the back, waiting. But my office and the telephone were only yards away, and there was something faintly silly about sitting out there behind the camera, squinting at the sun and watching the days away.

Whenever there are great crowds of professional extras there are bizarre stories. Our spectacular was a haughty young man who appeared at the set each morning in a chauffeur-driven Rolls. The car would stop, the chauffeur would get out and open the passenger door —and out would come this lordly young man, dressed in the tattered uniform of the POWs. He would issue instructions, and the driver would nod, get back into the car and drive away. Then the young man would saunter into the dusty prison camp. He made the papers on the second day, and from then on there was a group to watch his act every morning.

At least I assumed it was an act, even though the stories made him out to be the heir of something or other, worth umpteen millions of dollars. Some publicist introduced us once, but he grinned and shuffled with the same blend of unction and hostility as any other extra.

I would have forgotten him quickly enough but for Vikki Dougan.

Who?

In the early '60s, that remote and innocent time, what made Vikki a hot column item and the butt of stand-up comic jokes was exactly that butt. Vikki became famous wearing a low-cut gown, cut deeply enough in the back to expose an inch or so of rear-end cleavage. When Vikki appeared, photographers and old men in raincoats ran around behind her. From the front she was an ordinarily pretty Hollywood blonde, but going away she was a scandal, a column item, the sound of flashbulbs popping.

By some marvelous coincidence she showed up in my office just as we were shooting the big bare-ass sequence in the prison-camp set. (Determined to force the camp commandant to give the men new clothing, Ryan makes all the prisoners disrobe in the middle of the parade ground and burns the rags they've been wearing. They get new clothes; he gets sent to solitary.)

The spectacle of several hundred men disrobing at once drew a lot of attention, of course—along with the customary warnings from the Code office. In fact, most of the men wore jock straps with body makeup smeared over the straps—but from the sidelines, as in the film, the illusion was as satisfying as today's hair-and-pore close-ups.

Sometime during that week of maximum glutei, Vikki Dougan showed up in my office looking for a job—making the rounds, an innocent tribute to poetic economy.

I had nothing for her and nothing in prospect, but the joke was too good to ignore, and we talked for an hour or so. When I asked her how she'd happened to come see me she said she was visiting someone on the lot and had heard my name mentioned.

I told my story in the executive dining room and got a few laughs but no takers. No one said, "Send her down to see me."

The shooting went on. The prisoners burned their clothes, rioted, marched and countermarched on the parade ground, buried their dead and finally broke out—only to be recaptured. We finished the sequences with the huge crowds and settled down to smaller scenes. Once or twice during the big days I saw Vikki Dougan on the set, watching. I waved; she waved.

A couple of months later I saw her again. My secretary buzzed the intercom, then, without waiting for me to answer, came in and closed the door.

"It's Miss Dougan," she said. "Do you want to see her?"

"Miss who? Oh—sure, why not?"

She didn't leave. "She's, uh, very upset."

"So?"

"I just thought you ought to know."

It took me a moment to understand.

"Forget it," I said, "bring her in."

There are some actresses who welcome the chance to weep in a producer's office—the Kleenex box being in some cases more effective than any other. But Vikki was not crying—or acting. She had a problem, and could I help her please?

I made encouraging, noncommittal noises.

"It's about my money," she said. "He worked for you for a while. You know—the fellow with the chauffeur?"

I remembered. It was a bit no one in the world would have taken seriously, but she did.

"Really," she said, "he came from a very wealthy family." And she told about mines and department stores and ranches. And also how he had managed to borrow several hundred dollars from her—something about a check clearing—and disappeared.

Even then she didn't disbelieve the story. She just wanted to know how to find him.

"It's not much money to him," she said, "but it's a lot to me."

Everyone remembered the fellow, but the trail ended in a confusion of names and identities. Whoever he was, the Guild card he used was either phony or someone else's.

She phoned me a few times after that, hoping for news. Then the calls stopped. I don't know if she ever found him or got her money back. Maybe he really was a rich boy. Maybe the Rolls-Royce finally came for Vikki Dougan.

And in that same, vague way, *Von Ryan's Express* slowed and began to stop. People whose faces were as familiar to me as my own would appear in my office in the middle of an afternoon to shake hands and say goodbye. Then they would be gone.

The parade ground was empty now. And every couple of days a piece would disappear or change—moved or altered for some other picture that needed an archway, a group of pillars, a section of barbed-wire fence.

We switched to night shooting. And one night, with a persistent, fine rain falling, Robson directed the last of the principal scenes.

That night he and I finally talked a little. While the crew was preparing, we strolled the parade ground in the wet darkness. It was not a long talk or a friendly one.

He said, "I hear you've been saying some things about me."

"Unfriendly things?" I said. "Yes, I have. You want to know why?"

We walked slowly, in step, not raising our voices.

"You tell me," he said.

"Sure. I think you've treated me like hell. I don't like it and I don't care who knows it."

We kept on walking. Second time around.

"This is a tough business," Robson said. "You had it easy compared to what some people get first time out."

"Okay," I said, "you asked me. Is that it?"

"No. Something else."

I waited. "I heard you said I was a lousy director and"—he picked his phrase delicately—"not much of a man."

He stopped walking, and so did I. They had gotten some of the lights into position now, and the arcs were coming on. I could see that whatever he meant was deeply serious to him.

"Look, Mark," I said, "I think you were a bastard to me and I've said so. If anyone asks me I'll say so again. I have never knocked your directing. For one thing, I don't know enough to knock what I saw you do—even when I didn't like it. I do know that you worked hard as hell and that it wasn't easy to do. Okay?"

"Is that what you've been saying?"

"That's it."

"Okay," he said. "Fair enough."

We walked back toward the lights, where things seemed to be getting organized. The rain was heavier, a steady drizzle. Since the scenes to be shot involved men climbing across rooftops, I wondered if we might have to cancel out.

"Not unless it gets quite a lot heavier," Robson said. "When you backlight this kind of rain it doesn't show up."

He was right, of course. The drizzle continued and the scenes were shot. *Von Ryan's Express* was finished.

The picture premiered on Broadway on July 15, 1965, and in Hollywood at the Chinese on July 28, 1965. Critics, constitutionally unable to evaluate Sinatra's work objectively when he played an adventure hero, were no more obtuse than usual, and audiences were delighted. It was an undoubted hit. I had hung on long enough to see my name on the screen.

Memory rearranges events into better designs, and I remember a casual conversation in a Spanish hotel lobby as if it were a postscript. It was with Sinatra and a couple of others, and the talk was idle— afternoon jokes about his feuding with Mark Robson. Some remark made Sinatra serious. He turned to me.

"I'll tell you one thing. Next time we do a picture with Robson we'll set it up better in front."

I was astonished. "Next time? You mean you would work with him again after all this . . ."

He laughed at my vehemence. "In this business you gotta stay loose," he said. "You never know when some bastard comes up with something you want to do."

23

§

Film Critics
and
Movie Audiences

"**A** NY GOOD?"
"Well . . . you know . . ."

It used to be that when people heard you worked in movies they were openly interested. What exactly do you do and did you ever meet and don't you think so and so would have been better in such and such than whoever? No more.

"Truth is we hardly ever go to the movies anymore. I bet we haven't been to a picture in six months."

General nodding. Nobody has been to a movie in six months. Pause. "Say"—hopefully—"didn't you do one called *Fantastic Journey?*"

"*Fantastic Voyage.*"

"Right. We missed it, but Velda's boy said he liked it a lot, didn't he, Velda? Remember Claude saying about *Fantastic Journey* . . .*"

They are not being mean about it. University populations aside, rudeness is not yet a way of life out among them and they don't despise you or feel challenged by you being "in pictures." In fact, the tone of the innocent zap is often apologetic—maybe they *ought* to see more movies. Most of us were raised in the belief that we're supposed to care about Hollywood. And a lot of people still do, but not in the old *RFD-Photoplay* way. As I say, they don't despise us, not yet, but they've found out that they should, and discomfort is setting in. Everyone gives reasons—subject matter, parking problems, ticket prices, television, the goddam kids, all good reasons but not good enough. What people really seem to be saying is that they have the feeling that what was once their own is their own no longer. Culture stirs and values are imposed on dreams. Not everyone's up to it, and the great audience, respectful, wistful and inarticulate, is sneaking out of the tent and off the midway.

The prestige of cultural shamans has never been higher, and conformism in the name of liberation is the rage. There's a tidal wave of sexual reassurance books to feed an apparently limitless appetite. "Dr. Havalook N. Eatitt tells you what you've always wanted to hear about sex in plain everyday language," a stream of bestselling comfort: Relax, the whole world's kinky.

No doubt. But the price of reassurance is authority; the other face of the smiling, unzipped guru is the cultural commissar. And they are everywhere, ubiquitous as candy bars.

Whether or not you've got the gall to know what you like, no one with a radio or television set or a daily paper has any excuse for not knowing What's Good. And not simply What—equally important, When to Applaud.

Everyone remembers the critical acclaim for those "delicious satires," those "witty spoofs," the James Bond pictures. But local legend says they didn't start that way at all. Of course, it is not unheard of in Hollywood to launch one kind of picture and collect for another. The campaign announcing *The Wild Bunch* as an ultimate statement against violence was one such triumph of When to Applaud, but it was an easy run around one's own end by comparison to the transformation of James Bond into a kind of George Bernard Flynn.

Ian Fleming's spy adventures had been around awhile before lightning struck in the form of an offhand endorsement by JFK. President Kennedy's memory has been mayonnaised by the stableboys of Camelot—but what other politician could have sent us all racing to the paperback racks? Nevertheless, no one said it was delicious spoofery—certainly not Ian Fleming, who took it all with grace, many interviews and, one hopes, gratitude.

Doctor No was made on a budget, with a leading man who had not scored in several tries, a second-rank sex queen and transparently earnest intentions. If not Stanley Kramer earnest, at least Harold Robbins earnest. Wax-museum gore, but real wax.

According to legend, the preview was a disaster. They laughed where they should have gasped, howled at shudders intended. (I doubt it, as you'll see, but that's the story.) And so hysteria. Producer vomiting in the lobby, director fainting in the street and so on. Then the transcendent stroke: *Let's cut it to the laughs!*

And the critics went mad with delight and the money poured in, right? Wrong. Early reviews of *Doctor No* were as caustic and unappreciative as the first reports on the Beatles. But in both instances the kids went ape, the registers rang and the critics saw the light, grabbed the flag and went to the front chanting slogans. We found out we were enjoying delicious spoofery.

When to Laugh is what movie criticism is all about. Now that cultural dowsing is everywhere, They catch up with everything sooner or later, and, since critics are sprouting faster than art, nothing people will pay to see or do is likely to remain unculture-coded very long. From the soup cans to the tangerine-flaked etceteras, it's all being nicely and profitably sorted and graded. And gutted.

The technique is loving contempt plus embarrassment.

Suppose the people who made those dreary, banal and phony Hollywood Flicks were as hard and insensitive as the diamonds on their pinkies. Still, they churned all of it out, Andy Hardy (At this writing, Andy Hardy is still unmined for Statement, but the people who've made Jerry Lewis a culture hero on one continent, Jerry Rubin on another, should not be counted out) together with Bogie and Lombard and Laurel & Hardy and—what do you suppose High Culture was saying then? Same as it's saying now—yecch. But who listened? Movies were a subculture not to be taken more seriously than western novels, auto racing, rodeo or beer drinking—all of which are now on their way to the academic block. But movies were the most insistent and had to be coped with first. So the language of loving contempt was invented.

Sometimes not so loving, either. Before the verse of SDS and the chorus of Black Panthers, modern political insult just wasn't up there with movie criticism. Given the right target, a critic in good shape can add a touch of unbearable condescension not easily injected into a condemnation of the bloody-handed imperialist pigs. I can't remember an organized critical attempt to Solve the Hollywood Question, but neither do I recall Hitler's having objected to the very existence of Jews more vehemently than onetime *New York Times* critic Renata Adler objected to the existence of *The Green Berets* and John Wayne.

Language can be stretched only just so far in the service of passion before it comes to copulation or murder. But when Miss Adler and *The*

New York Times called the Wayne movie "vile and insane" nobody said, "Hey, the Adler broad has blown her cork," or suggested that the language was a little excessive.

Let us snivel together: If you make movies you're supposed to shrug off the barrage of insult which comes your way when someone doesn't like your work. The line runs that you cry all the way to the bank, where you count the money, select a smuggled cigar and light up, dreaming of new insensitivities.

It shapes up as selective breeding for insensitivity, which is what you're complaining about in the first place.

When *Our Man Flint* was being reviewed, Pauline Kael loathed it concisely in *McCall's,* her right and duty, but went on to offer an extraordinary warning to any reader who might see a favorable review of the film somewhere. She pointed out that the studio (20th Fox) had taken a bunch of journalists on a junket to Jamaica where the picture was previewed, and suggested that any favorable comment was a direct result. In other words, the nice lady was saying that anyone who said he liked the movie was probably paid off.

I can only assume she was beside herself with that critical fury which comes from having been spoken to by the suckling pig whose only function was to hold the goddam apple straight on the critic's platter. Kael had blasted *The Sound of Music* and the studio had complained —why not? They *loved* it. And besides, they needed the money.

Whatever the reason, she had behaved like a shark in a feeding frenzy and slashed at fellow predators. I reprinted her magazine piece and broadsided it to reviewers without reference as to whether they'd been on the junket or liked the movie. Along with it I inquired whether a reviewer's vote could really be bought that way. Send prices, please. Quite a few answers arrived, many of them copies of letters addressed to Miss Kael or the magazine. Of course there were also many (chiefly from college papers) who were unhappy with me for touching the hem of Kael's garment. But most were upset with the lady for treating fellow journalists as if they were producers.

Shortly afterward I read that Pauline Kael had been separated from *McCall's* and was told that she'd made an embittered address to a group of film publicists, accusing the studio of having "gotten" her in that treacherous way.

I was appalled then and now at the possibility that my effort at table-turning might have cost Pauline Kael a job. If we must have critics, may they at least write as well as she. And may He who made the anopheles mosquito explain it all in His Good Time.

And yet. Though untaintable by junket freebies, the lady demands and gets private screenings. Moviemakers hate that because the timing is always off and the hoped-for contagion impossible. Roadrunner cartoons look a bit slow in those dark, empty rooms. But the major critics demand and get the pictures without the pollution of the audiences for whom they were made. Kael's ambitions, of course, go beyond most. She sees herself as a Cinema Influence, and to exercise that function she has even criticized films shown to her in rough cut. This is quite a lot like having the basketball coach turn up at the maternity ward to pick prospects, but it seems normal to a Cinema Influence. It has been a long time since anyone suggested to Miss Kael that a lot of what she writes so well is simply silly. Nobody laughs. Her good opinion is courted by directors, agents and actors, and movies are shoved a few steps further down the alienation road. I think junkets are better.

When I produced *Fantastic Voyage,* Kael found the film dismayingly banal (one of her complaints was that the film [a sci-fi adventure inside a human body] was too timid to venture below the waist). "Up the Alimentary Canal with Rod and Gun." She was not alone with the joke; I found it in about forty of the sixty-odd reviews I saw, including the one by Brendan Gill in *The New Yorker.* I wrote Gill, giving him my box score on the quotation by way of suggesting that my crummy movie was more original than his crummy review. Mr. Gill wrote right back—but his subject was not the movie or the review, it was the poor grammar and poorer syntax of my letter. I tried again, and we did this for a while, finally tiring of what both knew and neither would admit—that his function, like mine, was entertainment, but that mine was appointed to feed his.

Why do they do it? The NBC-TV *Today Show* features a critic by the name of Gene Shalit. Mr. Shalit, who looks exactly like the late Jerry Colonna in a fright wig and glasses, comes on grinning hugely and raps various movies with an air of intense enjoyment of his own jokes. Those jokes run to a bald capsule version of the plot, interspersed with killing asides: "At this point the angry farmer rushes in and he strangles our poor hero, which is a mistake because he surely should have strangled the producer of this little horror instead." Shalit finishes beaming and creaming, generally to the accompaniment of loud offstage titters from the newscaster, who comes on shaking his head in wonder and amusement. "Boy, when he doesn't like a picture he really doesn't like it."

Of course, Shalit likes some pictures, too. Those seem to fall into two categories—uplifting or crude. Like almost all the TV critics (most of whom ape him anyhow) he takes lofty moral positions—deplores "needless" violence; mocks war heroics; favors "tasteful" sex, young love and the obvious nobility of the downtrodden. Safe, safe. Like all of them, he *adores* the coarsest kind of imitation slapstick. Mel Brooks' ancient burlesque crossovers are hailed as "inspired insanity," and praise is smeared like peanut butter all over sophomoric and inelegant sight gags which would have made Stan Laurel vomit. Not to begrudge the great Mel Brooks—no one can pay him enough for his two-thousand-year-old man—but criteria?

And yet. Shalit is clearly literate and probably thinks of himself as a kindly person. In the worst of his clowning there's none of the deliberate sadism of John Simon, the Dr. Mengele of the group. Watch Shalit when he deals with books, especially children's books, and you can see what might be and never is in film criticism—useful and illuminating guidance. It's an oddity. Books, plays and music of all kinds are treated with some respect and some decency by people who reserve the language of utter contempt for feature films.

Shalit has expanded the cheap shot into a career, and his success has unleashed a horde of imitators on every channel—ha ha boys, drugstore condescenders, pipe-smokers and ladies in funny hats. People whose feet should be sticking to the floor in a neighborhood movie house are leaning forward—telling you how it really is. Right here in the Movie Capital of the World, there's an assortment which allows a viewer a deep look into Wasteland's wasteland.

It is a privilege to be engaged in a profession where a parasite with a gift for insult comedy can make a good living by urinating on you from time to time.

Writing in *TV Guide*, Judith Crist defended reviewing in general and TV-movie reviewing in particular as useful. But minus her belligerence (what every critic shows when you ask to see his chauffeur's license) she offered only the horse-racing rationale: To improve the breed, amuse the customers and make a buck for the owners.

On the tube especially, the argument limps. Except for those mules bred especially for TV, the crudely edited film you see in your living room represents a race long since over. Do you suppose moviemakers read TV reviews of the butchered corpses of their movies for guidance? Uh-uh. Guidance is the point, but only for the TV viewer. But since the real verdict on the movie—the public's verdict—was in long before, why doesn't *TV Guide* tell you that?

If Judith Crist or your local feinschmecker says, "Don't waste a rainy evening watching *The Mothersmokers,*" but the record shows that millions of people loved it and it made a fortune for Peristalsis Pictures and a star out of Al Banal, wouldn't you be inclined to have a look at it anyhow? So why don't they tell you? Because the critical premise is very fragile. A Seeing Eye Dog is a noble animal and a nobler concept—but who wouldn't rather see for himself?

Reviewers often get the facts wrong, but never care. If the filmmaker whimpers that the reviewer is ignorant, if he points out that the actors don't make up the lines, that the director is not the editor, that the extraordinary pastel color was a lab mistake, that the brilliantly enigmatic ending was enigmatic because the studio pulled the cameras before the last sequence was shot, that the transparently fake sets were really unretouched Elsinore and the sound of the muted heartbeat really a defective BNC camera—he will be met with the joke about omelets and rotten eggs or some such. If you tell a critic that his attributions are simply dead wrong, that he is canonizing some coffee-carrying, ass-kissing flunky who knifed the real talent in the back of the front office, you are peddling garbage and the critic will point impatiently to the credit sheet and ask if you expect him to be psychic.

The problem is that movies are both collaborative and functional, unlike any other art except perhaps sex or public architecture. But they are reviewed as if they were sonnets.

Many months ago I visited several campuses with a picture called *Skullduggery* and talked with students and teachers who care about film—a large, shaggy, opinionated group. Had I been a building I'd have been bombed in Madison, Wisconsin—but I was less surprised by the stagey hostility than by the private questions. A few wanted to know how you get a job in pictures, but most of them had a quite different ambition. They wanted to know how you get a job as a critic.

Or, to put it another way:

> *I am disheartened by the erroneous point of view from which criticisms are written. . . . I am not complaining of bad criticisms . . . but there is such a tendency to look upon the author of a bad or an unsuccessful play, not as a poor devil who has tried his best, but as a man who has committed an outrage against nature. The critics attack him as if he were a scoundrel of the worst type. . . .*

W.S. Gilbert
Evening Dispatch
Edinburgh, Scotland
October 1897

24

If Faust
Had Had an Agent,
He'd Have Renegotiated

"**Y**OU FAUST? I'm Meadows. Freddie Meadows? Nice to meet you. Hear nothing but good—sure, sure, what can I tell you? These things get around, you know. Bankables—you know Rick and Edie? No? Well, they were over the other night and Rick brought up your name—that's why I thought you knew him. What? The show, of course—last week, wasn't it? Oh, come on, what's that, modesty? Lot of people saw it—*lot* . . . of people. Started a lot of talk —*lot* . . . of talk. About you. I don't know, something—a touch. Class. You can't hide it even if the money looked a little—now I hope you don't take it personally—a little *hungry,* y'know? Hey, wait—nobody thinks it was your—after all what'd you get to spend on it, one eight, one nine? You're kidding! One four and a half? Jezuss, what a buy. Too damn bad they didn't get you another mil, you could have—well, I didn't mean to get into all that, I just wanted to say hello. What? Look, I don't want to knock a good little agency, but *we* would never have let it go in for that. Hey, gotta run. Look, think it over, take my number—here—this one just rings in the inner office. If you ever think of making a change . . ."

It's an article of faith out here. If Faust has a good agent he avoids damnation; he renegotiates. A good agent is not a contradiction in terms unless the point is moral.

The late Walter Wanger made several distinguished films and one distinguished joke. Wanger went to prison for the parking-lot shooting of Jennings Lang, a prominent agent who was supposed to be romancing the beautiful Mrs. Wanger, actress Joan Bennett. (Gossip has it that Lang was hit in the groin, but that's the kind of neatness our gossip demands.)

When Wanger got out, he talked a lot about prison reform, made some movies on the subject and told his joke. He said, "Everybody talks about agents, but I'm the only one who ever did anything about them."

It was a shot in a lost cause. His target went on to become a solidly successful producer/executive high in the MCA constellation (a guy who can say "yes"), and Wanger, who died in 1968, narrowly missed seeing the whole Industry taken over by agents. Columbia, Universal, 20th Century-Fox, MGM and Paramount are all run or dominated by ex-agents—if agents can ever be said to be ex.

And why not? The price of everything is the agent's stock in trade and the other half of Wilde's aphorism—the value of nothing—his strength. The package is the deal is the power.

During the studio years, the agent's changing status could be measured by the changing stereotypes. I was raised on Manny, the semiliterate, funny and sometimes contemptible shyster of the Arthur Kober stories, and on F. Scott Fitzgerald's dying laments. But sometime in the '60s we began to see another kind of agent, world-weary, long-suffering and much put-upon. In TV drama these agents generally got to play a climactic scene—the good man at bay:

"All right, boychick, you want the truth? I'll give it to you plain and I hope you're man enough. No, listen to me. The money's gone. *Gone.* They don't want you back. You know that part you say is an insult? Listen. I had to *beg* them for it. You hear? Don't walk away from me. Listen. You know the dough it took to get rid of that poor little girl in Ensenada? That wasn't the studio. No. It was me, Arthur the bloodsucker. . . ."

And so on. The natural nobility of agents began to shine through as their sun rose. One of these days I expect to see an agent beat a star at tennis.

I have never heard an actor, a director or a writer admit that an agent got him or her a job, and the people who cling most tightly to their agents tell the most venomous agent stories. It's axiomatic in those stories that all agents are crooked, but when one of us fires an agent it's usually because "the son of a bitch hasn't brought me anything in six months," while the new agent is hired because "the bastard would rob his own mother and I need someone like that."

I had produced three successful pictures in a row at 20th—*Von Ryan's Express, Fantastic Voyage,* and *Our Man Flint;* a track record like a Roman candle. I was not allowed to gloat, however. Between Harris my Agent and Zanuck my Leader it had been worked out so I was not a participant in profits. Nevertheless, I was a hit, and agents stirred in the murky depths, smelling blood.

My friend Jim Moloney was an agent. He wasn't my agent, of course, and he often reminded me of the fact while marveling at how little Harris my Agent did for an important fellow like me. Jim was and is all charm, white smile and flashing cufflinks. One day I thought he was dreaming out loud.

"Listen—would you consider taking a job as studio head?"

"Well, I'd rather be Secretary of State. I like to travel and I think I get along good with foreigners."

"That's funny," Jim said, "but I'm asking you a legitimate question. Something's come up."

"Okay. Tell me."

"Not on the phone," Jim said. "Can I come over?"

"Sure. Lunch tomorrow?"

"How about right now?"

"Universal."

The studio had been taken over by MCA and was operating under an uneasy policy of phasing out the old regime, the young men in black suits still keeping a low profile while everyone waited for a bloodbath.

Jim said, "The job is yours if you want it. Will you take a meeting?"

"With whom?"

"My boss, Andy Slavin. It's his deal."

Slavin turned out to be a shortish, swarthy fellow with a very crisp manner and an elaborate suite of offices—apparently very new. The furniture, pictures and plants seemed to have arrived together—matching sets. But the liquor was genuine. My friend Jim brought out the Jack Daniel's for me, explaining to his boss that "he learned to drink the stuff from Frank when they did *Von Ryan.*" Slavin just grunted and got right to it. He explained that having once been one of the top MCA agents he retained close ties with the new owners of Universal.

"When Lew told me they were thinking of a change, I remembered Jim talking about your terrific record at 20th and I mentioned your name. They like the idea. Will you take a meeting?"

"Wait a second," I said. "What do you guys get out of it?"

Something flashed between them. Then Slavin said to Jim, "I thought you discussed it with him."

"I did," Jim said, grimacing an appeal. "I told him this kind of deal isn't commissionable in the ordinary way."

Slavin turned to me. "You agree?"

I glanced at Jim and went along. "Sure." I had no idea what the exchange meant. "You know I'm with Harris, don't you?"

"Yeah," said Jim, "and a hell of a lot he's done for you, right, Andy?"

Slavin shook his head. "Three straight winners and no profit participation? The guy's killing you."

"He's Zanuck's friend," Jim said.

To be told that you deserve more than you're getting is hard to resist—and I was not resisting. It had already occurred to me that Harris the Agent had collected quite a fat fee for an introduction and I was restless about not participating in the profits of pictures I'd produced. Still . . .

"Zanuck's tough," I said, "and Harris isn't. After all, he would profit too if he could get me a participation."

"He's Zanuck's friend," Jim said. "He stands to gain more from being his friend than being yours."

"Maybe. But what happens if this works and he insists on a commission?"

"We split," Slavin said. "Probably. But I don't think it'll come to that. He has to do business with Universal too."

"All right," I said. "Set it up."

"It's set," he said. "Can you see Bill Yetti tomorrow?"

"Yetti? Who's he?"

He looked to see if I could possibly be joking. "He's important. If you and him can get together you got a deal."

I remembered all the scare stories I had heard about MCA.

"Why not with Mr. Wasserman?"

Slavin was patient. "How would it look for Lew to be in a meeting like that if you don't make a deal?"

Studio head. When Howard Koch took the job at Paramount they rebuilt the office suite for him. He bought a big house with white pillars in the middle of Beverly Hills, called in the carpenters and wound up with a real soda fountain in the living room and a new projection-room wing added to the house—all probably paid for by the studio. Studio head. "Who's calling? Mr. Zanuck? Tell him I'll get back to him when I can."

Bill Yetti was a pleasant, voluble man who radiated cheery enthusiasm. "Know all about you," he said. "Great track record over there. Great. Used to be a publisher, right?"

"Editor, actually," I said.

"Doesn't make any difference. Good background."

He gestured. "Let's sit over there."

We sat in a pair of facing armchairs. Jim, who accompanied me, sat a discreet distance away, arms folded, beaming attentively.

"Wanted to get some of your ideas," Yetti said. "Big job. Important to know how you feel about things."

I was not quite sure what I was supposed to say, but it didn't matter. Yetti flowed on—jokes, anecdotes and opinions tumbling out in an attractive jumble, voiced in the side-of-the-mouth style of actor Walter Catlett, the barker's barker.

The offer was apparently real, although not quite straightforward. They wanted me to come over there right away, but—"Set up your own unit. Learn the ropes. See how it goes. Comes April, we make the change."

My own unit! To a staff producer with no points, the words had kettledrums behind them.

Yetti was looking inquisitively at me. Jim spoke up. "I'm sure he can get out of his deal at 20th, Bill. Dick Zanuck has told him he'll let him out any time he really wants out."

"That's true, Bill," I said, "but even if he wasn't serious, I think he'd let me go for something like this. As a courtesy between studios, don't you suppose?"

Yetti just looked blank. Jim jumped in. "Of course he would. Dick wouldn't want to stand in the way of something like this."

"It's easy enough to find out," I said. "Why don't you just get Dick on the phone and ask him?"

Yetti squinted at me, shook his head. "No, no," he said. "Not the right way. You two guys are friends, you ask him as a friend, right? He says yes, you give me a call and we go, right?"

He stood and spoke to Jim. "Tell Slavin to call me and we'll get the deal worked out."

In fact he had already discussed the kind of deal they wanted to make with me. What I remember about it is only that it amounted to several times what I was currently earning and was full of references to Ross Hunter's deal, full of zeros, stock options, percentages. Fortune!

"Well, you can put in a pool if you insist, hon," said the lady I had married, "but don't expect me to be a baby-sitter for all the kids that might want to use it."

"A pool would be nice, Dad, but why can't we move down into Beverly Hills where all the kids are?" said the girls.

"I'm going to do you the biggest favor of your life," said Dick Zanuck. "The answer is no. You're going to stay right here."

I mentioned reciprocal courtesy between studios.

"Fuck that," Dick said. "You're a pain in the ass but you're a valuable studio property. Forget it."

The projection room was glimmering away.

"I don't think that's fair, even from you," I said. "Goddammit, I don't even have a piece of the action here."

"How long has your deal got to go? Eight, nine months? Tell you what. Bring it up again in six months and we'll renegotiate." He laughed that high-pitched giggle.

"Look, Dick," I said, hating myself, "I thought we were friends."

He got up and paced. "We are." Up on his toes now, finger stabbing. "You don't know what you're talking about. Those people would eat you alive."

"That's my lookout."

He sat down again, fiddled with things.

I just sat.

"All right," he said. "Let me think about it overnight."

I got up.

"You just don't know when you're well off," Dick said. "You'd be lost over there. Without me you're nothing."

"I'll call you in the morning," I said.

I arrived early, but my phone was ringing as I entered the office.

"Get down here right away."

As I entered through the double door (two doors separated by about a foot and a half like an airlock) I could hear him on the phone. When he saw me he gestured and covered the mouthpiece. "Get on the extension," he whispered. "I want you to hear this."

When I was seated he waited, then indicated the precise moment for me to lift the receiver, uncovering his mouthpiece and speaking simultaneously so as to cover the telltale click. He loved to have people listening in when he was going through some charade or playing a practical joke on the person at the other end.

"Hello, Bill?" I looked at Zanuck but could read nothing. "Me again. Sorry. I wanted to get something to take notes with."

I heard Bill Yetti. "Notes? What for, Dick? It's just a misunderstanding. The guy must have misunderstood."

"Yeah, I know, Bill—but he's kind of hardheaded and I just wanted —you say you never got in touch with him at all?"

"Hell no," said Yetti. "You know I wouldn't do that. After all, he's your guy, I mean—hate to have you do that to one of ours."

"Right, right," said Dick. "So he got in touch with you?"

"That's it. He got in touch—I mean that kid agent who works for Slavin called me and told me the guy is free and looking to make a change. And what the hell, he's got a good track record, so I tell this kid—what's his name, Mahoney? I tell him sure, have him come in and tell me what's on his mind, y'know?"

"Just take it slow," Dick said. "I want to be sure I've got it straight. Right. You know, he came in here and told me you were looking to put him in charge. Can you beat that?"

"In charge? Jezuss, I don't know what ever gave him a wild idea like that. Our guy's still got six months to go on his deal. Hell, I thought your guy was a free agent, Dick, and I just let him come in."

I had heard enough. I put the phone down again and started to leave. Dick gestured fiercely at me to stay put. I didn't listen to the rest. But eventually it was finished. Zanuck turned to me.

"All right, you lying son of a bitch," he said. "Let's see you get out of this one."

I choked out something or other.

"I ought to fire your ass off the lot right now. But I'm ready to forget it," Dick said. "Just go back to work and I'll pretend nothing happened."

"The hell I will."

He stood up. "Look. You just lost your head. I'm really doing you a favor. Those people over there would chew you up in six months. Forget it." He became impatient. "Tell you what," he said. "Just to show you what kind of a guy I am, you come back in six months and we'll talk a new deal with a percentage."

Later on, I asked an attorney about it all and he laughed. "I can imagine," he said. "All Zanuck had to do was call Universal and threaten them with an induced breach."

"All right," I said. "But we were supposed to be friends."

"Who knows? Wasn't that just after *Our Man Flint?*"

"Sure."

"Weren't they dying for a sequel?"

"I suppose. Sure."

"And could they get one without you?"

"Legally yes, actually no. I'm pretty sure Jimmy Coburn wouldn't have done the sequel if I wasn't on it."

"There's your answer."

Maybe.

Actors don't like sequels too much. If the picture in point made them important the problem gets even tougher, because the contract is usually far below the new market value. When an actor becomes a star, he finds it hard to be everlastingly grateful. After all, he knew all the time.

Jim Coburn was by no means an unknown actor when he went into *Flint,* but he was not widely considered to be a leading man. *Flint* changed all that for him, but he was never very proud of the role and by the time the sequel rolled around he had expressed his restlessness in several public appearances. A deal was a deal, of course, and there was no doubt he was going to do a sequel for the studio, but there was also no doubt that his reluctance would have been worse if I had disappeared. So I was an asset of the studio, as *Flint*/Coburn was an asset. The studio policy toward such assets was a bewildering alternation of blandishments and threats—the threats tending to dominate. Attorney Harry Sokolov, representing the studio, once put the case trenchantly.

"Look, David." Harry is a short man with a loud voice and a crinkly, friendly manner which changes without warning to a hard, loud and insulting bray. "Guys like you think you can just crap around any way you want. So let me tell you, David. Look at that contract. You'll see we own you and what you do. Own you. Got it? "Read what it says. It don't matter at home or in the office or on the goddam toilet. You're under contract to us."

With an actor, of course, threats are restrained, held back until the end. But then it is the familiar "You'll-never-work-again-we'll-tie-you-up-until-you're-seventy-years-old-you-ungrateful-prick."

Coburn's discontent was not that serious. So we made the sequel called *In Like Flint.* But the worm was well into the bud, and what the sequel really did was get me liberated. Fired, that is.

25

§

The Stuff That
Legends Are Made Of

THERE ARE NO producers' footprints in the forecourt of
the Chinese Theater, and unless you are confused with a director or a wicked baron, you can hope for Rich but not for Famous. You
have one other chance—to become the subject, object or point of a
good story. The producer who occasioned the wisecrack about setting
the son-in-law business back twenty years is famous in this community
for that reason. All things considered he would have preferred obscurity.

Who directed *The Wizard of Oz?* Mervyn Leroy? Nope. And who
directed *Gone with the Wind?* Selznick? Uh-uh. Both were directed by
Victor Fleming—a man who never makes the auteur lists and whose
work is therefore a reproach to serious cinéastes.

Maybe his obscurity is a bitter injustice to Fleming. If so, these years
of auteurism and the extravagant group aggrandizement of the Screen
Directors Guild have more than made up the lag. When I was compiling
the screen credits for *Logan's Run,* I had to get a special dispensation
from that guild in order to put on the screen the title "Director, Texas
Film Commission." The DGA says that it owns the word "director" and

nobody can be called a director unless he's a member. I'm not sure what would happen if some producer's name was Director, as army privates are sometimes named Major or Sargent. When Leon Uris' novel *Exodus* was heading the lists and filling the windows of your drugstore, El Al, Israel's airline, decided to run a tour of their country under that name. Leon threatened suit. "Sure it was in the Bible," he said, "but I made it famous."

Nobody becomes David O. Selznick anymore. Stanley Kramer and Irwin Allen, two of the most successful and well-known producers of this time, have used their clout not to lick but to join 'em. Both became directors.

A boyhood friend with an ear for the harmonics of words used to say it this way: "There is a destiny that shapes our ends rough. Hew them as we may." My rough end was a public stab at repunctuation. For a few hours, I reminded 20th Century-Fox of Belshazzar's feast.

The 20th lot is probably the most pleasantly situated of all the studios. It sprawls over a large knoll just west of Beverly Hills, and during the summer there's a breeze from Santa Monica and the ocean. Most studios are hell in summer. Warner Bros. squats beneath its red tile roofs under the shoulder of the hills rimming the south end of San Fernando Valley; Columbia, once a tight-packed jigsaw behind a stucco wall on Gower Street in tatty old Hollywood, now occupies a couple of Ramada Inn–style buildings at the back end of the Warner Bros. lot. The amalgam is formally known as the Burbank Studios, but nobody working there is fooled and the two studios retain absolutely separate identities, a dog and cat sewn together in a sack. Universal, the studio that made the trains run on time, is located a mile or so from Warners/Columbia, backed up along those same hills, abutting Forest Lawn cemetery.

Only Paramount hangs on in what was once Hollywood, still making movies in a vast, ramshackle collection of splintery stages and odd buildings cut through with passages and gangways. There's a Jewish cemetery on one side and an endless plain of body shops, secondhand stores and tire rebuilders on the other. MGM, whose main entrance is also flanked by a mortuary, is a short distance from 20th, but the distance is all downhill. Culver City, home of MGM, is to Beverly Hills as Yonkers is to Scarsdale. Culver City looks as if there should be a feed store on the corner of State and Main.

But the 20th Fox lot is pleasant. The studio streets are wide and the whole lot is dotted with little parklike islands. There are trees in your eye line most of the time. The buildings themselves are mostly the Tom-Mix flavored Spanish you see around Beverly Hills—rough stucco and rounded corners. During the reign of the Son, the buildings were repainted in popsicle colors to celebrate the studio's burst of renascent success. At that time too, the "Think 20th" campaign was launched.

It was a major publicity effort, spearheaded by a huge sign—free-standing gold letters illuminated from behind at night—crowning the tallest building on the lot and proclaiming to the world, "Think 20th!"

This was followed by a series of advertisements in newspapers. Each ad featured one of the creative ornaments of 20th in a pose suggesting a combination of deep thought and vigorous action—pointing, mostly. On the ad the headline shrieked, "Producer Lex Talionis Thinks 20th!"

Some of us, studio assets and half-assets, found the series embarrassing. When my turn came I stalled, was screamed at and finally did what I was told—managing to wear dark glasses in the picture. My friends thought that was terribly affected.

As the years turned rancid, Think 20th began to loom. Like a boyhood friend who used to talk back to road signs (" . . . -ly," he would mutter when the sign said GO SLOW), I took to mumbling, "Think 20th"—and one day I knew I had been put there to get a comma into that sign. It would read "*Think,* 20th" . . . a reproach by day and a pillar of neon by night. Mene, Mene.

Meanwhile, there was another *Flint* to make. *In Like Flint* was a sendup of the women's movement before there really was one. In it, female militants have been programming women via beauty parlors—hypnotic tapes in the dryers. Harmless. Like many sequels it suffered from a lumpy, scattered script and the pressing need to find new grace in a flight of nonsense which had been exhausted first time out. What it had for me was a final joke which I had come to love.

At the end, the hero, Flint, apparently lost in space and being mourned by all Good Americans, is discovered to be alive and well, having a ball in a Russian satellite staffed with females. Okay? Here's the joke: With communication reestablished, the chief of American Intelligence (Lee J. Cobb) shouts his question over a radio which is being listened to by everyone alive. "Flint, Flint—what have you learned?" And Flint answers, "Men and women are *not* brothers!"

I thought it was funny then and I think so now. Dick Zanuck did not. When the lights went on in the screening room he asked, "What the hell is all that? Any damn fool knows that men and women aren't brothers. Ridiculous. Cut it."

Whereupon I instantly made matters worse by explaining.

All this flowered into badly strained relationships and a final version of the movie which not only stripped off my beloved joke, but effectively demolished every other pretension it had along those lines.

All in all, about three minutes was chopped out of a film which may not have been an immortal masterpiece anyhow—but which had made more sense before surgery.

"Men and women are *not* brothers!" In that heated air I had been able to imagine people coming out laughing and marveling as they did at "Nobody's perfect"—the zinger of all time. Gone. What would Pauline Crist say? "Like so many sequels, without distinction or wit"—and there was all that distinction and wit on the cutting-room floor. I was in a self-righteous frenzy about it all by the time the film was previewed.

Arthur Knight, critic, teacher and friend, saw the movie in his capacity as critic for the *Saturday Review*. As a friend, he phoned and asked me about some of the more obvious bald spots. I poured it out, superjoke and all. Bent on suicide, I offered to prove the point by sending him the two cutting continuities—before and after the three-minute massacre. Could he print any of it? Sure.

Still a friend, he phoned again after reading it. "Are you sure you want me to use this?" I was sure.

As I remember, the magazine appeared in New York on a Thursday and it contained an article called "The Missing Three Minutes." Someone read it to Dick Zanuck on the telephone and before the office closed that day I had been told to be off the lot by five o'clock, Friday.

"You wanted out? You're out."

That left me with only hours left to do something about "Think 20th!" I had already been working on the project for some weeks.

The sign was made of gilt metal, the letters about four feet tall. Each letter was backed by a neon tube and fastened to the block wall near the top of the building in such a way as to leave a space of about six inches—so it cast a deep shadow by day and glowed like redemption by night, inspiring anyone on the south side of West Pico Boulevard. Since the south side of the studio faces a golf course which is deserted by night except for couples who are not necessarily looking up, the main effect of the lighting was to impress the people who put it there, but with us that's always half the battle.

Frontal assault? In a studio, that often pays dividends and starts legends. There is the story of the two young men who scaled the fence at Universal and set up shop in a vacant office, bluffing their way into acceptance and (so the story goes) eventually into production. And the legend of how a large yacht being used for filming at 20th was stolen by a nervy group with a big truck who simply told the cop at the gate that they were there for the yacht—and got some help in loading it. No matter how tight the security at a studio, high-handed behavior will usually get you past the guards, since the penalty for letting Jack the Ripper into Ladies' Wardrobe is not likely to be as severe as for not letting someone with clout past the front gate. Studio cops are professional survivors.

When the people in the shops told me the sign had been installed by professional sign people, I checked with them but the cost of the job was too great. "Be cheaper if we do it on a weekday," the man said. "Why does it have to be on a Saturday anyhow?"

But during the week, in broad daylight, the chance of failure was too great.

Commando time.

The place for the comma was just barely reachable from the window of the men's room on the fourth floor. It was a slit of a window, a steel casement which opened toward the sign. But the crank was missing. Easy. I bought a crank, a can of oil and a wire brush, stayed late one night, sneaked up to the men's room and, working only by the light from outside, got the thing to operate. By cranking the casement all the way open and by hanging onto the window with one hand and onto the ledge with my feet, I could touch the spot!

The obvious way to do it was to drill a hole in the concrete block, set some kind of lug in the hole and slip a comma, properly bored, into place over it. I tried. I brought my quarter-inch drill and a couple of masonry bits and an extension cord. But in the night silence the drill made a hell of a noise, and the position, hanging out there in the dark, trying to drill into concrete with the drill held in one hand, was too much. After a couple of scary tries, I gave that up.

Glue.

You have seen those ads where one drop of glue holds an elephant as he's hoisted into the air? I made a wooden comma, gilded it, fastened it to a block to hold it the right distance from the wall, waited for a nice dark night and tried the elephant-hoisting glue.

The comma dropped like a shot and smashed on the pavement below. I crawled back in, closed the window and pelted down the stairs to pick up the broken evidence—and that was all for that night.

I tried the stuff where you smear both sides, wait for each surface to dry and then slap them together. *"Be careful how you position the pieces because once placed together they cannot be moved."* They moved. That comma hit, broke, bounced into the street. Before I could get out of the window a studio cop rolled around the corner on one of those electric go-carts they use, stopped and looked around for the source of the noise. Luckily he stopped the cart right over the broken comma. When I emerged from the dark building holding the brown bag in which I kept my materials he looked at me oddly but settled for my brisk goodnight.

Studio cops have seen a lot of people do a lot of strange things. Bizarre behavior from a producer whose pictures are making money is quite likely to be overlooked by a cop who has already outlived a lot of spectacular nuts, so the cops making rounds who saw me going in and out of a dark building late at night a couple of times a week just shrugged it off. If they checked the building after I left they would have found only that I had gone to the fourth-floor men's room. Eccentric at that hour, but nothing special.

Weeks passed. It took time to make new commas in my home workshop. Each one had to be glued to a block and gilded, time-consuming stuff. I tried the double-sided tape that holds pianos to the wall in commercials. It didn't hold the commas. No matter how light the wood, it seemed to be too heavy for the job. Then I got an idea. Styrofoam!

That weekend I made the last of the commas, a masterpiece of plastic. I filled the pores of the stuff with spackle, sanded it smooth, varnished it and then sprayed it gold. Beautiful. But how to fasten it? Pretending casual interest, I went to the studio art department and asked one of my friends if he knew of any kind of glue or tape that would hold such a block to the face of a concrete building. He smiled.

"I think I got just what you want," he said. "It's a sort of a mastic— comes in coils, see?" It was a serrated coil of grayish, ropy, sticky stuff which stuck to my hands and to everything else.

"Perfect," I said. "Can you let me have some of it?"

"Take it all," he said. "We don't use it."

"Well, how come?"

"Just take it," he said. "I hope it works. I was going to give it to you anyhow. But if they find out, don't tell anyone I helped."

So much for secrecy.

"Who else knows?"

A shrug. "Nobody."

That was on a Wednesday, I think. It was the day before Arthur Knight wrote his story for the *Saturday Review,* twenty-four hours before someone read it aloud to Zanuck, twenty-four hours and twenty minutes before I was fired.

"Be off the lot by the close of business Friday."

I finished packing by noon, said all my goodbyes and waited for the Bekins truck. It came, the boxes went, and by four-thirty I was walking down the corridor for the last time.

Just before I got to the elevators, an office door opened behind me and someone hissed at me to wait.

I turned. It was Tony Hope, Bob Hope's son, a pleasant young man with whom I had one of those "Hi, how are you" acquaintances.

"I heard what happened," he said. "Give me the comma."

I stared. "What comma?"

"Oh, come on," he said. "I know about it and I'll get it up. Give it here."

I was too surprised to ask any questions and he was in a hurry. I led him down to the parking lot where comma, mastic and all were concealed in the trunk of my car. We bent over like stage conspirators, I opened the bag a crack, he nodded and took it. We shook hands and he went back into the building. I closed the trunk and drove off the lot.

On Monday morning the comma was in place. "Think, 20th," it said. To all the world. But I never saw it. Instead I got a photograph—a good clear shot of the sign with the comma where I had dreamed it. "Think, 20th." With the photo came a note which said: "It lasted until noon. One of *Them* spotted it. They knew right away it was you. Regards."

26

§

"That Kid Don't Know
What Good Is"

MY FATHER was born in one of those remote mud-and-plank villages on the Russian-Polish border and died, a few years ago, in a modern hospital in Coral Gables. Even in an age of astronauts, his was a long trip. He was a stubborn man. I have one of those sepia enlargements of him in the uniform of the U.S. Navy, lips compressed, looking straight out. Stubborn. When he enlisted he had been in this country only a couple of years and hardly spoke English. I asked him once what he did during his year in the Brooklyn Navy Yard and he told me he had shoveled a lot of coal. But he had decided to be an American—and if that meant shoveling coal for a year in the company of men whose jokes he could only guess at, why, that's what it meant. Tenacious.

Like the others, he brought his politics with him—that odd, messianic socialism of the immigrants. The word salads of my childhood are full of talk about Kerensky and mensheviks and all those last-syllable-accented words ending in "ist"—Sozial*ist*, Tzion*ist*, Capital*ist*. The first time I learned that this was not the table talk of my classmates was in a social-studies class in Forest Park Junior High, Springfield, Massachusetts, when Miss Hodges asked us to stand in turn and tell which candidate our families supported and why they liked him. When I said "Norman Thomas" it got very quiet. Then some kid began to giggle, thinking I had made a weird mistake; maybe Norman Thomas was in the vaudeville show at Loew's.

But Miss Hodges stopped the laughter pretty quickly. "Norman Thomas," she said, looking at me. "That's very interesting, isn't it, class?"

The class knew enough not to respond, and we went on to other things. But I felt my father should have warned me. I could have said "Roosevelt." But he wouldn't have. Stubborn.

We were a kitchen-table family, of course—and every Sunday morning saw us together for breakfast. In those days my father worked five and a half days and came home too late for dinner (called supper) on five nights. What was left of Saturday was the Sabbath. But Sunday morning was an assembly. At odds with every other immigrant father I knew, mine was devoted to the health and strength recipes of Bernarr MacFadden—a pioneer health-food nut who preached the gospel of carrot sticks and whole-grain cereals. My father was so impressed by MacFadden's ideas that he persuaded my mother to add bran to potato pancakes. It made them crisp and somewhat dry, mahogany-colored and slightly shiny—a bit like floor tiles.

Wanting the best for us, he naturally insisted on a breakfast which began with a great hot glop of oatmeal or wheat meal or buckwheat groats—the coarser the better, according to MacFadden. Never having heard of cholesterol, my father would drench the whole thing with sweet cream and hand the pitcher to me. I would put it down, preferring milk. Father would purse his lips and reach for the honey, which he ladled onto the whole rich mess. He would then hand me the honey and I would say, "No thanks, Pa." I preferred salt.

"Try the honey."

"I don't like honey on cereal."

"You won't even try it?"

I would sit mute. My father would look at me, sigh and turn to my mother in resignation.

"That kid don't know what good is."

Maybe it wasn't a thousand Sundays but that's the way I remember it. Summer sounds and green grass out the window and my father shaking his head.

"That kid don't know what good is."

I sailed out of the auto gate that day at 20th, and my father's curse never crossed my mind. If someone had said something funny . . . but

instead there was decent Stan Hough, shaking his head. Stan said,
"Don't do it—huh? I've talked to him—he doesn't really want you to go.
Just go back in and say something like you're sorry. He'll forget it, I'm
telling you. . . ."

He'll forget it? No qualified injustice collector could pass that up.
"Well, I won't!"

Glowing with martyrdom, puffed with injustice, throbbing with recti-
tude, I left the lot, having proved my father's point to Zanuck's satisfac-
tion.

The lady of the house said, "I'm sure you know what you're doing,
hon. Anything else lined up?"

And Harris my Agent tried to be brave, but the disconsolateness
showed through. "Do you think he'd take you back—I mean, I could
talk to him? . . . Well, give me some time, I'm sure I can find you
something." Then he said, "Why don't you go away for a while? Think
things over. Give him a chance to cool down."

I said that sounded like a good idea and he sighed with relief.

"We'll sit down and have a talk when you get back."

"Look, Harris," I said. "Under the circumstances I have an idea we'd
better split up. I mean, you're a close friend of Dick's, and—"

He interrupted, cheerful for the first time. "Right, right, right," he
said. "No hard feelings."

"No."

"Good, good. Uh—"

"Yes?"

"Have a nice trip."

Slob time.

"I'm sorry," I said, "I mean, we've been together a long time—"

His pale gums glistened. "Nothing, nothing—I was just lucky enough
to introduce you two guys."

Noblesse, baby.

"Look," I said, "I'll write you a letter. Appreciation for all you've
done."

"Be swell if you would."

And that was that. Humble, appreciative Harris my Agent, happy to
have been of service. I went home and wrote him a valentine which
spoke of his inestimable value. He treasured the note—brought it into
court later on when he sued me successfully for a share of my winnings.
"He says right here he couldn't have done it without me."

After nearly five years of constant, overlapping production I was free,
just as I wanted to be. It took me about forty-eight hours to get nervous.

"Look, hon," said the lady of the house, "if you think you made a mistake why don't you call him up?" I glared, she shrugged, picked up the little dogs and clickety-clicked across the terrazzo floor to the imposing double doors of that house.

"Later," she said, and the Cadillac convertible slid down the long driveway into her busy daytime world. "I'll be at the Beverly Wilshire for lunch in case you're looking for me. . . ."

I thought it was an invitation, and I shaved, put on a jacket and went down to the hotel. She saw me instantly.

"What a nice surprise," she said, in a voice that made everyone look.

I waved, came to the table and was introduced to her friends, none of whom I had ever seen before.

That night she said, "You were pretty quiet at lunch, hon. Everyone noticed."

"Well," I said, "I didn't know any of them, and I never really figured out what anybody did. . . ."

She shrugged it off. "This and that—the best they can. Want a drink?"

"Sure."

From the wet bar in the corner she said, "What were you doing there, anyhow?"

"Doing? You said you'd be there, and I—"

She laughed and dropped ice cubes into the glasses, smiling brilliantly. "Just wondered if you were checking up. . . . Here, this all right?"

"I'll tell you what I think," she said. "I think you need a job. Why don't you let Jim find you something?"

Jim was Jim Moloney, old friend, new agent. Loud, gusty, sentimental —a bright smile to break down a door combined with a powerfully manic imagination. One night, Jim got the idea that he'd been born to sell Nikita Khrushchev a touring country-and-western trio—Sons of the Sagebrush or something—and the next thing he was on my extension phone calling Moscow, wheedling, commanding, inventing credentials until he actually got to make his pitch to some minister or other in the Kremlin, who told him to send a letter.

"They'll fall all over each other when I tell them you're available," said Jim. "You know what you want?"

I didn't.

"You want me to talk to Zanuck? Guaranteed you can go back with a better deal."

"Why the hell does everybody tell me they can get me back to 20th? Won't any other studio give me a job, for chrissake?" ("Without me, you're nothing.")

"Of course they will! You're the hottest name in town! Just give me a couple of weeks to look around. . . ." ("That kid don't know what good is.")

"Hey," said the lady of the house, "you're spinning your wheels, aren't you?"

I was, of course.

"I'm going to go away for a couple of weeks," I said. "Florida Keys. I'll go fishing."

"Great idea."

"Just what you need."

"Been working too long without a break."

"Time to look around."

"Relax."

"You know Frank is shooting in Miami? *Tony Rome,* I think. All your buddies will be there."

It was arranged immediately. A lady who could keep ashtrays emptied at parties had no trouble with travel arrangements.

"You can touch base with the leader, catch a fish and maybe play some tennis, huh?"

Agent Jim said, "Guarantee I'll have a couple of good things by the time you get back. And I'll see what's doing at 20th . . . anyhow."

"Tell you what, hon," she said. "Let's have a few people over for Saturday brunch. Say goodbye."

"Great idea," Jim said.

Just before noon on Saturday, the cars began pulling up in the long narrow driveway, dropping off guests in California sports-weekend clothes (it was just before denim) and backing down between the rows of cypress and oleander. Her brunches were highly regarded by our friends. There were parking boys in red jackets.

By three the house was full and noisy—people were sitting on the floor and jamming the terrace and the music churned the bloody marys and the maid was scooping dead peanuts into ashtrays and freshening the bowls of dip and the dishwasher was going and it was indeed a party when the doorbell rang and someone called me. Two men in uniform coveralls. Behind them, motor running, a small moving van.

The shorter one, apparently the leader, held one of those clipboards with a sheaf of papers on it. He looked at the papers, then back to me.

"Mr. David?"

When I nodded, he shoved the clipboard at me, pointing to the top sheet, a pickup order.

"We come for the sectional sofa."

"What?"

"It says right here." He tapped the paper. "See? Green, sectional. Four pieces. Curved."

The other one had been looking past him into the living room, where people were milling about, some of them looking at us curiously.

"In there, Les. I think that's it."

I looked and suddenly understood.

"Wait a minute," I said. "That green sectional sofa in there is bought and paid for—it came off the set of *Our Man Fli—*"

Somebody shoved a glass past me. "Hey, Bekins, you want a drink?"

"No thanks, sir." He turned back to me, obviously embarrassed. "Maybe I better call the office."

I took the clipboard and rooted through the papers. The third one down was an order from the 20th Century-Fox prop department. It said, "Bekins to pick up Flint sectional. Saturday *afternoon.*" The time was underlined.

"Stay right here," I said. "I think I can straighten this out."

"Yessir."

I found Jim out on the terrace, smiling, flushed, telling one of his stories at the top of his voice.

"Can I talk to you a second?"

He excused himself and turned to me. "Swell party," he whispered, then he laughed loudly. "Jesus! Did you see what that broad in the lace top was doing when you came over?"

"No," I said. "Jim, think a minute. Were you at 20th any time this week?"

He had trouble focusing on it. "Sure—sure, I was out there a couple of times. Lunch or something Thursday . . ."

"Did you talk to anyone . . . ?"

"What?" He peered at me, slung his arm around my shoulders and leaned in close. "Listen, buddy—don't you worry about a thing. They just want to save face is all."

"Jim—forget all that. Did you tell them there was a party here today?"

Jim beamed. "How'd you know? Did someone show up?"

"No," I said. "But they sent regards."

When you buy a prop or a piece of furniture from the set of a movie, you sign a paper saying that the studio can, with proper notice, borrow the item from you in the event they need it for pickup shots or a sequel.

The picture and its sequel had been finished some time before, but when they heard I was having a party, the chance was too good to pass up.

By the time I got rid of the movers, all the guests had heard the story. They loved it, of course, and later when I heard it retold, it had become a pitched battle in the driveway—guests vs. movers in a tug of war over furniture, with chair arms and legs torn loose in the melee. Everything but Laurel and Hardy.

But I was not in condition to applaud incoming jokes, and I raged, threatened reprisals and finally moped off to Miami. Now there was no studio limo to pick me up, no driver to carry my bags, no VIP reception at the counter—"I'll check those for you, why don't you go right up to the lounge. . . ."

The Sinatra Company was living in the Fountainebleau and shooting in a grand, moldering mansion somewhere on the ocean front. Everyone was happy to see me. . . .

On a location, visitors are always in the way. Any movie company is a closed and obsessive society, tense with its own concerns, full of inside jokes and secret understandings and alliances as passionate as they are short-lived. Take that same company on a distant location and it's all heightened into a kind of Us-against-Them xenophobia. In the evenings away from home, arguments flare, friendships grow ferocious and the leading man often feels compelled to keep proving his role after work. Visiting writers love the atmosphere, but if you're a moviemaker yourself, visiting someone else's location tells you what it'll be like when you can't get a job anymore.

Director Denny Campbell asked me to share his enormous suite—a plum-colored string of rooms full of bamboo wet bars and television sets. "I got a couple of broads lined up for after," Denny said—but for some reason or other they never showed and we turned in early. Sometime during the night there was a banging on the door and suddenly the room was full of laughing, yelling drunks. "Where the hell is he?" "Get up, goddammit—it's drinking time!" Finally someone switched on a light and, when they saw me, the laughter died. "Oops, sorry—didn't know you had company." The last one out the door reached back in and switched off the light. Campbell yelled something after them and laughed. "Every night," he said. "Last week they carried me out of bed and all and this broad is screaming, 'No—put me down!' "

"Anybody I know?"

"Who? Oh, the broad? Kid on the picture."

Somewhere out in the hall I could hear doors slamming and more laughter.

"Let's get dressed and go down to the bar."

Next morning I rented a car and drove south into the Keys, hoping to catch a tarpon, even though it was past the season.

A lot of people just shrug when you tell them you like to fish—or more exactly, go fishing. But so far no one calls you a heartless murderer or says things about "macho" and "blood sports." To most of my friends, fishing is a kind of old-timey affectation, something like wearing sleeve garters. It's odd—in spite of home aquariums and those assorted tropicals you see in every dentist's waiting room, fish have not caught on as an oppressed minority. The people who will fling themselves across the bows of a tuna boat to keep the fishermen from killing one more porpoise don't seem to mind being beastly to the tuna. There may be a mammalian brotherhood waiting to be discovered.

The Keys are a string of not very attractive little islands which stretch out in an arc toward the Gulf of Mexico. Flat, dry, covered in rank marsh grass and mangroves where mosquitos breed, and connected by a narrow concrete causeway built by WPA, the Keys, except for Key West itself, are without exotic character. There's a string of motels usually called Captain Something-or-Other's Dunrovin Cabins or Bud 'n' Thelma's Fishing Camp. Dr Pepper is sold here along with the local specialty—Key lime pie, a pie which allegedly tastes different because the shrunken yellow limes were grown in the gravelly decomposed coral of the Keys. Raunchy, roadside America. I love it.

The romance of deep-sea fishing escapes me. The machinery, the chair and the heavy gear—lines like hawsers—and the whole professional, chrome and mahogany, tub-full-of-beer-and-money feel of it don't grab me. I like to fish from a small boat or from the bridge abutments using light tackle. Nighttime is the best. When the tide is running from the Gulf to the sea and the fish are feeding, I smear myself in mosquito lotion, hang a flashlight around my neck, set my pailful of live shrimp down carefully so they won't topple in the dark, put one on and toss it out into the incoming water. On one crazy night I caught twelve different varieties of fish—but the real prize is a tarpon. When you hook a tarpon he goes straight up into the air, landing with a splash like a grand piano—and right up again. If there's a moon, you can see his eyes shining orange when he breaks. If you're lucky or good at it, you finally bring him in to where you're standing. A big fish for shallow waters—three feet long is the biggest I ever caught that way. That's when you use the flashlight. You switch it on, leaving it hanging around your neck, so the bobbing light will help you see well enough to grab and gill the convulsing fish and hang onto him while you twist and pry the hook loose. Then you throw him back.

During the day you can lie around, drink, play tennis (if there's a court close enough) or go bonefishing. Bonefishing is really hunting bonefish; it's expensive and takes great skill. You hire a bonefish guide, who takes you out in a skiff, which he poles, quietly, standing up and peering into the shallows where the torpedo-shaped bonefish hang. When he spots one, the customer is supposed to delicately flip the bait out so it sinks in front of the bonefish. Too much splash, a noise—no bonefish. But if it works, the fish seizes the bait and takes off in a straight line in an explosion of speed which makes the reel whine and can scare the fisherman right out of the boat. Ted Williams made the sport popular, sold a lot of fishing gear with his name on it and created the bonefish guide. Given good luck and bad, it costs about four hundred dollars to catch a bonefish. One day I wandered out to a sand spit, put a bit of bait onto a hook, cast it out about thirty feet, wedged the pole into some rocks and forgot about it. Hours later, when I reeled it in, there was a small bonefish on the end of it. I was so impressed that I had it stuffed and mounted—at a cost of about thirty-five dollars. A terrific bargain.

Bonefish are not eaten, any more than tarpon. Conspicuous nonconsumption.

After about ten days the spell was broken. I think the island was Marathon. Wherever it was, I had just checked into a Howard Johnson's motel when the manager came to the door. "There's a call for you, sir."

It occurred to me that the room phone wasn't working.

"You want me to come down to the desk?"

"No, sir," he said. "It's Mr. Sinatra for you. Frank Sinatra."

It wasn't, of course. It was one of the Companions, Miami branch—a big, soft-spoken man whom Sinatra had introduced, "if you need something down here."

"Jesus, Dave," he said, "I had a hell of a time finding you. I checked every yacht harbor from Miami to Key West. What the hell boat are you on?"

I explained. No boat.

"Your car break down? What're you doing in a Howard Johnson's?"

There was no way. "I'm writing a piece on motels," I said. "Anyway, what's up?"

"He wants to talk to you about something."

"Should I wait?"

"No, no—he just wanted to know when you'd be back in town. Nothing urgent," he said.

"Day after tomorrow."

"Good, good. I'll tell him."

He just likes to know where everyone is. . . .

———————

The only one excited by my reappearance was producer Aaron Rosenberg.

"Whaddya say—how do you feel about being replaced?"

I explained that I had been out of touch.

"Harris," he said. "He went out of the agency business soon as you left. Now he's a producer, sitting in your old office and assigned to your properties!"

Without me you're nothing. . . .

27

—§—

My Brief Encounter With ABC Features

MOST OF US need someplace to go in the morning even if we don't go there. There are men raised in other traditions, of course, but to most of us a man who never goes to a place of business is like someone who has never had to ask how much anything costs. An object of overt envy, covert contempt. Actors between jobs stay home; directors, producers and screenwriters rent little offices in odd buildings around Beverly Hills so they'll always have someplace to go. Most keep those offices for years and years—even if they're too busy ever to use them. Writers are great goal-setters who talk about going down to the office and turning out "my ten pages a day" with the smug piety of joggers describing their morning mileage.

But a free-lance producer—an independent looking for a deal—has no growing page count to keep him feeling morally fit. Even though he hustles like an anteater, there will soon come a day without an appointment, a time when all his projects are "out under consideration" and his agent has a lunch date. Such a man, idly glancing into shop windows on Beverly Drive at an hour when only women are on the street, is subject to day sweats and bleak fantasies about never working again.

Once seized, the victim will grab at anything. Celebrated directors, world-renowned screenwriters, have been known to accept several jobs at once—just to make sure. The director will leave the omelet for his agent to unscramble; the screenwriter will tell his agent but no one else. Screenwriters mostly have such a high sense of self-worth and Original Virtue that they feel perfectly moral about cheating several producers simultaneously, convinced that each of them is getting better than he deserves.

A while ago, at a cocktail party full of famous faces, I was greeted by Irwin Allen, resplendent in a white suit. He clapped me on the shoulder and said he had been hearing good things about me, and I thanked him and made a mistake.

I said, "What have you been up to lately?"

He stared. "What have I been up to? *Where have you been living, in a cave?*"

I was being absent-minded, not insulting—but he was right to think otherwise. Everyone in that room knew that Irwin Allen had announced fifty or sixty million dollars' worth of deals that week, and if I didn't know that, what the hell was I doing there saying hello to Sue and embracing Peter and kissing Raquel and Liza, for chrissake?

The bridge to 20th was burned while I was fishing, but Agent Jim was not daunted.

"Glad to see you back—million things to discuss. You look great. Rested. Everybody wants to talk to you." The white smile, the ringing cufflinks, the rising voice. "Everybody!"

It was almost true. Everybody was willing to talk to me, and what it came down to was, "Terrific piece of manpower, Jim." Then, to me, "What've you got?"

Walt Disney himself spent a few minutes with me.

"I liked *Fantastic Voyage*," he said.

"Thank you."

"You could have done it a lot better here."

Probably.

A week later Agent Jim told me Disney had made a proposal to him for my services. "It was a lot of money," Jim said. "Twice what they were paying at 20th. But I told them to forget it."

"You what?"

"Take it easy," Jim said. "We can always reopen if that's what you want."

We were in my living room. Glass all around—Mrs. Jim and the lady of the house laughing and making kitchen sounds from there, the little girls and the little dogs scrabbling around on the brick patio near the olive tree, throwing a chew stick into the ivy—"Go on, find it. Find it!"

"I told you," Jim said. "Be a snap. But first we listen to everybody."

I wavered. Three years at those numbers was quite a lot more than I had earned in ten years at Bantam. Jim brushed all that aside.

"Grant you it's good money," he said, "but they wanted too much for it. Exclusivity. You'd be stuck for three long years."

He laughed the laugh of an agent whose client is hot.

"Don't worry. We'll do better. Way better."

SOUND: IN BG, A MOCKING CHORD.

Hearing nothing, I said, "Right. We pass."

When the trade papers call something an exploitation picture, they aren't trying to flatter it.

Studios used to be brand names whose products were as easily identifiable as Mars Bars or cola drinks. When Harry Cohn said he could tell a movie's quality by whether or not he fidgeted in his seat and Herman Mankiewicz made the delighted comment, "Imagine! The whole world wired to Harry Cohn's ass!" he was only exaggerating. That part of the whole world that watched Columbia's pictures *was* attached to Cohn that way.

Now, the studios and the managers, deal makers and packagers who run them are homogenized so they spread easily, Mrs. American Housewife, at any temperature. Almost all. Until recently, two were still unique: Walt Disney and AIP—American International Pictures, Inc. Each of them made movies which are instantly identifiable, for very different reasons. The Disney product comes from a concept and an operation which is only technically a part of the other Hollywood—I have heard studio heads turn down picture projects by saying, "It would be great if it had Disney's name on it." But AIP was gut Hollywood, a tent show that never turned into a concert—a carnival that stuck to its freaks and geeks even as they shimmered and turned into astronauts, monsters, rock music kids and ornate murderers, whatever was drawing a crowd on the midway. And AIP has one other distinction. It was the only major motion-picture production/distribution company always run by one of the men who founded it, Samuel Z. Arkoff. Alas, AIP is now RIP.

"Just for laughs," Jim said, "like you to take a meeting with Sam. You'll like him. He's got a proposition."

"What kind?"

Jim made an agent's answer. "See if you like him first."

I liked him. Arkoff is a rotund, jowly man who chain-smoked cigars, lamented his bad back and groused about having to go on a rigid diet "if I want to survive, he says." Then, still growling around the cigar, "He didn't see the first-quarter grosses, I guess."

We drank quite a lot of iced tea and talked about movies.

"I suppose you'd really like to direct too? Yes? Why not? We use a lot of first-time directors—works out pretty good too—most of the time. Think about it."

The discussion with my near and dear ones rapidly turned sociological. "Well, hon," she said, fluffing an immaculate pillow, "it's up to you, of course—but AIP?"

"You think it's chintzy?"

"Tacky, more like."

I said, "So nigh is grandeur to our dust, so near is God to Man—and all that."

She said, "Bullshit."

"You think it would be a comedown?"

"Without a parachute."

Jim said, "It's not what *I* think, it's what the town will think."

"For chrissake—the whole thing was your idea, wasn't it?"

"Sure," he said, teeth and cufflinks dazzling in a conjuror's gesture. "But now I got a better idea."

"What?"

"Can you take a meeting with Selig Seligman?"

"Who?"

"ABC Feature Films. They're going into features. Heavy."

"And?"

"If you guys like each other," Jim said, "I can get you the biggest production deal in the history of the business."

"What the hell are you talking about?"

SOUND: TA DA!!

"How about three hundred thousand per picture and fifty percent?"

"You're kidding!"

"Three pictures firm!"

"When Duty whispers low, *Thou must,* the youth replies, *I can.*"

"What's that?"

"Emerson. It's on a statue in Providence, Rhode Island."

"Yeah, great," Jim said, looking puzzled.

"He means he loves it," said the lady of the house.

Robert Frost is very good on the validity of walls, but when he talks about two roads diverging, in that wonderful, rueful stanza, he is only encouraging astrologers. That fork in the road always looked like a seamless freeway to me.

The American Broadcasting Company has traditionally played poor cousin to the other networks, and, until quite recently, the West Coast offices looked it. Now the executives are housed in a kind of cathedral of lofty wooden halls, dreaming clerestories and padded stairways—in the ABC Entertainment Center in Century City, which is an enormous park of office buildings, green belts and fountains on the western edge of Beverly Hills; but then they were scattered around Old Hollywood in nondescript buildings mostly converted from older failures.

Most visitors to Hollywood barely see it. The tour buses pant through Beverly Hills and Bel-Air and the tourists stand in long lines to take the Universal Movie tour or the Burbank Studio tour—both as synthetic as Disneyland. The closest they get is a quick stop at the Chinese Theater —Sid Grauman's Chinese Theater, which is now called Mann's Chinese Theater because it was bought by a Midwestern theater operator with a strong sense of himself. A quick swing up Vine, "This is the famous corner of Hollywood and Vine," past the Brown Derby, "The walls inside are covered with autographed caricatures of all the most famous stars," and forget it. The Hollywood Brown Derby is *not* the one shaped like a derby hat. That one is miles away on Wilshire Boulevard in an area of insurance buildings and clothing stores. There too is the immense old Ambassador Hotel, shabby-grand, set back from the boulevard by a city block of landscaping, nonworking fountains and winding paths—home of the Coconut Grove nightclub, where everything used to happen long ago. The tour buses don't go there anymore. They don't wallow down through the crowded grid of narrow streets to the south of Hollywood, Sunset and Santa Monica boulevards. There, in miles of plain, two- and three-story ocher-stuccoed buildings, are the old studios where silent films were made, cramped little stages showing every addition demanded by technology and the fire inspectors; production offices each with a window air conditioner dripping rust into the ivy which chokes off the light from ancient casement windows long since painted and rusted shut. But this is magic land. The buildings in these treeless streets house every kind of technical speciality—the film labs, special-effects houses, optical specialists, property warehouses, costumers. The tour buses couldn't get through the streets—besides, what's to see?

Immense contract and all, I went to work for ABC Features in an old building on Vine Street, once a local radio station and still a functioning theater for quiz shows and game shows with a gaudy cutout sign out front telling you when you can get the free tickets for the taping of BRIDE FOR AN HOUR!! PRIZES!! LAUGHS!! 4TH STRAIGHT YEAR!!

Upstairs is a clutter of offices. I got one just vacated by a former football star who had become a sports commentator. It was dark because the only windows in it opened onto a corridor. The football star had done it up in ankle-deep, blood-red carpet, shielded little lights and cabinets that became bars when opened. I got a new desk lamp, an imitation Eames chair and a pussycat—a pretty red-headed secretary named Carole who affected itinerant agents the way a quail affects bird dogs.

No one could dislike Selig Seligman. He was a big, bulky man whose speech sometimes overran itself into a stammer. His cheeks shone when he smiled, and when he walked with you he would touch you on the shoulder; not quite an embrace, more a reassurance, to himself as much as you. His office was a monument to family life—pictures of his wife and kids everywhere; scholastic trophies were on his shelves and framed classroom art on the walls. This is not unfamiliar in Hollywood, but in Selig's case it was no pretense. His home, a Tudor-Gothic mansion high in the hills above Old Hollywood, had been built, he said, by Adolphe Menjou. It was full of beamed ceilings, unexpected staircases and nooks. Great paneled doors on chased-brass hinges, flagstone hallways—the baronial works, all of it filled with children, relatives, dogs, cats and visiting friends. I was there several times at different hours but it seems to me music was always playing and the barbecue grill was always smoking. The tents of Abraham.

My meetings with Selig always ran into lunch. "Gee—it's nearly twelve-thirty. You got a lunch date? We can talk there."

"There" was a Chinese restaurant called the Shanghai. Selig loved spicy Chinese food, and on days when the temperature hovered in the nineties he would scoff up great bowls full of "hot and sour" soup, gesturing, laughing, telling stories as he ate—the perspiration raining down from his face.

"Go ahead, try it—try it," he would urge, and then, laughing, "Too hot for you? Here—some rice. No, don't drink water—the rice will cool you off."

So I enjoyed the lunches, learned to eat hot Chinese food and never got to finish a conversation about a project. The months slid by, my red-headed secretary announced that she was going to be married, and I became restless with no production in sight. The world was changing, old certainties seeming to crumble at a touch. *Playboy* magazine stopped reprinting "ribald" stories from the *Decameron* and began selling an irresistible vision of a liberated Youthcult which combined Penrod's and Tom Swift's dreams of gadgets and long pants with a kind of sexual delirium like a Moslem paradise: psychic uplift, hi-fi speakers, white wine with dinner, and afterward the houris of the centerfold.

Suddenly a movie industry that had banned the use of the word "pregnant" and fought over an ad showing Carroll Baker sucking her thumb was confronted with *The Fox,* which contained one scene which set censors and civilibertarians ablaze. Masturbation!

People who make movies for a living talked about nothing else. The trade press flamed with essays pro and con, until you might have supposed that the proper spelling for that Constitutional guarantee was the Fist Amendment.

Carole made the most telling comment. Since her fiancé was a publicist, she saw the movie long before I did. When I asked her how she had liked it, she shrugged.

"Okay, I guess."

"Okay? Is that all? I mean, what about the—uh—masturbation scene?"

She shrugged again. "I suppose it was artistic," she said, "but that's not how you *do* it."

All the same, I was liberated along with everyone else, and I persuaded Seligman to read a wonderful satirical novel by Vercors, *Les Animaux Dénaturés*—a story which had been repeatedly optioned, once performed as a play, but never filmed because of its outrageous premise. Vercors asks: What if a tribe of "missing links" were found somewhere, manlike enough to be trainable for labor, animal enough to be classified as draft animals and exploited? Now imagine a scientist who becomes so inflamed against this "slavery" that he takes the only course open to prove the creatures are human—invokes the scientific dictum that only animals of the same species can interbreed! Right! Like the Young Man of Dundee. And, in this case too, "the outcome was horrid." The scientist murders the offspring and demands to be tried for murder—thus proving the creatures human.

I loved it, and, to my surprise, so did Seligman. We assured each other that the possible implications of bestiality could be handled tastefully, and ABC bought me the novel and allowed me to hire a first-rate, high-priced screenwriter, Nelson Gidding. We called it *Skullduggery.* With two L's. A pun.

We turned in a full treatment. Seligman criticized a little, laughed a lot and authorized the next steps. Then, after some weeks, he approved a draft screenplay and asked for a budget. I countered by urging a location hunt first, unless ABC wanted the picture to look like one of those Tarzan pictures made by trucking potted philodendrons into Bronson Canyon.

"Where do you want to look?"

I rolled the dice. "The story is set in New Guinea," I said. "Why don't we look there?"

"New Guinea! Are you kidding? You know what it would cost to ship a crew and equipment to New Guinea?"

"Sure, sure," I said, "but we wouldn't do that, we'd base ourselves in Australia. You can shoot for about fifty percent of U.S. costs."

The Australian figures were well known. Cost-conscious U.S. picture makers were already shooting some TV-western episodes there. Seligman was impressed. "So you'll have to survey Australia too, right?"

I agreed that it was a sound idea. "As long as we're going to be there anyhow."

"We?"

"I think Nelson should come along. He's been there several times and he's very friendly with the Chief of Staff of the Australian Armed forces. Might come in handy."

"You've got a lot of style," Selig said. "How long do you guys figure to be gone?"

"About a month."

He thought about it. "Okay," he said, "but what about the small acrobats—to play the Missing Links? You going to use kids?"

"Don't know. You know how it is to work with kids. . . . "

"So . . . "

"I've been thinking—maybe a troupe of Japanese acrobats . . . ?"

Seligman stared at me then roared with laughter.

"You mean you might as well stop off in Japan, don't you?"

"Selig," I said, "you've got a hell of an idea there."

"Stop off in Hawaii on your way back. Might as well look around there too," said Selig.

"Hawaii?"

"Good place to shoot," said Selig. "A little expensive, but damn good for jungle stuff."

"Why not? Maybe we could use that fern forest on the big island. . . . "

"Just what I was thinking," said Selig. "Now when do you figure to be there?"

"Hawaii?" I calculated rapidly. "Sometime in the fifth week, I imagine . . . it's hard to be exact. . . . "

"Do you think you might be there by the tenth of the month?"

"Sure." Dawn was breaking fast.

"Good, good," said Selig. "You do that. It'll just work out great."

"It's a deal," I said. "You bringing Muriel and the kids?"

"Just Muriel."

Off we went on a glorious Pacific tour, feeling like Hecht and Macarthur.

The Japanese acrobats were too tall and muscular for our imaginings, but Kyoto and Nara were delightful, and Nelson had friends in Japan too.

New Guinea, at that time still being administered by Australia, was a place of extraordinary beauty, discomfort and sudden frights—a naked, painted man with a bone through his nose and a stone ax in his hand is a disconcerting sight when you're wandering a few feet off the trail, looking for tree orchids—but the worst of it was the miles of red tape tangled around every request for cooperation. Warm smiles, vigorous Australian handshakes, pukka colonial afternoon tea parties given by the DO's wife who "never met any of you film blokes before"—but no permits. "Have to be careful about these people, you know—the bloody UN watching every bloody move we bloody make here."

We needed connections, so we flew to Australia and visited Nelson's friends. The results were not magical, but there was movement. We went to Canberra and shuttled from office to office, always invoking Names, and finally got permission to film in New Guinea. Three days to spare. I sent a triumphant cable and we flew to Hawaii.

There were no hotel reservations awaiting us in Hawaii. I telephoned Los Angeles and was told that Mr. Seligman was out of town; New York, she thought. Had he received our cable? She wasn't sure but she thought so.

"*Skullduggery* is in trouble," Nelson said. "Somebody hates it."

"Impossible. They all read it and approved."

"New York too?"

"Absolutely."

Nelson gave me one of those up-under-the-eyebrows squints. Slightly stooped, gray-haired and ruddy, wearing one of those huge, shaggy WWII RAF mustaches, Nelson often looked like Jean Hersholt doing a takeoff on Oscar Homolka. He said, "Well, somebody's dragging their feet."

Somebody was. Next time I saw Seligman he was friendly but preoccupied. He glanced at our photos of New Guinea, nodded at my recitation of permits granted, provisional budget figures, Australian facilities and timetables.

"Sounds good. I'll get back to you."

I said, "I don't want to rush you, but you understand about the rainy season down there? If we want to get the picture made this year we have to be able to get started in eight or ten weeks."

"Of course. Leave the stuff with me."

After a week I asked the secretary, who told me she would tell him I called.

Nelson shrugged. "I'll start looking for another picture," he said. "If it goes, and you need more work, call me."

The weeks passed. I sent memoranda, increasingly crisp summaries of the problem. Selig didn't exactly avoid me, but our lunches stopped. The contracts that had to be made were not drawn, the Australians who had been provisionally engaged began writing sardonic letters and the rainy season approached.

Agent Jim said, "I think Selig has some problems inside the company."

"What kind of problems? Does he want to cancel the project? Why doesn't he say so?"

"I dunno," Jim said, "but that's not the reading I get."

"So why's he stalling?"

"I dunno."

A few weeks later he called with that big-things-urgent sound. "Not on the telephone," he said.

We met for lunch.

"Would you like to take the picture somewhere else?"

"Why? ABC wants out?"

"No," Jim said, "but there's another proposition that I think you ought to consider."

I waited.

"Universal," said Jim.

"Universal!? You're out of your goddam mind!"

"Not so loud," Jim said. "Some of the network guys eat here."

"Never mind that. You want to get me killed?"

"It's a new setup."

"You're insane. What about the ABC contract?"

"The option comes up in a couple of weeks," said Jim. "It's a year already."

"So? Are they going to drop it?"

"No," said Jim, "but *you* are—if you like the other deal."

"I? How?"

Jim's laugh boomed. He leaned in. "Did you ever *read* your contract?"

"Just the numbers."

"Well, read it," Jim said. "The option to continue is yours under the 'failure to perform' clause. I checked it. It'll stick."

"Do they know it?"

"I notified them," Jim said.

I was uncomfortable. "I'm going to have it out with Selig first," I said. "They've got a hell of a lot of money in this thing. Maybe I can get him off the dime."

"He's out of the country. Berlin."

"I'll wait till he gets back."

"You can't," Jim said. "There's a two-week notification clause. Why don't you just go right to the top? I'll call Leonard Goldenson in New York and tell him you want to come in."

"Shouldn't I tell Selig first?"

"Don't worry," Jim said. "He'll be told."

The ABC headquarters in New York must be a hive of activity, but the top floors were eerily quiet and empty. The day I was there may have been a holiday, but whatever the reason the whole floor seemed vacant except for Goldenson and his chief operating executive, Sam Clark.

The meeting was pleasant and came rapidly to the point. I explained what I had been up to during the past year and brought out a sheaf of memoranda to buttress my complaints. Nothing I said seemed to surprise either man, but they went through the exercise, looked at the papers, asked a few questions, looked at each other and nodded.

"The position is pretty clear," said Goldenson. "What do you want to do?"

I answered that I wanted to make the movie for them if they still wanted it but that I had lost confidence in Seligman's will to get things moving.

Clark spoke up. "What if we moved you out from under Selig? What if you reported directly to me?"

"I'd be delighted." I said.

"All right," said Goldenson. "We'll see what we can do. But I have to speak to Selig about it. If he agrees, that'll do it."

It was apparently the end of the meeting. I stood.

"When can I expect to hear from you?"

"Hear?" Goldenson looked surprised. "Selig's in Berlin, waiting for my call. If you'll wait outside while we talk to him . . . ?"

I wandered around the empty floor for some twenty minutes. I had found a long, all-white executive dining room with cupboards that opened at a touch, revealing glassware enough for an ocean liner when the secretary found me.

"They're waiting for you, sir."

They were both standing when I came in. "I'm sorry," Goldenson said, "but Selig refused. He insists you remain in his division." He shrugged. "It's up to you now."

28

Complete Artistic Control!

*"Federal law requires that early withdrawal
be penalized by a loss of interest."*
—Bank commercial

*I*N THE INDUSTRY, it's not quite a federal law, but there's no doubt that premature hubris flattens as many trajectories as premature ejaculation. I was recruited for MCA/Universal by a quick-spoken, curly-haired, perspiring young executive named Ned. "I think you should take a lunch with him," said Jim the Agent. "He's close to Lew."

"I think you ought to hear what they have to say," said the Lady I Was Married to in Those Days. "After all, what can you lose listening?"

"She's right," said Jim the Agent. "Don't forget, we're in a much stronger position this time."

I liked Ned at once. He was both earnest and offhand—an attractive and flattering blend. He referred to the people he represented as Them, not We.

"Look," he said, leaning forward across the table at Musso's, "I know what happened the last time. But let's face it, you're in a much better position now."

"I won't deal with Bill Yetti no matter what."

Ned laughed appreciatively. "Who would if he didn't have to?"

He beamed. "And you don't have to!"

"Good."

"In fact," Ned said, leaning back and dropping his voice to a banker's level, "you don't even have to deal with Lew."

Jim nudged me. His face was shining. "Big things happening over there," he said. "Changes."

Ned's voice dropped still lower, and he spoke almost without moving his lips.

"Lew-may-not-be-staying." He waited for that to sink in. "You'd just be dealing with me—and Berle."

"Berle?"

"You'll like him," Jim said. "He's your kind of guy."

"When do I meet him?" I asked. "You know, I never met Lew that other time."

"Anytime," Ned said. "What the hell, you're going to be one of the family."

"If we can make a deal."

Ned and Jim both laughed, appreciating my acumen. "I heard you were tough," said Ned, sticking out his hand and rising. "We can make a deal."

We walked out through the kitchen and into the parking lot. "Let me have your ticket." Ned's car was a new Porsche, maroon with a black top. Ned himself was in a black lightweight suit; he wore a tie and his shirt had cufflinks. He read my look.

"Keeps 'em guessing," he said. "They don't know whether to believe the suit or the car."

We watched him drive the Porsche out of the parking lot, turn left and gun it up the street. Jim turned to me smiling, palms up, a successful conjurer.

"They really want you, pal," he said. "Ned wouldn't talk that way if he wasn't ready to do it all."

His exhilaration was contagious, but I tried to be cool. "I don't understand the setup," I said. "Didn't you tell me he's close to Lew?"

"He is. Lew's been like a father to him," said Jim.

"But he's Berle's man?"

"Evi*dent*ly," Jim said. He looked thoughtful.

"There may be quite a lot going on there."

I nodded, without too much interest. Jim the Agent had a passion for cabinet-level corporate intrigue. He loved to talk of lines of credit, debentures, syndicates of new money—all the wheeler-dealer talk that's both irritating and meaningless to me.

"How do we know that they'll like the stuff I want to do?"

"I sent him scripts this morning," said Jim. "I have a feeling this is going to work."

"Not if they hate the project."

"They'll love it."

"He loved it. It'll be your first picture," Jim said on the phone. "You doing anything this evening?"

"Nothing special, why?"

"Could you fly up to Vegas for a couple of hours?"

"You're rushing things a little," I said. "Wait till there's something to celebrate and we'll all go—"

"No, no," said Jim. "It's about this deal. There's someone up there would like to talk to you."

"In Vegas? Who?"

"Look," said Jim, "I'm in a phone booth and it'll take me nearly an hour to get there if I leave now. Okay?"

"Okay."

"Six o'clock at Western," Jim said. "I'll have the tickets."

The elevator to the Penthouse was not automatic, and the operator asked us our names, spoke them into a microphone and got an answer before we started up. The Penthouse was simply the top floor of the hotel, a combination home and office for Mr. Melville—austerely and sparsely furnished with white furniture on a gleaming, hard, black-and-white tile floor—large blocks like the floors in a Vermeer. There were alcoves in the room, each shadowing a piece of slim white statuary on a fluted pedestal.

Stanley A. Melville, a famous labor lawyer whose picture often appeared in *Fortune* magazine, was pleasant, soft-voiced and crisp. He offered us drinks, drank nothing himself and made idle talk about movies until we'd each had our second sip.

Then he asked me, "Who represents you in this?"

I was puzzled. After all, there sat Jim the Agent.

"No—I understand that," Melville said, nodding briefly at Jim, who had the look of a cripple at Lourdes. "I mean your attorney."

I decided against mentioning the fellow who handled the ex-wife skirmishes.

"Nobody," I said, adding somewhat lamely, "not right now."

"Good, good," said Melville, clearly not surprised. "You mind if I make a suggestion?"

Jim and I answered together, "Of course not" and "Wish you would," when the phone rang. Mr. Melville went to it, shrugged apologetically. "I told them not to ring through unless it's important." Jim and I made those broken flutters you make when you're in someone's office and he gets an important private call, but Melville waved us back into our chairs and picked up the phone.

"Who? Oh. Yes. . . . Go ahead. . . . No, don't worry about Cincinnati. All right, I'll call him. . . . I'm telling you not to worry. The bakers won't go out. . . . That's right. And the maintenance people have already agreed. Last night. . . . All right. If there's a problem call me."

He put down the phone and returned to us. "You know," he said, "most of these problems are really misunderstandings. I try to get into it before people get angry."

He sat down facing me. "Do you know Nathan Mittleman?"

"We've been introduced. I know who he is, of course."

"What do you think of him? For you, I mean."

"I'd be flattered," I said, and I meant it. Nat L.

Mittleman is one of the major powers in the Industry, attorney, power broker, maker of governors and speaker at fund-raising dinners. Like Greg Bautzer, Paul Ziffren, Milton Rudin and a few others, he's an adviser to major stars and studio heads—listed on the left-hand side of invitations to Industry Events. These men are quite different, of course—ranging from flamboyant to discreet in personal style and in the coloration of their clients. All of them are very social and are as likely to be found on a yacht at Cannes during the festival as in their offices. And none of them actually tries cases. They negotiate, they discuss, they settle.

Melville was pleased. He nodded, got up and went to the phone again.

"Nat Mittleman," he said, "at the first number."

Mittleman must have been two feet from the phone.

"Me again, Nat," said Melville. "I hope you haven't sat down to dinner yet. Sure, but I know how Doris—yes. Just now." He glanced over at me, smiling. "He says he'd be flattered, Nat. Just a minute." He turned to me again, holding out the phone. "Here, you might as well get to know each other."

It was simpler once. The flash roll, the diamond pinkie ring and the stickpin went out, replaced by the foreign car and the cashmere jacket and the column inch break—but when Adidas became Bootmaker to the Stars the identification game got complicated. Party lists were once a guide, but a student of such matters might conclude that Charlie Manson was at least B list. What's changeless is representation. The important agents are very careful about whom they represent—but agencies usually house subagents too, and some fairly nondescript clients wind up claiming majestic agency representation. But if one of the Great Attorneys takes you on, that's it. These are princes—and if one of them will represent you, it follows that you are a principality. Contracts are drawn between corporations, yours agreeing to "furnish the artist's services," theirs agreeing to "compensate as follows."

The contract, or treaty, between MCA and me was a work of Bismarckian iron, fitting product of Mittleman's clout and my grandeur. It began with a statement of intent to give the producer "complete artistic control" and went onward from there. Complete Artistic Control—Call Me Ishmael!

Agent Jim busied himself with similar but more practical matters. "I got them to reopen the Rachmil bungalow for you," he panted. "The Rachmil bungalow. It hasn't been used since he left."

"Why not?"

Jim's face blazed. "There was nobody important enough till now!"

The Rachmil bungalow, so-called after Milton Rachmil, the last head of pre-MCA Universal, had a bathroom with a shower, a small kitchen and two offices. Mine, the large one, was heavily paneled in some dark wood and graced with a large, intricately carved fireplace and mantel in some smooth, purplish stone. With its tall, narrow windows and the solemnly shining walls, it looked like a set for *Death Comes for the Archbishop,* but I didn't have the heart to say so. I looked and nodded in awe.

Later I heard Jim on the phone to Ned. "He's thrilled," Jim said.

The tragic consequence of hubris is one of those mean, moralist inventions, and we millions of lip-smackers forget that the sins may have been pretty good sinning. Moral history is a kind of police blotter anyhow—a record of failures, and who knows about the others? Out here, success is retroactive ennoblement—the idiot who becomes head of a studio doesn't just learn that he's right about things, he learns that he has always been right, even when nobody could see it. Is it possible to resist learning that your judgment is sound?

I moved into the paneled office and plunged into preparation. The secretary was a pretty, efficient girl named Sandy, my parking space was about fifty feet from the door of the little house with my name on it, and the cops at the main gate knew my name without having been introduced. One day, a few days after moving in, I saw a familiar-looking fellow sunning himself on the steps of the next bungalow. Cary

Grant. I looked, he waved. It was like walking on pine needles, soft underfoot and aromatic. Heady.

My friend Ned, red-lipped, busy and shining, had introduced me to Berle—a small man, quick as a bird, brisk and cheerful. They both loved the project. "Just the kind of picture this place needs," Ned said. "It'll shake 'em up."

"If there's anything you need and Ned can't do it for you," said Berle, "just give me a call. Here or in the New York office."

I still had not met Lew Wasserman, head of the studio. "Does he know I'm here?"

Ned laughed. He had gotten into the habit of dropping into the bungalow late in the afternoon for a drink and a few laughs. He and Sandy were obviously old friends, and she'd come in, perch on the arm of the leather chair and have a drink with us. She always called me mister, no matter how informal the talk got to be. "If I used your first name I might forget sometime and use it on the telephone or in front of one of the executives," she said. "This way there won't be any embarrassments."

She and Ned exchanged a look of understanding. "He knows you're here, all right," said Ned. "When he read your contract he screamed like a wounded eagle."

"Ned," I asked, "are you telling me that Lew Wasserman objects to my deal here?"

Ned's wet mouth quirked. "It's the first time he saw a deal where he's got no say, you know. . . ."

"You mean he hates the whole thing."

"He'll get used to it," said Ned. "Look, if it bothers you, talk to Nat. Those guys are old friends. Nat must know the score."

Nat Mittleman shrugged at the question. "It's business," he said. "He'll get used to it. You want some coffee?" In Mittleman's office when you asked for a cup of coffee it arrived on a tray, in china.

"No thanks."

"You can't expect him to be ecstatic. It's not his deal. Why? Does that bother you?"

"He's the head of the place," I said. "I hate to start out on the wrong foot. You know, I never even met Mr. Wasserman that other time."

Mittleman peered at me. "Don't be nervous. I thought you were supposed to be pretty tough." He nodded his understanding, hesitated. "You ever have a talk with Bill since coming on the lot?"

"Bill Yetti?" I must have raised my voice. "Hell, no! I told you what he did to me that other time."

Mittleman shrugged again and relaxed. "Well," he said vaguely, "why don't you just let things work themselves out? You getting all the help you need?"

"Absolutely. Ned's terrific. We're getting to be pretty good friends."

"That's good," Mittleman said. "And how's Berle?"

"Pleasant. Haven't seen him much."

"Script going all right?"

"I love it. Nelson's doing a wonderful job. It's about time to start shopping for a director, I think."

"Got somebody in mind for it?"

"Couple of people," I said. The problem was still nagging at me. "Has Wasserman ever discussed the project with you?"

Mittleman sighed. "All right. Yes."

"And?"

"He doesn't understand it."

"You mean he hates it."

Mittleman looked at me with a tinge of irony. "He doesn't have to love it. He's a realist. You love it, Ned loves it, Berle loves it. Don't they?"

"Okay. Okay," I said. "I get the point. The contract will protect me?"

Mittleman smiled with genuine warmth. "Complete artistic control," he said gently. "Just what you wanted."

But I still had sense enough to be disturbed, almost enough to worry about regular reminders that I was tough—but not quite. Outspoken, candid, direct, frank and honest? Sure, I could see that. But tough? Aw, shucks. Not with people who could see how right I was all the time.

So it came to pass that the screenplay was finished and everybody I talked to *loved* it and I offered it to a director whose work I admired and he *loved* it and I met with him and we admired each other and I phoned his agent and told him I wanted to hire director David Baker.

The next morning I got a phone call from the tower. "Can you talk to Mr. Wasserman?"

"Of course."

"He'll be with you in a moment," she said. Then, "Would it be convenient for you to come to the office instead?"

"Right now? Sure."

When I looked up from the phone, my secretary was standing in the doorway.

"You know where it is, sir?"

"Of course, everybody—" But that wasn't it. "What's the problem?"

She actually blushed. "There's a necktie in the closet, sir. . . . "

The Black Tower of MCA is an Industry metaphor, as striking to people who work out here as the De Mille Gate of Paramount is to audiences around the world. But while the De Mille Gate is an eye-catcher by any measure, the Black Tower is simply a tidy, modern office building, only fourteen stories high, one of a small cluster of commercial buildings arranged in a little plaza along Lankershim Boulevard, just off Ventura, where Hollywood and the San Fernando Valley come together. Almost immediately behind and on top of a steep hill is the Sheraton Universal hotel and the tour center and the rest—all of it far more visible and striking than the black-glass building below. But the MCA Black Tower is a monument in the landscape of the mind.

History applauds Caesar Augustus who found Rome a city of bricks and left it a city of marble; we never hear about the Romans who bitched about the change. But "Old Universal," a studio of stucco bungalows surrounded by trees and topped by red tiles, is instant nostalgia out here—a memory of endless summers and long-term contracts and pleasant popcorn movies. The MCA takeover changed much more than the buildings, of course, but the change took time. For a while, the new black-glass building, filled with slim, quick young men in dark suits, stood there as alien and menacing as a spaceship, while orders flowed out to the stucco buildings and the casual people in them read and trembled, watching the familiar world disappear.

There's a lot of talk of ruthlessness, but Hollywood was always ruthless. What MCA brought was order, the kind of neatly ruled-off, bottom-line order which offends bohemian elan and wrecks comfortable illusions, chief among them the illusion of having fun. The new MCA Universal is profitable, orderly, efficient, but unloved. Fun is manufactured and shipped from there by people who are not having any.

The lobby of the Black Tower is curiously empty. There's a guard at a desk, a bronze bust of Our Founder and a bank of elevators. The guard checks passes, confirms appointments, and doles out the composition metal discs visitors must have to work the automatic parking-lot gates. Lose one on the way to your car and you must return to the lobby and beg one from the guard—who will then follow you to the exit to make certain you're not up to something. The interior of the elevators is all aluminum or stainless steel—everything ribbed, whorled, machined, dimpled and corrugated into optical confusion. It probably discourages elevator graffiti; most passengers look at the floor.

As you rise, the doors open and close on perfectly ordinary office corridors, tile floors, rows of doors with nameplates and the sound of office machinery—the rhythmic thumping of Xerox machines.

Until you get to the twelfth floor. Corridors have disappeared or widened into lushly carpeted indoor avenues, deep and soft enough to turn an ankle, so hushed that no one would hear the scream. The furnishings here are European antiques of immense value and astonishing discomfort. Everything is the wrong height—the great desks and ornate tables meant to serve people who either stood or perched on stools. There are wonderful cranky cabinets with doors, tall chests and short chests and doubled chests on chests with twinkling rows of little drawers and pigeonholes. Some things are covered in leather or cunningly inlaid with bits which have swollen over the years while others shrank. Appropriate ornaments grace shelves and lamp tables. There are rare old bindings and oddments of metal whose use is no longer apparent. They are not quite priceless, but you would not be surprised to look at those offices over velvet ropes. Ask the obvious question and you will be told that (a) these furnishings are the pride and passion of Mrs. Jules Stein herself, and, (b) that the value of every item has appreciated enormously in the last few years, making the furnishings a better investment than many blue-chip stocks, thus combining function, publicity value, status and aesthetics with rising value and tax considerations. Waste not, want not.

Wasserman's office was large but not especially ornate—tending to the austere in shades of gray, black and white, like Wasserman himself. He's a tall, spare man, silver-haired, fair and pleasantly hawk-faced. He was cordial and slightly impersonal and led me through some general talk about films—he favored the term "motion pictures"—into an assessment of current trends and the box-office hopes of pictures then in the field. His analyses were sharp but not especially original. What *was* unique was an apparently limitless grasp of the worldwide structure and detail of film distribution. Currency rates, booking policies, governmental restrictions, competitive practices, favorable and unfavorable seasons, and so on. He was not showing off for a visitor, he was discussing what he thought important.

Years before, on an errand for the book company, I had found myself at lunch with Aldous Huxley and some others, so seated that a lot of Huxley's conversation was with me. Unfortunately I was too awed and impressed to retain what was said. Somewhere in my head something kept saying, "Pay attention, this is really Aldous Huxley," with the sad result that I came away thrilled, proud but not especially wiser. The *event* of it was too much for me. But I do recall the encyclopedic range of his references and the insanely flattering way he had of implying that you knew what he knew. "You'll recall that when you come in off the street into the Uffizi, there's that little room just off to the right. . . ." All his sentences looped and garlanded with arcane facts and classical references interjected with "you'll remember" and "didn't you think?" and "don't you suppose?" Leaning forward, peering through the thick lenses, laughing and pausing for your opinion.

Another crane of a man, without Huxley's warmth and playfulness, but not a machine either. Those dreary numbers and percentages and schedules were passion and reality to him, and while he spoke (and I made proper responses) I was genuinely impressed. I'm familiar enough with the language of business to know that a lot of corporate talent is bluff and the manipulation of personality plus knowing how to use lawyers and accountants. This man seemed to be without an act at all —an atmosphere thin as the moon's, every detail visible in that airless clarity.

He changed the subject as abruptly as if a bell had rung for the end of the social period.

"I understand you've been looking at directors?"

"Yes, sir. As a matter of fact, I think I've found the right man—"

"David Baker?"

"Right. He loves the script and he seems to have some very good ideas about—"

He stopped me. "I want you to reconsider."

There was nothing rude about the way he said it, but he was not asking.

"Well . . ." I meant to be careful. "I don't know what—would you mind saying why?"

He did not mind. And as succinctly as he had explained Australian bookings, he explained that Baker was an undependable hysteric who had been taken off his last two pictures after he had wasted lots of money, irritated everyone, lied, stolen, disappeared, etc., etc. He used names, dates, places and estimated sums of money in making his points, ticking them off on his fingers as he spoke.

I was floored by the calm ferocity of the attack.

"I just had him in here the other day," I said. "He seemed perfectly sensible to me . . . and he loved—"

He interrupted. "Baker would love *anything* right now. He knows his hope of getting another picture is just about zero." He rose, stuck out his hand. "Don't worry, we'll find somebody."

By the time I got back to my office I had capitulated.

"Very sensible decision," said Mittleman. Agent Jim agreed. Ned laughed and Berle shrugged.

Baker's agent was annoyed but not combative. "It's true he's had a little trouble on the last show, but he had a big problem getting the script right. You know how it is."

"Yes," I said, "but it's past that. They just won't go with him no matter what. I'd hate to repeat what the man said."

"I can imagine. He doesn't pull any . . ." His voice trailed, then, "Will you talk to David, or shall I?"

"As long as you're playing it smart," said Jim, "why not go with somebody they like?"

"Like who, for instance?"

"Like your friend Richardson—he's here and I don't think he's got anything lined up."

I'd known Bill Richardson for years and counted him and Annie as old friends. I was a regular drop-in to their beach house in Zuma. I knew their dogs, their Mexican cook and the basic guest list of their parties. I knew they no longer saw my first wife. We were friends.

"Not a bad thought," said Ned. "We've got some kind of deal with the guy, all right. He any good?"

I named a couple of quite successful pictures Richardson had directed. Ned snapped his fingers.

"Sounds like you just might have something there. And smart."

Bill Richardson *loved* the script and there were no phone calls about him. The deal was made and we began principal casting.

It was obvious that the male lead was the touchstone of the piece and should be cast first. So agents were phoned and scripts went out to the super five who are offered everything all the time. Since the word was out that a big one was looking like go, the other agents were on the phone and in the doorway all day long, pitching clients they knew to be second or third choices at best.

"Sure, I know you saw that one, but let me bring you a couple of minutes from the one he's in now—*The Mothersmokers.* Yes That's right. Well, it's not a lead, but it's a hell of a showcase, and believe me he'll come off it. . . ."

Richardson and Nelson and I looked at bits of new film, saw a few actors, but nothing. The usual bizarre suggestions were heard. "Could he have a Russian accent, you think?" "Have you seen Francis X. Wishbone lately? He looks *great!*" The casting office made a few polite but unserious suggestions, and the talent department made appointments for their people to be seen. "Maybe not for the lead, but why don't you just take a look?"

I forget who first suggested Burt Reynolds. Whoever it was (and I seem to hear a female voice) kept saying, "I don't care what you've seen. This guy has got it." In fact, I vaguely remembered Reynolds from a TV series, something where he played an Indian cop and glowered a lot.

Casting is not exactly what audiences imagine and not at all what actors wish. The problem is that by the time you come around to it you've been living with a screenplay for weeks, months, even years—and you've been seeing someone in each part, a face, a voice, coloring, style, all with the blurred intensity of a dream. Actors rarely match those peripheral visions, and casting becomes a major accommodation, the first and biggest in the long series of compromises by which the words are transformed into speaking images.

Once in a great while there's an almost audible click in your head as an actor and a role seem to come together like Johanson blocks, flush and seamless, made, as they say, for each other. Now and again that click is probably valid; more rarely but still sometimes it leads to the particular actor getting the particular part. Sometimes the combination is successful. But the statistical failures of marriage don't diminish the impact of love at first sight.

All of which is to say that somebody finally showed us a lot of Burt Reynolds footage and the clicking was audible in the screening room. We *loved* him in the part. So the agent was phoned and Burt himself showed up after a while—very pleased, a little shy and with his now famous insouciance well under control. He wanted the job. We told him he had it.

"Gee," he said, looking around, "I never thought I'd see this place again." He shook his head. "Uh-uh!"

"Why not?"

"Oh, I used to work here," Burt said. "A series called *Riverboat.* You ever see it?"

Richardson had, I hadn't.

"Just as well," Burt said. "Anyway, we didn't part friends, exactly."

"So what?" I said. "They've probably forgotten all about it, whatever it was."

"Hope you're right, chief," Burt said.

We shook hands. "I'll call you about wardrobe," I said.

———————

Next day I was summoned again by Mr. Wasserman.

"Burt Reynolds? I hope you're not serious!" There were no preliminary niceties this time; he attacked as I entered the office.

"I sure am. He'll be terrific in the part."

"Reynolds, terrific? He's *nobody*. This is an expensive picture."

"He's going to be *very* big," I said. It did not seem an auspicious moment for the click theory.

"Him? He's a bum. We had him here and I'm telling you . . ." He was not yelling, but getting close to it.

I tried a little nervous grandeur. "You know, Mr. Wasserman, they told me the same things about Jim Coburn before I put him into *Flint.*"

"That's crap," he said. "Coburn wasn't a leading man, but he had done a lot of important things when you used him in *Flint.* This guy is a nobody."

He was right about Coburn, of course, but I thought I had the offensive. "Would you care to make a few suggestions?"

He fell right into it. "What about George Peppard?"

"He would be great," I said. "But I've already talked to him. He doesn't want to do it."

"He's under contract," said Wasserman.

"I know. But if the star doesn't like the part . . ." There was no need to belabor that point. "The fact is," I said, "we all love Reynolds for it and I've already made the offer."

He really stared at me, shook his head. His voice was calm again now. "Well, I'm sorry. You can't have him."

"Can't?"

"I'm not going to make a four-million-dollar picture with Burt Reynolds."

"Mr. Wasserman, according to my deal here, I can decide these things myself."

"I know your deal," he said, "but I'm sorry. I'm not going to make this picture with Burt Reynolds."

Luckily, neither of us had sat down. I started for the door. "I'm sorry too," I said. "But I don't know what to do now."

He smiled briefly. "You just go back and think about it," he said. "I'll come up with some other names and send them over to you."

He sat and I left.

On the phone I could hear Nat Mittleman sigh. "You told him what the contract says?"

"He knew it. He doesn't care."

"Does it have to be Reynolds? I mean, he certainly isn't a big star. . . . Maybe you ought to see what Lew comes up with?"

"Maybe," I said. "But I'm not sure that's the real problem. He pushed me on the director and I gave in. Now he's pushing on casting. What the hell good is the contract?"

"I know," said Mittleman. "That's not the way he's used to working, and the way things are going, he's probably pretty touchy. What do you want to do?"

In fact, I had been thinking it out and I had an idea. "Maybe this'll surprise you," I said, "but I'm willing to change the deal. I don't know what's going on around here, but if the head guy just won't honor the damn deal I think we're kidding ourselves."

"So?"

"So let's revise the deal. Give them the usual controls—principal casting, director, budget—"

"They have budget now," said Mittleman.

"Under that 'normal business control' clause?"

"You better believe it."

"Okay. So principal casting and director. Give it back to them in exchange."

"For?"

"Money. A lot more money," I said.

"The deal's pretty rich now," said my attorney. "Don't you think?"

"Yes. But I can't just give away what I fought for unless we really stab them for it."

"It would change the relationship if you did."

"I don't want to change it *that* much."

"All right," said Mittleman. "I'll try it out and call you back."

In only a few minutes he was back. "They're not interested in paying any more."

"You mean they think they can just push me around without paying for it?"

"I was afraid you'd take it that way."

"Well . . . aren't they in breach, then?"

"Just a minute, please." He apparently covered the mouthpiece and spoke to someone. Then he was back. "I'm sorry. Look, before we fly off the handle, why don't you call your friend Berle?"

"I think he's in New York this week."

"Call him. Let me know what he says about all this."

Berle listened very carefully and asked a couple of questions addressed to the detail of my conversation with Wasserman. "You sure he said it that way? 'I won't make the picture—I'?"

"That's what he said."

"O-kay," Berle said, sounding chipper. "Let me get back to you."

"When?"

He mumbled calculations. "Late tomorrow or day after?" Whatever he was thinking made him sound very cheerful.

He sounded gleeful when he called back next day. "O-kay. You've got your actor! Now what's the next problem?"

Burt was amazed. "Never thought they'd let me in the gate. Not after I threw that guy off the riverboat. Who-ee! Was he pissed at me!"

"You what? No wonder Wasserman's down on you."

"Yeah, no wonder," Burt said.

"Jesus. I wish you had told me."

"Don't worry about a thing, chief. He'll get over it," said Burt.

Nat Mittleman heard the news thoughtfully and asked an odd question. "Called right back the very next day? Just like that? No-o kidding. . . ." Then, "Poor Lew."

It was almost six months later that I heard again from Mr. Wasserman. In between talks, the movie had been filmed, and by then the roof was falling.

The filming was attended by a series of disasters. When I got off the plane in Jamaica (where all the first-unit photography was shot) I was met by a terrified driver.

"Mr. Sam is dead."

Mr. Sam was the island production manager and coordinator, the man who had made all the deals, above and below the table. He had died of a heart seizure on the way to the airport.

After I got over the shock I asked who was filling in for him and learned that a couple of his relatives were flying over from Alabama, where they lived, to straighten out poor Cousin Sam's affairs. They arrived late that night. The funeral was immediate. Poor Sam was hustled into the ground and everyone turned to the movie. It was almost instantly clear that Sam kept most of his deals in his head—and all of his records.

Studios are more worried about starting delays than about starting unprepared, for the basic reason that all sorts of contracts and expenses have begun to tick off on the Big Meter and film in the can—any kind —is the way you pay it off. The studio wanted to know if we *could* start, anyhow—and of course we could. We started.

I had filmed in Jamaica before and loved the island. But during the three or four years since my last stay the world had changed and Jamaica with it. People who used to smile snarled. People who used to work cheerfully and hard now threatened a strike a day, called one a week over issues impossible to understand. Someone explained that some bitterly fought local elections were about to be held and that our presence had been seized on by both sides—each telling the electorate that he would squeeze us harder than the other. The result was that scenes shot near a market or any other reasonably busy place would cause real, screaming riots—at which the smartly uniformed Jamaican constabulary would wade in with swinging truncheons. One of the assistants, a thoughtful young Black named Charlie, was aghast at the brutality and pleaded with me to call off the cops. "Let me go talk to them," he said. "They're my people."

"Go ahead."

So Charlie waded into the crowd and was swallowed by it only to reemerge in a few minutes, shirt torn, bleeding. The constables rescued him and we gave him first aid.

"I couldn't talk to them," Charlie said, while we mopped his face. "I couldn't talk to them."

Jamaican hotels are legendary, and the film had taken over an entire hotel for cast and crew—to make the stay as pleasant as possible. But illness struck immediately. Those of us who could make it to the locations in the morning usually arrived bent from the waist, clutching little bottles of paregoric and bismuth, Enterovioform, Kaopectate. We called a doctor, who clucked about the sanitation, shook his head over the refrigeration, scowled at the dishwashing. Management shrugged, pleaded a lack of facilities. The Board of Health people inspected regularly but could find nothing actionable. By the end of the first week the crew was holding meetings and threatening to go home. The studio called anxiously to say that union representatives were growling.

The actors were not only sick, they were scared, and the fear focused on the director. A little delegation called on me. "You gotta do something about him. He can't cut it."

Richardson was floundering, all right. Why not? A deliberate, thoughtful man who plotted out his next day's setups on paper every night, he was somewhat slow and indecisive at camera point. We were suddenly losing days at an alarming rate. As usual, the studio production department had informers on the crew and the front office was doing what front offices do, only quite a lot sooner than they usually do it. The phone rang a lot and the daily cables got longer.

I phoned my pal Ned. "What's the panic for? I think Richardson'll straighten out. Things are tough. . . ."

"I don't know," Ned said. "They're upset. They don't have too much confidence in Richardson in the first place. You're not going to go down ten days, are you?"

"I hope not. But we might."

"Better not," Ned said. "They'll take over."

"For ten days?"

"It's in the contract," Ned said. "Business controls . . . remember?"

I remembered. But to actually invoke such a takeover is just about unheard of.

"I'm telling you," Ned said. "They will."

Panic.

"There's only one way, you know—replace Richardson with someone they really like."

"Replace him after a week? Jesus, the guy's a friend of mine."

Silence. Then, "Well, maybe you'll pick up. . . ."

We continued to lose days. The actors were beginning to behave like zoo animals who smell fire. They did what they were told, but nervously, with much rolling of the eyes—mugging as actors do who have no confidence in the instructions.

Richardson listened to me patiently and, just as patiently, explained the difficulties. The crew hadn't settled into its work, the lighting cameraman was slow, etc. All true. He pointed to what was miserably obvious to both of us and wondered what all the fuss was about. I explained the agitation coming from back home. He listened skeptically and offered the hope that things would settle down soon. "Maybe we can start picking up in a week or so." He fiddled with his diagrams and tried to give me advice. "Don't let them rattle you. After all, the actors are on our side."

Normally, on a major film, that would have been a clincher. If it had been Paul Newman or Marlon Brando or Burt Reynolds *now* instead of Burt *then,* Richardson would have been quite right. The star's agent would have phoned the studio and said, "Listen, fellas—I don't want to butt in but I had a kind of disturbing call from Marlon last night, and if you don't mind, I'd like to make a suggestion. . . ." And things would quiet down. Richardson had directed major stars, and he knew. He didn't quite understand that his leading man was Nobody and his producer a Thorn in the Side. He also didn't understand that the actors who told him they loved him were telling me they were worried.

I got a phone call from Jim the Agent. "Gordon Douglas said to tell you he's available. He loves you, y'know—and he can move in without losing time."

Appalled. "You mean it's all over town?"

"There's a lot of talk," Jim said. "The tower doesn't love you, y'know." He hesitated. "I gave Douglas a script—I hope that's all right?"

"Oh Christ," I said. "Do you know how long I've known Bill Richardson?"

"I know. It's a bitch," said Jim. "But if they take over he's gone either way."

I stalled. "I'll talk to Ned."

"He's right here with me," Jim said. "I'll put him on."

"These things happen," said Ned, "and it's better all around to get the jump on them."

"But how do you know they'd go for Douglas?"

Silence.

"I've talked to them," Ned said. "They love the idea. They said he's the guy you should have hired in the first place. Put him in and your troubles are over."

"What about Bill Richardson?"

"What *about* him? . . . Oh, I see what you mean. I think we can find something else for him."

"You sure?"

"Promise."

Somewhere in my throat I could taste it. Ned understood that much.

"Would you like me to fly down?"

"No," I said, "It's up to me. But . . ."

"You want it in writing?"

And the ship went down.

"It would help."

"You'll have a cable from us in the morning," Ned said. "We'll assume full responsibility."

The cable arrived. I waited till the end of the day, drank a lot of brandy and told Bill Richardson he was fired. He didn't believe it. I showed him the cable, explained, apologized and writhed. Finally he nodded coldly and asked, "Have you told the cast?"

"No."

"All right," he said. "I'll tell them."

He began phoning the principals and I left. Later there was a farewell party at which tears were shed and the actors who had been demanding his head swore to him that they were all his—that he'd been betrayed.

He left and told people at home that I had sold him out. . . . You know how They are.

We haven't spoken since then. And I often wonder if he was right.

After that we worked like hell. Gordon Douglas arrived and instantly got sick and the direction was as often Buzz Henry's work as his. Buzz was sick too, but he was used to walking wounded. The food continued to be terrible; the crew kept threatening walkouts. Some of the cast discovered the joys of ganja—the potent Jamaican marijuana—and the acting became less than crisp.

The comic, a talented, nervous and very fat man whom I'd hired not only because of his acting but also because the role required someone grossly overweight, arrived on location having lost nearly a hundred pounds! At my howl of dismay he was terribly hurt.

"My God, don't you care anything about *me?*" He spread his arms, turned, showed off his more or less tapering figure. "Don't you know what kind of problems I used to have getting a *girl?*"

"But the part—"

He grabbed me by the shoulders, all earnest passion.

"Don't worry about it," he said. "I can *act* fat."

This line does not draw a laugh from actors. They all believe it.

The whole picture was like that. As some politician said lately, it was shuffling the deck chairs on the *Titanic.* The studio, human sacrifice digested, said nothing more.

With about ten days to go I got an unusual phone call from a man I had not met but whose name I knew. He was an important member of the MCA board, vacationing in Jamaica, and he wondered if I could break away for a few hours for a meeting with him. Of course I could. And with an unaccustomed flash of sense I asked if I could bring my assistant, a young MCA executive who'd been wished on me for the obvious purpose of eavesdropping but who had turned out to be both helpful and bright—a friend.

"Who? Oh, the Hyde boy—works for Ned? Sure, he's family."

We were driven up a winding road to what was known locally as the Dorothy Hammerstein estate—a beautiful villa surrounded by gardens and opening to one of those perfect Jamaican views. My host was relaxed and pleasant.

"Will you be back home by June?"

"Oh yes. We'll be done in a couple of weeks."

"Good," he said. "I think you should be there after the next meeting."

There was to be a board meeting in June. At that meeting Wasserman would step down and Berle would step up.

"When he does, we'd like to talk to you about taking over production."

I was astonished and showed it. He laughed.

"I'm surprised that you're surprised," he said. "Anyway, think about it."

We finished the filming more or less on schedule. We'd compressed some things and cut others and the deficit was not great. But we were all very glad to leave the island. We came back into a kind of quiet.

There was no more filming to be done—only a couple of matte paintings for special effects shots. Editing and scoring began and the whole focus narrowed down to the scoring stage, the dubbing and mixing and editing. My days now began and ended bent over the shoulder of the editor who was bent over the Moviola. By June, the first cut was nearly complete.

From my window one June day I saw the street alongside the black tower lined with expensive, sober-looking sedans.

"It's the board meeting," said Sandy, trying not to look meaningful. "They all go to lunch first, then they have the meeting."

It was nearly lunchtime when Sandy stepped into my office, looking odd. "There's someone here would like a moment," she said, standing in the doorway. Then she moved aside and there was my friend from the Dorothy Hammerstein estate. I stood up, went to him and shook hands.

"Here for the board meeting?" I gestured him into the room, but he shook his head.

"I've only got a minute," he said, "but I wanted to say something."

I waited.

"You remember our discussion in Jamaica?"

"Of course."

He nodded. "Well," he said, "forget it." He pumped my hand again, turned and left. A moment later I could see him crossing the studio street on his way into the tower. I turned to Sandy.

"What do you suppose that's all about?"

"I think Mr. Wasserman's not leaving," she said.

The marvelous and complicated corporate murder and revenge plot behind that moment was described in thrilling detail in the first issue of *New West.* It was a struggle for control of that great entertainment empire, far more filled with plot and counterplot, treachery and double agentry than any film made there. And the ending, a breath-stopping cliffhanger in which the plot was reversed and the plotters undone, had the sweep and style of social change in China. Berle, the appointed usurper, had stormed up the palace stairs on schedule, turned to encourage his troops—and found himself alone.

The newspapers simply said that Wasserman had agreed to continue to serve in his present capacity. But within hours the tumbrels began to roll. Reassignment followed resignation followed corporate restructure announcements. Berle shrugged and continued his cheerful patter even while packing. Ned stopped dropping into my office, then stopped returning my calls. "Don't worry about a thing," said Jim. "The contract is ironclad."

Nat Mittleman said very little. After the board meeting I was no longer invited to his house.

Finally the picture was finished and previewed at the studio. Then Mr. Wasserman summoned me to another meeting. Ned was with him. Wasserman was blunt. He loathed the picture, he had no intention of putting any money or effort into its distribution, he would teach me a lesson. He was another man. The cords stood out on his neck as he spoke —it was Rod Steiger in *The Big Knife,* but colder, more controlled. Ned said nothing that I recall. He was hunched over the table where we sat. I remember that at one point he clasped his hands over his head, elbows on the table, pressing his chin onto the wood.

It was all over, of course, and I thanked God for an ironclad contract. "We'll just take the contract to court and get declaratory relief," said Nat Mittleman. "They'll have to pay up what's coming under the contract."

"Great," I said. "Let's do that right away."

Then he called back. "They're playing rough," he said. "Did you get your copy?"

"No. Of what?"

"I'll read you mine," said Nat Mittleman. "It just arrived by messenger."

What he read to me was a brief, obviously hasty notification that I had been terminated and was being sued for breach of contract for various unspecified misdeeds "of which you are aware."

It didn't sound like anything much to me. "Well, to hell with them," I said. "They'll just make fools of themselves trying to prove any breach. Let's just get that declaratory relief."

I could hear Mittleman sigh. "That's just the point," he said. "You can't now." He paused. "Look, can you come to my office?"

In his office I learned that by charging me with breach of contract, the studio had changed the matter into issues of fact which had to be tried. Declaratory relief was now impossible.

"You mean they can just fire me, charge me with having breached the contract, refuse to specify what I'm supposed to have done wrong and they don't have to pay me?"

"Not till it's tried." He turned up his palms. "That's right. It could be months, maybe years."

Control. Appeal to his pride.

"But Nat," I said. "You drew up this contract. You must know some way . . ."

"Would you like me to try to settle?"

"For how much?"

He hesitated. "The truth is I already talked to them. They'll give you ten cents on the dollar."

"Ten cents!"

"I think I could get them up. Maybe fifteen—maybe even twenty."

"Is that what you recommend?"

He shrugged. "You're angry now. I think you should at least sleep on it. No matter how little it is, you'd be free."

Control. Control.

"Nat," I said, "you've known these people for half a lifetime. You're friends. Can't you talk to them?"

"About what?"

"About the charge. They know I haven't breached the damn contract. They haven't even charged me with anything, because there's nothing to charge. Can't you even get them to do that?"

"You know," Nat Mittleman said, "I knew that would bother you. So I already asked them."

"And?"

"I couldn't get to Lew," said Mittleman. "I spoke to Bill Yetti. You want to know?"

"Yes."

"Yetti said, 'Tell your guy we've got two, maybe three years before we'll get to court. Tell him we'll think of something in the meantime.' "

"That's it?"

"I'm afraid it is."

"And you advise?"

"It's up to you. I would settle."

"Well, I won't."

"No," said Mittleman, "I didn't think you would."

"It's outrageous," I said. "Don't you agree?"

"It's only business," said Mittleman.

I saw Ned just once after all that—during the taking of depositions. He perspired heavily, asked for a glass of water, didn't look at me, but rolled out his story without faltering. "I tried to warn him that it was a mistake, but he insisted on making us take that picture."

After a while Nat Mittleman phoned to say he wasn't getting any younger and hadn't been feeling well and that I really needed someone more aggressive to represent me. Unfortunately no one in his firm . . . He wished me luck.

The gestation period for the Virginian opossum is listed as 12.5 days, while the Asiatic elephant averages 645 days. Actual birth is relatively swift for all species, as getting there takes most of the time. Everyone agrees that it takes a lot of years to be an overnight success—but no time at all to flop. Up like a rocket, down like a stick.

Somewhere in the blur of days the lady of the house began to look pained at hearing about it and said, "I know you've got problems, hon —but I'd rather not talk about them in the morning. It drags my whole day. . . ."

After a while she too was gone along with the house and the bank account and the stock. The phone stopped ringing and the Great Silence fell.

29

$

Homage to Buzz Henry

THIS TIME there was no cheering section at the exit. Agent Jim looked scared and murmured about the villainy of it all. Besides, he was having marital problems. He was vague about new openings and talked a lot about "industry reassessments." It was clear enough. I was no longer hot.

I rented part of an office in an apartment building and crammed all those boxes of files into closets, one atop the other. There was no one to call; everyone already knew.

The only incoming call was from Buzz. *They* love stunt men. Even so, these gentle tigers were nearly done in during the spasm of national repentance which followed the assassination of Robert Kennedy. The virtuous fury of Good People everywhere turns on Hollywood whenever the face in the mirror becomes frightening, and out here the air went dark with the shrill fervor of screenwriters and stars denouncing screen violence. The direct result was unemployment among stunt men.

"Hey Words—could you come over tomorrow? The guys want to put an ad in the trades. Something about all this antiviolence crap, you know? We could use a little help with the words—hey Words?"

"Words" was his nickname for me that season, one which appealed to his sense of style—pithy, wry, laconic, playful. How a cowboy should be. Buzz Henry was at least a cowboy, and he did those disarming prairie zingers very well.

Tradition aside, movie cowboys are not laconic. Given a couple of friendly drinks, a new girl or a new living room, your average big hat will talk the shoes off a pinto. But the style's laconic anyhow—Henry Fonda in *My Darling Clementine,* enriched by Strip lingo. "When you say that, smile, bubbeleh."

It was a funny meeting. Even though they were serious and the problem was real, the attempts to write an ad endorsing the unthinkable led to comedy. After an hour of forging solemn pleas, the meeting began to send up slogans like "No Kill, No Eat—Support Simulated Violence!"

Voices got louder, drinks were served, and I began to hear Buzz's high-pitched giggle. Somebody named Cliff or Shorty did an artistic backflip over the sofa and scraped his head on the stone coffee table. The dogs began to bark happily, and one more crisis was over.

In Jamaica, when everything went wrong, when the food at the expensive hotel was so bad that twenty percent of the crew was constantly sick, when the hotel manager just shrugged his consolation and the local health officials rolled their eyes and the actors sent home sardonic letters to be printed in the trade papers, Buzz sorrowed over it all, drank a lot one night and threw all the portable hotel furniture into the Olympic-sized swimming pool. For some reason this impressed the manager far more than my threats of suit. Breakfast became edible.

Buzz had that effect on primitives. In New Guinea, natives who hated each other loved him without anyone understanding a single spoken word. In my living room a silver miniature poodle who had taken to savaging the drapes gave it up after a long nose-to-nose talk with Buzz —who got down onto knees and elbows for the meeting. Horses told him how they felt (mostly lousy, according to Buzz, who thought of all horses as dim-witted hypochondriacs), and infants would reach for his offered face with two hands. So a resort manager was not beyond his reach.

"What the hell made you do that?" I asked. I thought we'd have to pay the bastard.

He was almost apologetic. "It just seemed like it would *explain* things to the guy." Then, characteristically, "He's not such a bad guy."

"He's a shit," I said.

"Yeah," Buzz said, "but not too bad a guy."

Stunt men play kiss-kiss with stars, of course. The stunt man gets a lot of employment—to become a big star's stunt double is to work when he works and live as he lives when working. The star gets the sturdy comfort of belonging to the company of men who smell of liniment. Nobody loses.

Because Buzz was slim and quick, he doubled for lots of non-burly heroes. Once, to his everlasting glee, he was stunt double for a beautiful lady who was stabbed and fell down a flight of stairs.

Buzz choreographed all the physical stuff in the *Flint* pictures and figured as Jim Coburn's stunt double. When reviewers and fans marveled at Jim's "pantherlike" grace, a lot of what they loved was Buzz flying through the air in a shaggy, taffy-colored wig. And as Jim Coburn learned the stunt man's quick and easy movements, so Buzz began to reflect the "where it's at" lingo featured in the star's dressing room. "Right on" and "Like wow, man." I thought it was a sad way for a cowboy to talk and made jokes about it.

Months later, with *Flint* in the can and the jokes forgotten, I got a postcard from Buzz, all the way from the wilds of Sonora, Mexico—on location with wild Sam Peckinpah. The card said, "I may not know where it's at, but this ain't the place."

Good with animals, aborigines, hotel managers and girls. On a set, girls noticed him right away. Maybe it was that he never seemed to be recruiting (although he was)—or posing (he was not). Buzz openly and candidly liked girls. When a nine-pointer went by Buzz would look happy and get off his regular remark: "Okay, podner—I'll stand on her hair for you if you'll stand on her hair for me. . . ." And giggle. I never heard him on the subject of femlib—it didn't seem to exist for him. If he didn't think they were men, still it had never occurred to him to fear the difference. He once told me that he liked women a hell of a lot more than horses, which may not be altogether a sexist remark.

Saddlesores aside, the preference was not just bravery. A lot of working cowboys will tell you that after the fadeout kiss on the muzzle, they had to touch up Old Paint with a two-by-four to keep things serene. Buzz rode like a centaur, but only for work, considering a horse "a damn poor way to get from here to there." He loved fast and fancy cars, and his driveway flaunted them, with his changing fortunes, alongside the sober station wagon driven by his wife. Patty Henry, a tall, straight-backed, dark-haired, blue-eyed beauty, loved horses enough for both of them and won cups in jumping horse contests and shows. Buzz was proud of her. And a little in awe.

Stage coffee—hot, bitter, in Styrofoam cups. Buzz morose.

"Goddammit anyway. You know old Patty wouldn't let me in the *door* last night? Had to sleep in the goddam car."

"She think you were a burglar?"

"Shee-it no." Quavering martyrdom. "She knew who it was all right. Hell, man—it was after sunup."

Then the joke of it overtook him and his face creased and the high-pitched giggle spilled over in sorrow and admiration.

"Whoo-ee. Mad? I tell you that gal's *tough.*"

It took me a long time to get to know Patty, and I didn't understand the word until later.

I first saw her in Cortina, come to visit Buzz on the *Von Ryan's Express* location. We may have been introduced earlier, but I really saw her for the first time that night during a memorable explosion of horseplay. Sinatra and the Companions and the Visiting Friends Of had returned to the hotel late and hilarious, punching each other and shouting for a nightcap in the bar. The laughter got louder, the punching turned to siphon squirting and it became a bottle-smashing, pail-throwing waterfight. I came down to see what the noise was about, was instantly doused and took cover behind a pillar. When I got the water out of my eyes I saw Patty Henry, sitting quite straight on a tall, armless rococo chair, smack in the middle of a long wall, watching. The fight raged up and down in front of her, water was sloshing along the floor, and there she sat, feet tucked, hands folded in her lap, head turning politely with the action. A lady at a play.

We remembered that night not long ago and she laughed at my recollection.

"I couldn't think of anything else to do," she said. "After all, we had been to dinner together."

The calliope was going full out for Buzz and her in those days, and she was sitting the painted horses as she sat the real ones.

It is absolutely true that rodeo cowboys climb onto bucking horses and Brahma bulls wearing plaster casts, neck braces, adhesive tape and Saran Wrap bandages. In their case it was contagious; I once watched Patty take a jumping horse through a show wearing a smart green riding outfit and an arm-length plaster cast. Buzz noted that it was a damn fool thing to do before a show—break an arm, that is. But he was glowing as he watched her.

Buzz himself took breaks and sprains very casually. On one of the *Flint* pictures, after some stunt, I found him in one of the dressing rooms busily stuffing cotton into his nose, wincing just a little.

"Broke the son of a bitch again," he said. "Give me a couple of minutes, will you?"

It was easy to see Buzz as man-in-motion, harder to see him as the

234

owner of a home in Toluca Lake, a fellow concerned with swimming pools and the placement of shade trees in the yard. But over the years I saw him shift from the one to the other, without losing laughter. There was a baby girl, and on weekends you could find Buzz in the new swimming pool with her.

She was fearless, of course—before she could walk, Buzz had her swimming alone, balancing on his outstretched hands, laughing, laughing.

There's a traditional line of ascent for stunt men, and some of the great second-unit directors began the way Buzz did—stunt man to double to gaffer to assistant to second unit. It's a hard way to go—many a director's reputation was gained, in part at least, from the anonymous work of a stunt man on his way up.

"Got the job all right, but no credit. He said, 'Next time.'"

The stunt man/second-unit-director-without-credit learns not to complain and not to tell the story too widely. Directors are all-powerful in an industry where They pride themselves on knowing nearly nothing about how a movie is made—everything about Deals. With the flowering of the auteur theory out of critical hydroponics, and the arrival of the Agent as Picture Maker, directors have become supreme and their long, long thoughts are the new dogma. So Buzz made some heroes, learned a lot and got more practice than credit. In its own mean way, of course, it's no different from the master-apprentice system. God knows who painted backgrounds and bodies in those Rubens and Velazquezes and Tintorettos and Michelangelos. Stunt men and would-be second-unit directors. But of course they were not *promised* a credit. Our masters have added cheating to the lesson.

Buzz worked on all the pictures I produced, from the *Flints* to the ill-fated *Skullduggery,* and he made the work notable. Marvelous comedy fights—the orchestration of key action sequences, sequences in which he usually doubled the star or played a small role as assistant heavy. The credit became "Action sequences designed by," and the job offers came in for action sequences in pictures which were all action. He became a second-unit director in fact several pictures before he became one in name. Among those, his work in *The Wild Bunch* was notable. *Skullduggery* came along, and with it a full second-unit credit. And when the director fell ill, Buzz stepped into the first-unit job. The rodeo kid from Pagosa Springs who had made it twice to Hollywood finally directed love scenes with major stars. The picture was stillborn, but They knew, and when he took a second-unit job on *The Cowboys,* John Wayne noticed.

While the picture was being finished, Buzz dropped into my office one day. We swapped the usual jokes and gossip, but something was on his mind.

"Listen," he said, "I just have to tell someone. It's not set and maybe it's bullshit, but—listen, I wouldn't want anyone to think I was saying it's a fact, but—"

I waited.

"Duke Wayne. Goddammit, he says he wants to talk to me about directing one for him. *Wayne!*"

We pounded each other and swore secrecy. Then Buzz said, "And wait till you see what I got outside."

It was a maroon Ferrari. Buzz jumped in, shouted something complicated about the down payment, and the car snarled and shot out into the traffic. Buzz waved as he took the corner onto Sunset.

A few weeks later, just at dawn, the telephone woke me. It was Patty.

"Buzz was killed last night." The world unfolding for him, Buzz Henry went to a late and happy party. The maroon Ferrari flipped off the Golden State Freeway and he was killed instantly, "traveling at a high rate of speed."

30

My Year as
One of Them

THE FOLK heroes of the Blacklist have all the good stories
about what it's like to live in the Great Silence. An ordinary
producer on his ass with the word out against him is only a clown by
comparison; what's worse, he knows it. There are no fellow martyrs to
talk to, and he cannot pretend he stands for anything important. The
weeks became months became years and jobs just didn't jell—nothing
quite went together, sorry. There were many unreturned phone calls
and odd-sounding apologies. "Honest, we'd love to but Upstairs says
there's a problem and they just don't want . . . I don't really know,
maybe somebody at the bank . . ." And when it got to be years, really
years—"What was your last credit? Sure—terrific. Uh—nothing since
then?"

It took close to three years, just as the man said. The various threats
were meticulously fulfilled and the useless lesson learned. Then vindica-
tion on the courthouse steps, a chunk of money which was neatly swallowed by the debts and the divorce—and I became employable again,
and, in time, employed.

Everyone loves a good funeral. It's ideal for the kind moralizing that brings a shine to the cheek and it's butter on the commentator's bread, so there's a lot of premature burial. Officially dead myself, I got a job as story executive in the Tomb of the Capulets, MGM.

In a decade punctuated by some of the most public funerals in history, the burial of MGM stands out because of one difference—it didn't die, despite the eloquence of its mourners. Here's Rex Reed, in the introduction to his book *People Are Crazy Here:*

"I was having lunch . . . in the MGM commissary. . . . A few blocks from where we sat . . . bulldozers were tearing down Waterloo bridge, tractors were crushing Andy Hardy's house . . . Katharine Ross . . . was appearing in the last movie to be filmed on the old MGM sound stages. . . ." etc., etc. It's a good, sharp and colorful piece by one of the better writers about the Industry. It rings the changes on indignation—"It had to do with the even lower taste of the men responsible, men who had no interest in the history or perpetuation of the movies as a cultural heritage"—and sympathy—"June Allyson was supposed to play a Lesbian. Now June Allyson . . . didn't have the faintest idea what a Lesbian was." It's a fair sample of the indignant and colorful stuff written when MGM auctioned off a lot of famous props and costumes. Rex Reed, condemning Them for callousness to history, got a little carried away. The movie he was savaging as "a cheap potboiler that came and went without embarrassment" was a moderately successful mystery-comedy called *They Only Kill Their Masters* which starred James Garner as well as Katharine Ross, and you can check Rex Reed's verdict on your TV set. But it was not the last movie to be shot on MGM sound stages—which are churning them out right now; the bridge wasn't being bulldozed and Judge Hardy's house is still falling down out there among the dry weeds on Lot 2. The trouble was simply that MGM's epitaph was a lot more interesting than MGM's recovery. So it was buried alive when the ruby slippers were sold—an event which seemed to make millions of people feel that Cinderella's glass slipper had been recycled.

The executive head of a story department at a studio is not the head of the story department but rather the literary henchman of the head of production with oversight on the department itself. At MGM, as at most studios, story departments are ancient, union-crusted bureaucracies which are usually stuck away in an old wing or a basement where they can wallow in their immense filing systems, grind out their endless, pointless reports and brew rancor. Even the young people who become story analysts (that's the Guild name for this corps of first readers) take on the pinched and resentful look they all wear after a while. They are people who feel unused, misused, ignored and superior. While the last is arguable, the rest is not.

I took the job because I was broke, of course, thinking it a step backward and away from heart's desire. But I was broke—inside-out broke—and Dan Melnick, the darkly vivid young head of production who hired me, said something that scored. It was on a second interview, I think. We had met once and decided to "think about it." This time Melnick said, "Look, I've done some homework on you and I'd like to make a suggestion. Take the job. You know why? So you'll have a big building to come to every morning. You'll have a hell of a big office, people on the lot will call you 'sir,' and your secretary will be saying 'He'll have to get back to you' to people you haven't been able to get in to see. Take the job."

I could have blubbered.

He said, "How do I know? That's why I took the job, and it works."

The truth is, I enjoyed my year as one of Them and began to sympathize a bit with Mindless Destroyers of Talent, Soulless Hucksters and civil servants everywhere.

Item: The true and unhappy history of Sam Peckinpah's famous "destroyed version" of *Pat Garrett and Billy the Kid* as seen up close by an ambivalent observer.

Pat Garrett and Billy the Kid came into MGM as a completed screenplay by Rudy Wurlitzer, a writer with impeccable Eastern Literary Establishment credentials which include *The New Yorker* magazine. The producer who brought it to MGM was an upper-class type named Gordon Carroll who had good credentials of his own—and everybody said, "Sam Peckinpah."

There was a minimum of the usual rope dancing. We executive advisers read the script and made some suggestions for improvement which were politely received and cheerfully ignored. "Look," said producer Carroll, "if Sam wants to do it there'll be time enough to go over it, because you know Sam, he always wants changes."

Equally obvious but politely unstated was, "If Sam doesn't do it it probably won't go here so why should we waste a lot of time with changes that won't mean a thing?"

Studio head Melnick, who had produced the successful *Straw Dogs* with Peckinpah directing, made the submission to the great director and in a very short time the good news was all over the third floor. "Peckinpah loves it!"

And he did. I attended a ceremonial meeting which featured all the creative brass from J.T. Aubrey to me. Peckinpah was welcomed, enthusiastic predictions made and pledges of mutual admiration exchanged. After Aubrey left we got down to cases a bit more—I offered some suggestions for making this utterly original western a little more like familiar ones, but Peckinpah rejected them all, not without kindness.

"I understand what you're getting at," he said, "but this is one I don't think we ought to fuck with, fellas." Peckinpah is a man who lowers his voice when he wants to make a point in an office. "I just love it," he said. "Let's just shoot it."

Nevertheless, there were minor shifts and changes made, chiefly to accommodate budget considerations—matters in which great sums could be saved by minor substitutions and compressions. No sweat.

Off went Peckinpah, cast and crew. Before long film was coming back from Mexico and management's teeth began to chatter.

"What the hell's that? That's not in the script."

"Get Carroll on the phone."

Sam was rewriting the perfect script. Not just tinkering with it, but adding whole chunks, scenes and characters.

"I'll tell him what you said," said Carroll, on the phone. "He says he's feeling sick."

"Sick?"

"Yeah. He says if he doesn't feel better he may have to shut down for a couple of days."

Rage. Threats. Second thoughts.

"What's it up to now?"

"He'll be a million over by the end of next week."

Eventually it was done. They came back and everybody said, "It looks terrific, Sam," and waited. His version of the film was about two and a half hours long, full of those added scenes and lively as a coronation. There were meetings which got progressively more acrimonious. Finally Peckinpah refused further changes. Management recut the film to something just over two hours in length and released it with a lot of publicity—into a cloud of critical rage. It was not a success at the box office.

"They ruined it," said Peckinpah.

"It would have made a profit if he hadn't gone a million and a half over," said management.

One thing was reasonably clear. The final "ruined" version was quite close to the original screenplay—the one Sam thought we shouldn't fuck with.

31

Cohn and Mayer? Like Ya to Meet Ozymandias

THE PHRASE used to be "power and glory," but the words have separated. Glory is thin blue milk now, but power is pure cream.

One of the founding fathers, a giant even among Them, had a luxurious little screening room which opened off his luxurious large office. There, according to devout legend, he would watch rushes, and while he watched, girls would come in, give head and depart, faceless in the dark. Such screening rooms are gone now and we confine our tributes to special awards given in public. It takes imagination to know how to use power.

A hundred years ago Guy de Maupassant wrote a short story in which a peasant girl, working at an inn, is ordered to give herself to a drunken young lord who comes in out of the night. She does so, trembling and ecstatic—creeps into his bed in the darkness and there loses her virginity. But the next morning, when she must wait on the young man and his friends at table, she realizes that she doesn't know which young man it was. It's a movie story, and the man in the screening room would have understood it. But it is not getting easier. What to install where sin used to be? What does Linda Lovelace read?

Our jokes reflect the loss. Nepotism used to be a standard gambit, burnished to a high luster in that wisecrack "He set the son-in-law business back twenty years." The provocation, if there was one, is unknown.

Who said it? Probably a screenwriter. Most of our enduring savageries originate with screenwriters, are retold by actors and publicity men and attributed to directors. Screenwriters in groups are mean as fish. Show a new movie to an audience of screenwriters and the darkness is lanced with cruel and to-the-point jokes, often valid. After a few minutes of this, the movie staggers along like a horse in a stream filled with piranhas—shivering, dying, bare bones beneath the waterline.

Mankiewicz or Wilder? Just don't attribute it to a producer. Who do you think the jokes are about?

The problem of the clean shot. *They* established the Industry, pushcart to palace, in a couple of decades. By the time sound arrived They were western dynasts with large families begat on Rivington Street but nourished at last in Beverly Hills. But that tide of talent which rolled west after *The Jazz Singer* was mostly young and largely hungry. The Good Old Days began with a generation gap. Naturally, nepotism got a lot of attention.

Was there ever an establishment which looked more permanent and proved less so? In spite of all the angry novels and the cartoons, in spite of stereotypes which have endured, Cohn and Mayer are one with Ozymandias. They are all gone and no studio is run by one of their anointed heirs. The dynasts who had young either ate them like Warner or crippled them like Zanuck. In order to work, nepotism needs confidence, pride, self-esteem—something. It didn't work for Them.

The forms change. There was a time when children's birthday parties were competitive tournaments—sources of the real gaiety and gossip. There were nannies then and the parties flowed among the great houses. Clowns and magicians performed on newly mowed lawns and the sound of ice and thin glasses mingled with polite shrieks and the distant thwock of tennis balls on the next estate. But birthday parties are no longer for kids—as childhood is not for them either. Birthday parties are for us.

One I attended was a surprise party given by an agent for his wife. The locale was one of those dark, in-group restaurants concealed in a residence hotel out on Wilshire Boulevard. The place is informal, clubby and queened over by a tousled homosexual with a voice like an

emergency stop on a streetcar. He has only one name, of course—Tyler.
Ty-ler. He tells you the menu in that voice. They don't have a written
one.

As my date and I entered, Tyler was in full and happy cry. *"Just* my
luck to get *pregnant* by a *convict. . . ."* Screaming with laughter.

We were sent to the bar to await the other surprisers. Four of them
were already there—people I vaguely knew from other parties. As we
identified ourselves, our host arrived, beaming at his wife's joyful
squealing as she saw us. "Oh, I'm so *glad* to see you . . . I didn't know
. . . he didn't *tell* me . . . suspect a *thing . . ."* Party kissing and hugging
and fumbling with presents and over everything Tyler's happy screams,
"Everybody come to the *table.* Right *here,* luv . . . oh, *anywhere,* for
Gawdsake . . ."

The long table was set for ten, and eight of us were there. Host at one
end, birthday wife at the other—that was easy. The other four were
quickly and firmly seated along one side, my date and I on the other
—at the far end. The two chairs adjacent to my host were left empty.
I understood at once: Jack Haley, Jr., and Liza Minnelli, the enchanted
couple who had just married in a sunburst of international publicity—
she a brilliant headliner, he the producer-director of the year's smash
hit. Our host had ten percent of the bridegroom and of me, too. The
empty chairs glowed in anticipation. And looking around the room I
could see by the quick, nervous turning of heads that everyone had
guessed who was coming to dinner.

We ordered drinks, drank them, smiled and waited. Ordered more.
The place was noisy enough to spare us all the need to hear. We
mouthed things at each other, smiled and drank. The birthday wife
continued to be thrilled and surprised, the empty chairs remained
empty. My date and my stomach growled a little. I decided to stir things
up.

"Watch this."

My date nodded, understanding as I got up, drink in hand, made my
way to the head of the table, and plunked myself down in the empty
chair at my host's elbow.

"Hate to talk business on an occasion like this," I said, "but I thought
maybe we'd better discuss . . ."

His smile was agonized. Trying to pay attention to me and to the
doorway behind him at the same time. Down the table my date smiled
maliciously and half rose—as if to move closer. My host sweated, stammered. . . .

"Uh—yes, sure . . . that is—you—uh—know some others are expected
and I . . ."

His head twitched. The sentence trailed. I fiddled with the Important napkin with deliberate absentmindedness. My date waved.

"Hi down there," she called.

But his pain was too evident. I put down the Important napkin, straightened the Important silverware, got up and groped my way back to my chair. My date cocked an eyebrow. Chicken.

I put the smile back on and we waited. On my left the birthday wife kept going, but her attention too was flickering to the doorway. It was a long while and we drank, ordered and drank again while the proprietor brought baskets of breaded, fried zucchini cut into long brown strips which looked crisp but wilted in the mouth.

My date was beautiful, young and of uncertain temper when drinking. She suddenly reached flash point.

"Either we eat now or I'm going home," she said.

I passed the word to my host, who shrugged wetly, exchanged an unhappy look with his wife and sent for Tyler. They whispered for a moment, then Tyler straightened abruptly and glared down the table. His look was pure contempt, a sword over our drunken, miserable company.

"Nobody eats till *they get here!"*

People across the room turned to look. My date rose and laid the napkin across the plate.

"Let's go. Now."

My host squirmed and flashed a look of supplication at Tyler, whose lip curled as his ringlets bobbed.

"All right, all *right,"* he said. *"Give* me your orders then, loves."

But at that moment there was a stir and Tyler wheeled and screamed. There *they* were—lustrous, gleaming in the doorway. Chairs scraped and teeth flashed. All around the dark room, faces shone whitely as guests elbowed each other with pleasure. My host was on his feet, spilling smiles, cheeks shining with fellowship. Liza, hands outstretched —every movement a subliminal cut to large screens and music—trotted down the table to the birthday wife, who wept ecstatically as they kissed hello. Jack, having draped her wrap along the chair, shook hands, shrugged and smiled their apologies for being so late. They had been pinned down at so and so's reception—one of those things you have to attend, you know? We all knew. So and so's reception had been in the papers for days. He looked down the long table and as if on cue she straightened up, turned and smiled at all of us.

"And just who are all these lovely, patient people?"

Introductions. The ones where everyone knows one of the names and nobody cares about the other. She is good at it, of course, blurting out her name warmly and eagerly—repeating yours. A lovely, flashing lady and a pro at introductions.

In the background, Tyler's happiness reached a new crescendo. We turned to look and there came a waiter with the cake. It was rectangular, white-frosted, multi-tiered and bearing two lighted candles. As it passed me I could see that the top had been designed into two panels, each one covered with writing—like the tablets of the Ten Commandments.

One of the candles went out as the cake was set down. Someone produced a lighter and rekindled it while Tyler shrieked, "Read it. *Read* it out *loud!*"

The candles flickered and the birthday wife leaned forward to peer at the text. She gasped, straightened up and called down the table to Liza, who had nearly greeted and smiled her way back to her chair and husband.

"Oh, look! It's for you, too! Come and *look.*"

Liza turned, a little stolidly, I thought, and made her way back. She bent over the cake and for a moment the famous smile went utterly blank. In the background, Tyler screeched his paean of joy.

"Isn't it *mar*velous? Don't you *love* it? Half for you, dear, and half for *Them!*"

A birthday cake with guest stars.

Out here where we all trained on the same dreams, it's a drag to learn that power is an illusion. So we resist the information while choking on the fact. How else to make movies?

When I was still a visitor to Hollywood—the long-ago night when I stood in the hot, jasmine-smelling darkness outside Sam Fuller's Spanish castle—it was all as marvelous and funny as it ought to be. And the small, steely-mopped man inside, laughing, gripping my arm, peering into my eyes, and shouting "Ha, *ha*" was irresistible to someone raised on Howard Pyle and Maxfield Parrish.

Sam Fuller. By the time I moved west he was off the painted horse. Next time I saw him he was a little subdued and accompanied by one of those bright-haired girls who turn up after a divorce. He was living in a small bungalow in Hollywood, one of those square, shingled wooden buildings, squatting in the sun, jammed with army stuff, crammed with books. "Everything handy, working like hell," he said. "Pound on the typewriter all day, fall into the pool and then back to the typewriter. A terrific way to live," he said, "beats working at a studio."

I understood. "What happened to the house?"

He flashed the old fire and waved his cigar at me. "I *gave* it to her," he said.

Sammy Fuller. By the time I got my bearings in the new world he was out of it. Gone to Europe, someone said—implying he was running out the string on some of those coproduction deals where the main title credits combine a list of countries with a list of burnt-out Names and character actors from television.

Epitaphs. "Crazy Sam Fuller. You know how he used to shoot off a pistol on the set? Right. Instead of 'action'—bam! One time he does that—at Fox, wasn't it? Fox. Sure, he used to make those little—for Darryl. Anyway, they roll 'em and he shoots the fuckin' pistol and guess what? Someone drops a couple of dead ducks down from the grids. Laugh? . . ."

And that reminiscent shake of the head, an old-timer yarning in a dry town. Tumbleweed blowing over Sammy Fuller; a helmet I once saw impaled on a stump in a swamp in New Guinea. . . .

32

§

Ray Stark, George Segal, and Me

MGM WAS GASPING like a beached whale. Nothing worked. Critics loved *Slither* but hardly anybody came. When we beat the competition to a surefire hit like *The Man Who Loved Cat Dancing,* the picture came out boneless. One triumphant Friday we closed a deal for a wonderful screenplay called *The Sting,* but by Sunday night it was no longer ours. We were second-highest bidder for *Jaws.* A deal was made with Irwin Allen to do *Logan's Run,* the sci-fi novel bought some ten years before, subject of a dozen unfulfilled screenplays and production designs. But Irwin Allen had spoken too soon and too optimistically. At the height of his enormous success, the studio he was bound to wouldn't let him go and MGM would not sell the novel. The deal died.

People began greeting each other with shrugs, and one day when I went in to see Melnick with something or other that looked promising he just nodded without interest. "I don't think we'll be buying anything for a while."

Business in the commissary slackened, the parking lot began to look windswept, and the voice of the agent was no longer heard in the corridors. Somewhere on the lot, Michael Crichton was finishing his little sci-fi picture, *Westworld*—but at a million two and a new director what was there to hope? Cheerful, red-bearded Jack Haley, Jr.—a notch above me on the executive totem pole—continued to spend his spare time noodling away at an immense heap of clips from old MGM musicals. As things were going, there was more and more spare time. For anyone walking down the silent third-floor corridor, it was eerie and sad to hear the shrilling of his office Moviola—endlessly shrieking out the great hits of a long time ago.

All of us executives still came to work on time every morning, but lunches became quite a lot longer, mostly eaten off the lot—job-interview lunches. Executives in a dying studio are a lot like those leaderless samurai in the Kurosawa westerns—proud, treacherous and willing to turn their weapons against anyone for pay. Their contempt for the failing leader is limitless, and those lunch interviews are usually spiced with the kind of stories we're all good at, stories whose ultimate point is always the same: I tried to tell him but he wouldn't listen.

To my considerable surprise, I was first to be offered another perch. The caller, whose name was Feldman, reminded me that we had met years ago and said he would like to meet me at the Polo Lounge. "I work for Ray Stark," he said.

Raymond Chandler is quoted somewhere as saying that Ray Stark seemed to him like a flickering light reflected on a wall, a description which conveys to me the kind of nervous admiration generally felt for Stark. Chandler the writer was speaking of Stark the agent, not Stark the great producer and power-behind-the-scenes, so Chandler's contract probably didn't contain a clause forbidding him to discuss Stark after they parted. Mine did. Mine said that after leaving his employ I was enjoined against disclosing anything about him, his associates or business operations without his permission and granting him the right to sue me if I did "publish or cause to be published said information, including but not limited to, a fictionalization."

Even if Chandler had signed such a contract, it would have been dumb for Stark to sue him—and Ray Stark is not dumb. When one of his favorite writers, Jay Presson Allen *(Cabaret, Funny Lady)*, wrote a Hollywood novel entitled *Just Tell Me What You Want* about a fellow remarkably like a flickering light reflected on a wall, Stark tried to buy the novel for production and lamented when he didn't get it. Jay Allen said, "Yes, he made an offer, but he wouldn't meet my price." Someone else made the movie.

Jay Allen's novel was shrewdly titled. When Stark wants something or someone, his munificence is not just kingly, as they say, it is usually psychologically on the button. You don't have to tell Stark what you want—if he wants you, it's at your door in the morning with a funny, endearing, self-deprecating note.

A lady who gets a monthly check once suggested to me that I should never take a job where my boss is shorter than I. But in an Industry remarkably full of dynamic short men, that would narrow my opportunities unbearably—and I'm not quite five eleven. Stark is several inches shorter—an erect, ruddy, active, laughing, intensely gregarious and very lonely man. He is immensely successful, lives on a huge, handsome estate which looks out onto rolling green lawns studded with great old trees and large statues—a couple of Henry Moores. His parties are Industry milestones, his movies win awards and earn millions—with some exceptions, like *Fat City* (a box-office failure of which Stark remains proud), and one he hired me to produce, *The Black Bird.*

Holding a conversation with Ray Stark on a busy day is like trying to watch a television drama while someone keeps changing the channel. So it takes a while before you realize that inside all the jokes and games and subject changes, there's a tenacity like a snapping turtle's. Stark never really gives up on anything he wants. One of the things he wanted for decades was to produce a sequel to *The Maltese Falcon.*

After years of false starts and misfires, he came up with a screenplay by David Giler, a bright young writer with a notably offhand manner and a gift for oddly flavored comedy scenes which manage to be both endearing and sardonic in the same joke. According to Giler, he had transformed Stark's idea for a straight sequel into comedy and thus made a sequel possible. I loved the screenplay and was delighted to be offered the picture. Giler was tolerant but skeptical. He had hoped for another producer, a close friend and convivial thinker, but his real skepticism was for Stark's intentions. Baffled by his attitude, I made optimistic and tactful suggestions for getting the script into final shape and urged speed. He nodded a lot, laughed at my jokes, promised to "give it a try" and wrote nothing whatever. I felt pressed to justify my paycheck and began to nag, finally triggering an outburst.

"Look," he said. It was after a long, long lunch and his gestures were free, his curly hair damp and his glasses steamy. "I don't really mind your ideas but there's no point in my writing anything unless we've got a deal and the only way we've got a deal is if George agrees. So get off my back, okay?"

George Segal. Stark had told me the script had been sent to him, but nothing more. Learning that I knew Burt Reynolds, he had suggested I send him the screenplay too, and I had done so.

"You mean Segal's really involved in this?"

"Involved? He loves it. He wants to do it. He told me so."

"So what's the hangup?"

"I don't know," Giler said. "Maybe the deal."

"What does he want?"

"I don't know."

"What's his agency?"

"Same as mine, CMA."

"So what does your guy say?"

"He says he loves it. I'm telling you, he loves it."

And so on for a while.

I asked Stark, who shrugged. "I don't know if I want to make his deal," he said, "but if George doesn't do it we'll get somebody else. Your friend Reynolds, for instance."

I said to Giler, "Stark says he'd just as soon have Burt Reynolds as George."

"I wouldn't," Giler said. "I think George is perfect. Hell, we could have had Reynolds anytime. He loves it."

"You mean he's already seen the script?"

"Sure. We talked about it. He's dying to do it."

I telephoned Reynolds' associate, a pleasant, polite man named Clayton, and told him I had not been aware that he and Burt had already seen the screenplay.

"I don't know what's the matter with those people," said Clayton. "Burt did read it a while ago and we told them we had no interest in it."

So I said to Giler, "Something strange here. Clayton says they passed it up some time ago."

"That's crazy," said Giler. "I was right there when Burt said he loved it."

Stark said, "To hell with him. Segal will be better."

A person could lose his mind. No doubt about it.

No matter what Agatha Christie and Rex Stout proclaim to the contrary, there's just no way to get all the suspects and principals into one room for the purpose of unmasking the Truth. For one thing, they all have agents—even the agents have agents if they rank. They also have lawyers, business managers, buddies, wives, lovers, husbands, enemies —any of whom may be combined at any time for group or solo purpose and all of whom will speak for the principal about anything you want to know. If a writer's business agent runs across an actor's attorney at, say, the Beverly Hills Health Club, and the attorney says he thinks the actor's closest friend said he loved that screenplay about whatever . . . the writer will eventually hear glad green tidings and in a matter of minutes the news will have become his own witnessed fact. "He's dying to do it. Told me so himself." And he could be quite right, too. It's also possible that the actor, hearing on all sides that he loved the script, will come to believe it.

However it happened, Giler's analysis turned out to be the correct one; Segal agreed to do the picture and suddenly sets were being designed. Somewhere in all that euphoria Giler asked me if I had any objection to his directing the film, adding that it was "more or less George's idea."

Auteurists and other mystics elevate the director's function to the point where giving a new man a shot is tantamount to inviting the ward orderly to do brain surgery—but it's not that serious, and I thought Giler would probably handle the picture well.

Stark just shrugged. "If George wants him maybe he'll behave. George. Maggie. Besides, she'll be there every day." He meant Margaret Booth, the legendary editor of the great days of MGM.

"What do you mean 'behave'? We've had a lot of meetings with George and he's as nice as he can be. Laughs, loves the jokes . . ."

Stark agreed cheerfully. "He has been agreeable," he said, "but I hear a note. I dunno. Weird. I've known him a long time." I thought Stark was performing. In all our meetings George Segal had been playing pretty much the person you'd expect him to be, quick, whimsical and defensively debonair—the David Niven of the Borscht Belt. He giggled unexpectedly and sometimes broke into shouts of laughter over trivialities. The net effect was that of someone whose sense of humor is genuine but is also used as an offensive weapon. George seemed to me to laugh the way other actors strike silences—to impress and disconcert. But we got along well enough.

Still, there were signs. Once he flew into a rage at someone's saying, "Good old George." Quite unexpectedly he turned on the speaker and *shouted*, "I'm sick of that 'good old George' crap, goddammit!" and almost instantly stopped, shrugged apologetically and was charming to the offender. With me he did what I'm accustomed to—he talked literary. The conversations were pleasant enough and he wasn't one of those people who pretends to have read a book. But every once in a while he would jolt me with some obviously quoted, aphoristic line, usually in that hip/sardonic vein which has made rock singers into popular philosophers. Then he'd add, by way of attribution, "Eliot."

I know half a dozen Eliot tags, I suppose, and I'm familiar with the flavor—but I had never heard any like those. Finally, I said that whatever it was didn't sound a damn bit like T.S. Eliot—"to me, of course."

George stared, then shrieked with laughter and threw his arms around me. "T.S. . . . ? I'm talking about Elliott Gould, bubbe. Elliott!"

And on another day he said, quite unexpectedly, "Would you object to sharing a credit with me?"

"What do you mean?"

"Co-producer," George said. "I'd like to be a co-producer on this."

I thought he was setting up a joke. "All right," I said, "I'll bite. Why do you want to be a co-producer?"

George stopped me. "No, no," he said, "I'm serious."

"Why?"

He peered into my face and said, "Because I respect you," then whirled away, shouting with laughter.

I told it to Giler, who said, "He's serious, you know. I think they promised it to him."

Stark said, "Don't be ridiculous. You're the producer."

The sets were witty, the cast mostly perfect, and I was welcomed to the set by old friends on the crew. But one day into the picture, anyone could see it was going to be one of those.

Graceful, stylish George, charming George, wistfully-bent-but-wryly-unbroken George, absolutely-perfect-for-the-game-but-bedraggled son of Sam Spade, a schnook who never wanted to be a detective . . . funny and touching George decided the part should be played with *anger.* He yelled, he scowled, he raised red eyes to hulking Lionel Stander, who was forced to yell back. The wonderful, pawky jokes sounded less elastic than they read and the helium turned to hot air. What was almost immediately evident was that it all came from George. He wasn't just playing angry, he *was* angry.

At what, at whom? No answers, just that laughter and a series of peremptory demands. A bottle of chilled white wine had to be available any time he walked out of a set. It was, but once it wasn't properly chilled and the bottle was thrown. He took to arriving late, disappearing for long lunches and refusing overtime. Visitors to the set were sometimes embraced, sometimes driven away rudely: "Get that son of a bitch out of here. He's in my eyeline!"

He directed the director, of course—but that was expected. All the same, Maggie Booth would clutch the arms of the tall director's chair in which she sat, her lips working soundlessly as she watched George explain a shot to Giler. Now and again she'd climb down, walk over to the two of them and gesture what she thought was needed. Then she'd stalk back to the high chair, shaking her head. In her view, neither one of them had a clue. In their view, her ideas were devoid of contemporary chic, man.

Whatever Giler's innermost thoughts, he was trying to be practical, to serve the picture and his own career. On a shooting picture that simply means "hang in there with the star." All directors know that the star is the power, the star's affection the talisman and his rage the ultimate shield. And Stark was already disaffected and promising a bleak future.

All of which added up to the old refrain for me. "You go down there and tell those sons of bitches that they better pick up the time this afternoon or I'll throw their asses off the show."

Which translated on the stage into "Ray's pretty sore, and you've been in this setup all morning. Let's see if we can get a little bit ahead before we wrap today."

To which Giler would say, quite reasonably, "Okay by me. But George said he's tired."

And George would laugh, put an arm around my shoulder and say, "Don't worry. We'll get it done. You want it *good,* don't you?" And play it angry and leave early.

Inevitably it was seen as some kind of struggle between Segal and Stark—even though neither of them and none of us could say what the struggle was about.

Segal used a star's weapons. He asked me, quite soberly, to keep Stark off the set. "Just his being there irritates me. I can feel it. He breaks my concentration."

Stark said, "Concentration? You tell Jonathan Livingston Segal that it's my picture and I'll come on the set anytime I want."

So Stark came onto the set and Segal stopped work and we got farther behind. Stark's money, of course.

The mark-it-with-a-white-stone day came about four weeks in. When I got to the stage entrance I could hear the sound of shouting, and there were passersby standing still, watching. It was George, angrily berating one of the second or third assistants because the refrigerator in his dressing-room trailer had malfunctioned and a bottle of Coke had frozen, blown its top, and made a mess. The assistant was sort of hunched over a bicycle, just taking it.

I bustled up like your friendly neighborhood cop, spraying "hi" and "good morning" and "what's doing" like room deodorant, but nothing helped. George called heaven and me to witness that he had been abused and put upon, that the studio was the laziest, sloppiest bunch of inconsiderate thieves on earth and so on. I agreed with him totally, pointed out that the particular assistant had no connection whatever with the trailer, swore I'd get the matter taken care of immediately if I had to go right to David Begelman (then president of Columbia Pictures) and urged George to enter the stage and "get to work for chrissake, we're ten days down now!" George looked, nodded slowly, but didn't laugh. He gestured me into the stage ahead of him and, as we walked, he said softly, "I bet you wouldn't have talked that way to Frank Sinatra."

The set was the girl's apartment, and the first shot had George coming down an interior flight of stairs into the room, looking around and then fumbling at a locked sort of china closet where he knows she keeps the liquor. Not a heavy acting scene, but one requiring meticulous camera moves—fluid, first presenting, then tracking and finally disclosing action.

As George came down the stairs, the sound man stood up and called, "Hold it, I've got a squeak."

On investigation it appeared that George's shoes were squeaking as he flexed them on the stairs. Nothing special. It happens often, and a good sound crew is prepared. They have various kinds of felts and rubber pads they attach to the shoes, depending on the problem. So George handed over his shoes and sat down to await repairs.

A few minutes later they were ready and the sound man trotted into the set and proffered them to the star. George looked but didn't take.

"That's not the way they do it in New York," he said. Nobody knew what he was talking about.

"In New York they wrap the whole shoe."

This annoyed the sound man, a fellow with a lot of pictures behind him and a few awards too.

"Well, that's how we do it here," he said. He dropped the shoes in front of George and walked out of the set. George didn't make a move toward them. Instead he said, "Usually someone helps a star put his shoes on."

It got silent immediately.

George said, "I bet if I was Steve McQueen somebody would be putting these shoes on for me."

"Yeah, Ali McGraw," said someone, trying for a laugh and getting one, but nervous.

One of the assistants jumped up onto the stage and knelt before George, picked up the shoes and slipped them on him. George stood.

"What's the matter with everyone?" he called out. "Let's keep things happy and light."

No response. He shrugged, turned and went up the stairs again. Ready.

"... and action!" said Giler.

Once again George started down the stairs. No squeak. He paused, looked and continued. Then he slipped and stumbled down the rest of the staircase—about six feet. When he picked himself up he was raging, screaming, shouting denunciations of the studio, of Stark, of Begelman, demanding they be brought to the stage to answer for their crimes.

"Get that bastard Stark in here!"

He could tell the reaction was odd, so he looked where everyone else was looking. Ray Stark had been standing in the shadows behind the camera for the past ten minutes.

Segal peered, saw Stark and opted for brass. "Come on, Ray, get up here."

Stark hesitated, shrugged, and picked his way up onto the stage and stood facing George. "Okay, George," he said, "I'm here. What's your problem?"

Breath-holding time. Suddenly George's face creased into laughter. He threw his arms around Stark and kissed him on the lips. Stark reacted, shoved George away and spat. George screamed, unfastened his trousers and pulled them down, then galloped wildly around the stage, hanging onto his sagging pants, yelling, "Kiss my ass, Ray Stark!"

I grabbed first assistant Art Levinson's arm, and he yelled, *"Lunch, one hour. Save the lights!"*

Sometime during the luncheon break, George Segal went to David Begelman's office in the main administration building and broke all of Begelman's flower pots, littering the room with debris.

Eventually the picture was completed and a rough cut hacked out. Giler and Segal were sure it was a big winner, Stark was hopeful (he said), and I thought it a failure. The budget had gone quite mad, of course, with very little to show for the overages. Maggie Booth's verdict was pessimistic; moreover, she was depressed that the scanty coverage had foreclosed the hope of bailing it out on the Moviola. Stark spoke of retaliation. He hoped and intended to prove that Segal's conduct had caused the overages and meant to deduct the difference from Segal. I was instructed to write a kind of day-by-day indictment and asked to get corroborative testimony from others on the set. Very few wanted to put their opinions on paper—most of them had seen such things before. In the end I turned in a factual report, as dispassionate as I could make it, but damning nevertheless. Stark beamed when he read it. "We'll teach that son of a bitch a lesson."

But they still needed the son of a bitch. After fooling with the rough-cut film for weeks, Stark and the studio decided that it needed some extra scenes—a hilarious new ending. The hilarity was duly written and presented to Segal, who agreed to do it but just couldn't find the time. On three separate occasions I scheduled the work, ordered the people and then canceled at the last minute. George couldn't. . . .

The weeks rolled on and I grew restless. MGM had offered me *Logan's Run* and Melnick was calling, asking for projected start dates. The studio had rolled over in the fever and delirium of its dying and begun to live. The hotel in Las Vegas, rumored to be unfinishable, unfinanceable and unlivable, had opened at last and made a stunning success. Money began pouring in. Little *Westworld,* completed with little money and less hope, squirmed into theaters and started packing them in. And finally Jack Haley, Jr.'s home movie to end all such was completed and magical. Now money was available and it was spent, and *That's Entertainment* began building those lines around the block. It seemed like a good time to get *Logan's Run* off the ground, and, with Irwin Allen unavailable, I was next in line.

So farewell Ray Stark and *Black Bird.* Back I went to MGM to make a movie among friends. I heard that the new ending was finally shot— some kind of *Jaws*-type takeoff involving George and a shark. I never saw the final version.

A month or so after my return to MGM I got a message from Stark informing me that I would have to share a co-producing credit with George after all. I demurred. We corresponded.

Stark said, "You have always known it was part of George's deal."

I said, "I'll share a co-producer credit with him if he'll share a co-starring one with me."

Stark said, "I'm sorry you feel that way about it, but that's how it has to be."

I wrote to Begelman, who answered politely that it was up to Stark. I then wrote Stark and said that rather than share a credit I would prefer to withdraw my name entirely. He said he was sorry I felt that way but he'd comply with my wishes.

The final credits on the film list quite a few people as having produced *The Black Bird*—Stark's office manager and Mrs. Segal, for instance. George himself is called the Executive Producer. After a while I realized that was accurate enough.

But there are no clean shots out here. Even our epitaphs are subject to renegotiation. There was a day early in that movie, when I found myself having drinks in the Polo Lounge with David Giler and his guest, actress Stephane Audran. She had just arrived, having been cast opposite George Segal. Although I thought her all wrong for the part, I'm an admirer of her work and was happy to have been invited.

It was her first visit to America, she said. Her English was only determined, but she was far more at ease with such meetings than we, and she could readily tell when each of us thought he had said something clever. We were enchanté wiz 'er—we drank steadily, nibbled pretzels and impressed the waiter. She looked from one to the other, lifted an appropriate eyebrow, nodded on cue and laughed a lot. Eventually I looked at my watch and she rose thankfully.

I said, "I hope you won't be lonely here."

She smiled and shook her head. "Oh no," she said, "I go from here to my most good friends—also American. One of your most famous directors—very important in France. Maybe you know him, Samuel Fuller. He is preparing a great important movie. *Ze Big Red One.*"

On the morning of the third day . . . maybe it was a prop rock.

33

Wizards, Green Bananas, and the Rating Board

W E A R E W I Z A R D S—everybody says so. Conjurors. Rods into snakes, water from rocks, miniature dinosaurs weeping on command, and did you see those swords flashing?—laser beams, really! In fact, marvels come hard and are seldom what audiences imagine, and the attributions are never right, which is probably the way it ought to be. We make miniature sets which are exactly that, but we also make sets which are enormously larger than what they represent. The lung and brain sets for *Fantastic Voyage* filled half a sound stage each —but they were referred to as miniatures.

During the filming of *Skullduggery,* the company was working somewhere near the still-primitive middle of Jamaica. It was a scene in which the "apes" pull bananas from a low-hanging limb while scientists take notes. With everything in place, apes rehearsed and cameras in position, there came the unhappy prop man to say, "Jeez, chief—I forgot to put the fucking bananas on the truck."

When they call you "chief," you must assume the worst—it's the opposite of "boss," as in "Right away, boss"—the sound of aggressive competence. In fact, a prop man who has forgotten to put the major scene prop on his truck is a man already halfway home in disgrace. A prop man's truck and the prop boxes on it have a significance hard to describe. On a location, they are the Ark of the Covenant, holder of the Sacred Scrolls. It results in an obsession. If it's not on the truck it doesn't exist for the prop man. He would die of thirst in a rainstorm if he had forgotten to put drinking water on the truck.

But here we were in the center of the banana-growing world—"work all night on a drink of rum, load banana till de mornin' come," remember? So I said, "Forget it. Just buy a couple of ripe stalks from one of the farms around here and hang 'em up." There is probably no place in Jamaica from which you can't see banana leaves growing.

"Right away, boss," he said. Reprieved. That's what I call a real producer. Nothing stops him.

"And hurry up. The light's changing."

About fifteen minutes later he was back, dangling a stalk of green bananas.

"The best I could get," he said. "Set me back five bucks."

"Take it out of what you're ripping off Local Purchase," I said. And to the cameraman, a crybaby: "Well?"

"Pretty green."

"I can see that. Will they work?"

"Have to put 'em up to answer that."

So the stalk was tied to the branch and the reflectors moved and the lights lit. The cameraman peered and shrugged. "Can't see 'em."

I looked through the lens. The bananas had vanished, green into green.

"Impossible." The cameraman had sunk down onto the little shooting stick he carried. Mr. Dejection. The actors waited, exchanging looks. The "apes" rehearsed scratching and sniffing. They loved it and had no idea what was wrong.

Then the assistant prop man whispered to his leader, who brightened and nodded. The assistant trotted off, reappeared in a moment dragging a cylinder of compressed air, a spray gun and some paint cans.

"Yellow paint, boss. Have 'em ripe in a minute. Okay?"

Why not?

Green bananas sprayed with yellow paint look quite a lot like green bananas sprayed with yellow paint, but the light was changing. As soon as they stopped dripping we turned the cameras. The little apes jumped and grabbed the bananas, getting yellow paint on their palms, the scientists did their lines, we went in for the close shots, and it all went well enough.

"Okay," said the director, "move it around for the reverses."

But of course we were out of bananas by now. Time to kill the prop man. Why the hell hadn't he had enough sense to get at least two stalks? But the prop man had vanished. No fool he.

Goddammit—

"Hold it!" One of the assistants was pulling a young, grinning Jamaican forward. "This clown says he can get us another stalk in a minute. Wants ten bucks."

The loneliness of command. "Give it to him."

In a few moments the young man was back with a huge stalk of beautiful yellow bananas.

"Hang 'em and let's roll."

"Places, everyone."

"Oh, shit," said the cameraman.

"What now?"

"They don't match," he said. "Way too yellow."

The operator nodded gloomily. "Look like hell."

Then, on cue, reappeared the prop man with the compressed air and the spray gun. "It's a cinch, boss," he said. "I got some green paint here."

And that's what we did.

We are magicians, all right. Cynical, drunk on Old Know-How. Manipulators of Public Taste, Corruptors of the Young. Now you take the ratings system. It's not perfect, but can you imagine what those people would do if there wasn't someone to ride herd on them?

Colonial America was apparently not a fun place, but in those days you could get the ducking stool for being a common scold. Nowadays, in a libertine age, you become a consumer advocate or the head of the Film Rating Board instead.

In *Logan's Run,* a confectionery science fantasy about a distant future devoted to mindless pleasure, there was a sequence called "The Love Shop." To be well over onto the safe side, it was filmed as a kind of dream sequence—slow-motion, heavily filtered lenses, intermittent strobe lighting and so on; choreographed by a genuine ballet choreographer named Stephan Wenta. The dancers looked nude, but they were not. The sequence lasted a couple of minutes—just long enough for the Boy and Girl to chase through, followed by the Heavy.

Everybody liked it, although there was some grumbling that it was too arty—not sexy enough. But what the hell—the movie was for kids. . . .

The studio executive who regularly dealt with the Rating Office had no qualms about it. "PG," he said. "No question about it. Not exactly Disney—but PG for sure." This in answer to my concern whether the sequence ought to be showed to the Rating Board before it was cut into the film and scored. "You'll just call attention to it that way."

So the sequence was cut and scored and the finished film sent to the Rating Board with very little time to spare. "Don't worry about a thing," said the Executive in Charge of Those Matters. "It's a PG."

It was not. It came back with an R rating because it "contains an excessive amount of sexually oriented footage."

Oh my God!

Fevered meetings. "We've *got* to have a PG!"

"Can we bluff them?"

"No way."

"But what exactly does that mean?"

"Exactly? They don't say."

"Well, can you ask them?"

"Sure."

"Okay. Ask for a meeting with them—with whatsisname, Heffner. See if you can get them to say exactly—"

"Maybe it's just a couple of feet here and there."

"Sure. That's it—a couple of feet. Ask the guy to be reasonable."

"Absolutely not," said Mr. Heffner, head of the Rating Board. "I will not point out any specifics. If you want to change it I'll look at it as often as you like. But I have no suggestions to make."

Try reason. "Look, Mr. Heffner—we sincerely thought it was PG. We weren't trying to sneak something over. So our problem is, we don't know what's troubling you so we don't know where to fix it."

"I'm sorry," said Heffner. "I'll look at it as often as you like."

"But Mr. Heffner . . ."

"Look," he said, "I'm in a hurry. I'm sure you know what's offensive as well as I do. So you just do what's necessary and when I come back from New York I'll look at it again."

Panic on the third floor. "How long will he be gone?"

"A couple of weeks."

"A couple of weeks! We'll blow the release dates!"

"You gotta get him to be specific!"

"Look, Mr. Heffner. You say 'excessive,' right? That means there's too much. Would you help us understand what kind of too much? What if we print the whole sequence down six points? It's pretty dark now— and if you print it down six points, it will be a dark night scene in the average theater—and in the drive-ins they'll just barely see something moving—"

"If you want to try that, go ahead," said Heffner. "I'll look at it before I leave."

"Have the lab make a rush print. Overnight or better. Never mind what it costs!"

The brightness of the image on the theater screen is subject to a number of variables, including the distance from projector to screen (the "length of throw"), the actual reflecting surface of the screen itself and how old and smoke-browned it might be, the kind of projector— whether arc or xenon lamp—and so on. All of these factors are supposed to be considered and harmonized by the individual theater owner who is expected to "read the light" from time to time and make adjustments as necessary, according to a numbered scale of foot-lamberts read from the projection booth. It's a simple system designed to assure you that wherever you see the movie, you'll see about the same as everyone else.

Let's say the desired number is about 14 FL. If the projection light is off by two or three points, anyone would know the difference. Film-makers care like hell about getting the light correct—they fuss over the printing of individual scenes and sequences, believing that those differences mean everything to the mood and tone of the movie. But with rare exceptions, exhibitors don't give a damn. Even in Hollywood, where a man with a film playing in one of the major theaters may be assumed to show up every couple of nights to see how it's going, it's commonplace for the light to be down fifty percent. When you see a movie of yours somewhere out in the Fifty States, you usually think you're seeing it underwater. Most exhibitors just don't give a damn.

So when the printed-down sequence was ready, I looked at it and my heart sank. Mud. Our classy little ballet looked like one of those under-sea shots of turtles moving through a bed of kelp.

"Show it to them that way," said my Superior. "We gotta get the PG. If it's too dark we'll correct it in the release prints."

I phoned Heffner again. "We have the new print," I said, "and we feel sure it will meet any objections. But just in case, could we look at it together and you people just point or make a noise when . . . if you see something objectionable . . .?"

A long silence. Followed by a heavy sigh. "All right," said Heffner. "Just this once."

Three of us went over to the MPAA office with the reel of film, Producer, Editor and Executive, grateful and ready to take notes—

hoping for the best. Heffner led us to a lush little screening room, introduced us to the other members of the board and waved us to our seats.

"Just one thing," he said. "We'll make our comments while it's running and you can take notes. But you are not to answer or argue. Just listen."

I said, "But—"

"No buts, no nothing," said Heffner. His board, each of them seated by now, looked at us blankly.

"Okay."

The lights went out and the screen lit up. Before fifty frames had unrolled I yelled out, "Stop it! Lights!"

The film stopped and the room lit up. Heffner was staring at me in a rage. But I didn't care.

"For godsake—did you ever *read* that screen? I bet it's eighteen or more!"

Heffner sighed heavily. Clearly he didn't know what I was talking about. I explained about the FL scale, pointed out that the national average was about 11 FL—that we had printed for 13. But here, in the little room, the dark, mysterious footage was lit up like a bathroom in a bus station. Things I had never seen before were visible, even stage nails in the set walls. Incredible.

"I don't see what that's got to do with it," said Heffner, in his Eastern prep school intonation.

I tried again, watching his impatience and contempt and disbelief rise as I spoke. "Wait a minute," I said, "while I ask the projectionist."

The projectionist just peered at me and shrugged. "They like it bright," he said. "I dunno exactly, maybe twenty."

Heffner heard me out impassively, shrugged. "Do you want to run it or don't you?"

Licked. I nodded and sat down. The lights went out and the film rolled.

And now in the darkness, the Rating Board gave tongue.

"Tits, I see tits."

"Nudity, full frontal there."

"Buttocks. On the right. Buttocks."

"Breasts again."

"What's he *doing?*"

"Sexual writhing."

"Breasts."

"Crack in the ass visible."

"Breasts."

"Buttocks."

"Asses."

"Tits."

The voices went on and on for the couple of minutes—rising constantly higher and more quickly in the darkness like some crazy word orgy. Finally just the words, shrilling and snapping, intermittent hiss of breath—"Breasts . . . Asses . . . Tits . . ."

Then it was finished and the lights came on again. The board relaxed, breathing audibly in the silence. Finally I said, "Can we discuss possible cuts?"

"No," said Heffner. "We told you what we think. The cuts are up to you."

"You know," I said, "time is really pressing. And unless we have some clue as to what will satisfy you, we won't make the release date. You've just got to give us some idea of what you're after."

Silence.

"Well," I said, "let me put it this way. Will *anything* help? Is there any way we can preserve the sense of the sequence and get a PG rating?"

For the first time one of the Board spoke. "What's the place in the movie called—The Sex Place, right?"

"No. It's called The Love Shop."

He nodded, looked around at his fellows. "See what I mean?"

"Then it's the *idea* you're opposed to?"

Heffner jumped in. "No, no—we have nothing to say about thematic content or artistic values. We just comment on the film we see."

"Does that mean you don't differentiate between a nude on a museum wall and a nude in a porno?"

"I told you." Heffner was annoyed. "We don't make any comment on artistic values."

"But surely that's the whole—"

"Look," Heffner said. "You agreed not to argue with our comments."

"But—"

"I'm sorry. We went out of our way to be helpful."

He was turning to the door. I made one more try.

"Can I ask one question?"

He turned.

"What about that full frontal nudity you kept pointing out?"

"Well—what *about* it?"

"There wasn't any," I said. "They may have *looked* nude, but—"

I never got to finish the sentence.

Back at the studio I said, "Why don't we take a chance—fight it?"

Silence. Then the Executive in Charge of Such Things said, "I don't mean to be critical—but I think you antagonized him."

"I wouldn't be surprised."

"Well," he said, "maybe you better let me handle it from now on."

And that's what happened. What was finally left in the film was less than thirty seconds long. Jerry Goldsmith's music was chopped into mere sound and the few people who commented on the sequence said, "I suppose you just *had* to drag in that *pointless* little sex bit. You people."

I wrote Heffner an angry letter, of course. In order to do it, I had to telephone his office for the correct spelling of his name.

"H-E-F-F-N-E-R," said the secretary. "Be sure you put in the two f's. He hates it when people confuse him with the other man—the one from *Playboy* magazine."

"What's the matter, doesn't he want to be famous?"

"But he is famous. He has his own television show, didn't you know that?"

"No, I didn't. What is it?"

"Well," she said, "it's a sort of interview and discussion show—on PBS, you know. You can see it on Channel 28."

"What's it called?"

"The Open Mind."

34

Epilogue to
the Industry:
Some Parting Jots

THERE ARE some movie scenes which escape their contexts and enter our memories as if they were real and private. Those two cigarettes, the moist blonde in the hand of the giant ape, Frankenstein's monster catching sight of the little girl on the riverbank and so on. Everyone who saw the original *Lost Horizon* was imprinted by Margo's death. Remember? She is beautiful and forever young as long as she remains in Shangri-la. But, addled by her passion for a sulky young American who just wants to get away from all that happiness, she attempts to flee with him. And at the icy exit from Paradise the magic disappears and Margo shrivels, withers, dies—becomes ancient, ancient before our horrified eyes. Like other such indelibles it has been repeated many times and it rarely fails.

As I write, the radio tells me that the bitterly fought actors' strike is coming to an end. The major issue in that strike was the question of fairly dividing the loot being earned from techniques of movie exhibition which were not invented when I started the first chapter. And the actors doing all the shouting and breast-beating were all stars of television. For all the grosses of *Star Wars,* the big screen is no longer where it's at, and the sleazy little newsmag at your supermarket counter is featuring the juicy depravities of TV stars, not Academy Award winners.

Generations of fruit flies—future shock is now. Given a moment of bad luck, a certified Winner can watch Margo's death scene in his shaving mirror on any morning. Or hers, of course. It's that quick. When we're admiring someone out here we say, "The sonofabitch is a survivor!"

Cineasts to the contrary notwithstanding, movies are a gross art. The subtleties we often claim are only a sledge hammer handled with finesse, and all the real shadings are in faces, faces. . . . Crazy. At one end of the scale there's Fellini, hiring absolute amateurs who are asked only to mouth the multiplication tables—il signor Regista will dub in voices and lines later on. At the other end, Wendy Hiller and Paul Scofield saying Robert Bolt's wonderful lines in the prison farewell scene in *A Man for All Seasons*.

But it is not a medium for thought. Possibly not for thinking.

And intellectualism is not a survival value, although there are as many genuine intellectuals hacking each other to pieces in the movie business as in Academe. It's just that they don't confuse the values. That's the critic's job. There's no penalty attached to reading Proust and the Partisan Review as long as you understand that those are after-dinner values.

Money, sex, power and all the myriad amalgams are behind the cameras. In front of them, add sentiment.

Money first. The great attorney, Nat Mittleman, once described the Industry as institutionalized thievery—and he was not being censorious. The bizarre headline stories about David Begelman which scandalized the *Wall Street Journal* made people in the business certain the poor man was ill. "With all his opportunities to grab it off the top forever, you mean to tell me he wrote someone's name on a *check?* Hadda be a death wish."

There was a great eruption, of course. When the stories hit the papers something *has* to happen. It's traditional. But what happened was also traditional. The reformers swept in; Begelman was swept out—but not without picture production commitments worth millions. The smoke died down and, suddenly, another spasm. This time the reformers were out—accused of all sorts of mis- or malfeasance in a pleasant, unofficial way. By the time the earth stopped shivering, Begelman was the new president of MGM, the ousted "Bad Guy" Reformers had taken command of 20th Fox and the Academy-Award-winning actor who had blown the first whistle was unemployed. A fellow I used to know well until he became an Important Figure was given to chanting a slogan during the days of adversity. "All we need is a hit," he said. It's our ultimate truth.

If you make movies people will assume your home is furnished from the sets—and it happens. People who work in studios and on films generally seem to regard all property as portable, and, when they make off with something, they don't think of it as stealing. One well-known production supervisor who was making a picture budget for me asked how much I proposed to skim off. "Just give me an idea what to shoot for," he said, "so I'll know where to ease up."

A famous young actor, as likeable and decent a fellow as I ever met on a movie set, once came to me while on a location to voice a complaint. "I'm going broke down here," he said. "I can't get by unless I spend some of my per diem!"

When I understood that he wasn't joking, I said what was obvious— that *that*'s what a per diem allowance was *for.* He was patient.

"I know all that," he said. "But I always send mine home."

Drugs? Sure. Pot, of course, and cocaine if you've got the money— and people you hardly know may ask if you've got an extra Quaalude. But Tim Leary is not the mayor of Beverly Hills. If high colonics were in, there would be a boom in bathrooms and the people who wear those little gold spoons would be wearing darling little fountain syringes instead.

Nothing is compulsory—not even to be in. You're as free to practice your own notions of morality here as anywhere, but you'll be thought a fool if you make an issue of it and a damn nuisance if you preach. Under the circumstance, virtue *has* to be its own reward.

Brad Dexter, whom I knew as Frank Sinatra's best friend and the Man Who Saved His Life That Time, finally made his move. I heard about it from Howard Koch, who shook his head, not sadly.

"Brad's a goner now," he said. "He's going to be Frank's producer on *Naked Runner.* Sid Furie, y'know?"

Since that was not long after Sidney Furie had made a stunning success of *The Ipcress File,* I thought Brad had scored a coup.

"Uh uh," Howard said. "Can't work. Sooner or later there's got to be an argument and Brad's going to think he's a real shtarker and back the other guy. You wait . . ."

Sure enough. Stories filtered back from wherever they were shooting and insiders began to say, "Brad's out." But there was nothing more than that. No lawsuits or spectacular dismissals. The gossip subsided.

Months later I saw Frank Sinatra again. I don't remember where but it must have been an Industry Occasion because mind's eye says he was in a dinner jacket. I do remember that he was as warm and cordial as always, with that gift of making a brief meeting seem personal and important to him. But he had something he wanted to tell me.

He said, "You know Brad and I aren't together anymore?"

I nodded. "That's what I heard. I'm sorry."

"One of those things," he said. Then, taking my arm, "One thing though . . ."

I waited.

"He didn't really save my life. It was an old guy on a surfboard."

In Sinatra's case, survival is a pretty feeble word. When he announced he was quitting, a few years back, a lot of my generation suddenly felt that old sunset glow. Then Frank changed his mind, came out again looking and sounding better than ever and I'll bet there was an instant boom in hairpieces and gym enrollments. "Don't push, kid."

It's a glorious illustration of the problem of the Clean Shot. It looks like a brass ring and it keeps coming around. But while you're leaning and grabbing you can't tell if it's The Second Coming or a remake. Soon at a theater or drive-in near you—*The Son of Déjà Vu.*

Index